PRAISE FOR *EXPECTING THE WORLD*

When managers of the World Bank hired a twenty-three-year-old French major, they thought they were hiring a typist. Little did they know that this American "girl" was a third-generation feminist, starting with her suffragist grandmother. In the next thirty years of her career, Jerri Dell carved out a corner of the male-dominated international bureaucracy, empowering herself and thousands of women in the developing countries she worked in. *Expecting the World* is an inspiring story of how one determined woman can make a difference.

> —Veronica Li, co-author of *Viking Voyager, An Icelandic Memoir*

Expecting the World is a story of women's empowerment at several levels: a journey from a world of men and "girls," bosses and secretaries in the World Bank, a large, complex international institution, to one where many women demanded and often came close to something approaching equality. It's a story of the women at the grassroots, working together to surmount the many barriers that face them. And it's also Jerri's story of living this transition and, in the words of Mary Catherine Bateson, "Composing a Life," with guts, setbacks, love, misunderstandings, growth, and adventure. The memoir offers both the living reality of the World Bank's rather reluctant transformation and a woman's journey through life.

> —Katherine Marshall, author of *The World Bank: From Reconstruction to Development to Equity*

Jerri Dell's immeasurable charm and grit are palpable through every page of this book. Her unique experience—and voice—at the World Bank takes the reader by the hand on both a personal and universal journey through what it's like to be a woman—to be *women*—navigating a man's world. She demonstrates with passion and vivid stories, with courage and humility, that women in "left-out places" have more to teach us than a man's world ever imagined. *Expecting the World* weaves a global village of thoughtful women (and yes, men), rich and poor, powerful and seemingly powerless, but all willing to constantly learn from each other, to make a difference. As someone who came to the World Bank a decade after Jerri,

I am eternally grateful for the path she cut that enabled those who followed to move one step closer to a world where everyone's voice counts.
—Linda McGinnis, Poverty Economist and former World Bank
Resident Representative for Mali

The World Bank works in countries that are stuck in poverty, inequality, and mismanagement. But the World Bank itself has been stuck at times—in hierarchical rigidities that undercut its critical poverty-fighting mission. Both the countries and the Bank would do better if they unleashed the power of women, and *Expecting the World* tells the story of Jerri Dell, a career World Bank professional, who advanced this cause in the countries and within the institution.
—Tim Carrington, author of *The Year They Sold Wall Street*

Anyone who has worked in international development will identify with the stories that make up this highly readable, deeply personal, and remarkably detailed book. Full of colorful episodes, it describes the jealousies, distrust, and even sexual dynamics encountered—and fought—along the way. This memoir is highly pertinent to the state of the world today, where countries from Afghanistan to Zimbabwe are turning away from democracy in favor of male-dominated, top-down authoritarianism. Author Jerri Dell shows that other outcomes are possible, how by collaborating with grassroots women she discovered the leadership, innovation, and persistence that makes those outcomes come to pass.
—Mark Nelson, former Director, Center for International Media
Assistance (*CIMA*) at the National Endowment for Democracy

Jerri Dell has written a poignant memoir of her thirty-year career at the World Bank. It is a brilliantly written book and captures fully her passion for work on the advancement of women both inside the World Bank itself, and as well, the programs that she helped to design and implement for women entrepreneurs in developing countries. A fabulous read.
—Richard Cambridge, former Advisor to the World Bank Regional
VP, Africa Region

EXPECTING THE WORLD

Learning from Women in Left-Out Places

Jerri Dell

EXPECTING THE WORLD

Learning from Women in Left-Out Places

Jerri Dell

Sidekick Press
Bellingham, Washington

This memoir represents the author's recollection of her past. These true stories are faithfully composed based on memory, photographs, diary entries, and other supporting documents. Some names, places, and other identifying details have been changed to protect the privacy of those represented. Conversations between individuals are meant to reflect the essence, meaning, and spirit of the events described.

Published 2021
Printed in the United States of America
ISBN: 978-1-7365358-6-8
LCCN: 2021916180

Sidekick Press
2950 Newmarket Street, Suite 101-329
Bellingham, Washington 98226
sidekickpress.com

Jerri Dell, 1951-
Expecting the World: Learning from Women in Left-Out Places

Cover design by Creekside Collaborative, LLC
creeksidecollaborative.com

Back cover photo by Larry Merrill

To Minou

The World Bank is a big, important place, full of important people who've gone on to be presidents, prime ministers, and winners of the Nobel Prize. I wasn't one of those people. But I did some things they didn't do.

This is my story.

Photo by Larry Merrill

New Girl

March 1, 1974

It was raining as I climbed off the bus to head for my interview. Three soggy blocks later, I arrived at an imposing grey stone building at the corner of 19th and H Streets, a few blocks from the White House: The World Bank.

Washington, D.C.'s humidity was not kind. It made my hair even thicker and frizzier than usual. The linen jacket I'd bought with money I didn't have was wrinkled. This was not the look I was going for to impress a recruitment officer. I wasn't sure what clothes World Bank secretaries wore, but I was pretty sure they were less damp and rumpled than mine. But there I was, anyway, an enthusiastic recent college graduate, heading toward the world's most powerful international organization, hoping to get a job.

In fact, I'd hoped to work for an international organization since I first visited the United Nations at nine years old. I could still remember, clear as day, walking through tall, double-glass doors into an elegant lobby, then looking up at the canopy of flags from a hundred countries or more. A steady stream of men in dark suits and African robes and women in saris and colorful cotton dresses with matching headscarves came and went.

An African security guard smiled at me as he directed my parents' friend, Gerry, to the information desk, where an Asian woman with long, shiny, black hair gave me a floor plan and I led us to the fourth floor, where we took our seats at the back of the room. In the dark, we watched a large group of important-looking men sitting at tables on a brightly lit stage. The men wore earphones and spoke into microphones. Their strong accents and complicated words made them hard to understand. I was restless and ready to leave when I noticed a glass booth a few rows down. Four women sat in the booth, almost invisible in the dark. Like the men, they wore earphones and spoke into microphones. I asked Gerry in a whisper who these women were. She whispered back that they were the interpreters, the ones who translated the men's speeches so that everyone could understand one another.

I'd never met anyone who spoke even two languages, let alone many. Instead of watching the men on the stage, I watched the women in the booth. They might have been nearly invisible, but from what Gerry said they were important. I wanted to be one of these women. I wanted to work for the UN. I'd go to college, learn a language, maybe two. At nine years old, I was already mapping out my future. I was that kind of kid.

In 1974, as I walked down 19th Street, I was a little more realistic about what being a twenty-four-year-old college graduate looking for work in a UN agency meant. I'd been to New York already, learned that speaking French fluently didn't qualify me to translate or interpret for the UN. I'd have to get a certificate from Georgetown University. It would take a couple of years. In the meantime, I'd get a job—any job—that would let me pay the rent, eat, and get my certificate as translator/interpreter.

I'd been warned about how big the World Bank was, several buildings spread out over twenty city blocks. My first task was to find the Flag Entrance to the F building. Standing in the circular drive, I passed two uniformed limo drivers, waiting, eyes trained on the big glass doors, as if someone of consequence might appear. They barely gave me a glance. High above the limos and opposite the front door of the grey building, flags representing one hundred countries were displayed in a glass case. This must be the place.

I tugged on the heavy glass doors and entered the World Bank lobby for the first time.

A guard at the front desk smiled at me broadly. When I asked how to get to Personnel, he explained that I was in the F building and must take the elevator to the tenth floor. Then I'd have to walk down the corridor to the D Building. The directions sounded simple enough.

As instructed, I took the elevator to the tenth floor, turned right, then right again, then headed to the end of a corridor. No D Building. I returned to the elevator and tried turning left and walking down a different hallway. Still, no D Building. I tried again. After many wrong turns, I ended up back at the elevator where I had started. If finding the recruitment office was this hard, maybe I didn't belong at the World Bank. Maybe I should forget the interview and get back on the bus.

The elevator dinged, and the doors opened. The guard I'd met in the lobby stepped out.

"A little lost?" He grinned.

"Yes. *Very* lost." I was almost giddy with relief to see him.

"No problem. Follow me." I kept up with his long strides through a corridor, across a breezeway to a different building, then down a hallway to yet another building, then to another. My head was spinning.

"Here you go," said the guard, pointing to the sign that read "Recruitment Office."

"I know it's confusing, but don't worry, you'll figure it out." He grinned again and left.

I entered and stood awkwardly in the office, waiting for someone to notice me.

"Please, sit down," said a petite woman with a pronounced French accent. "My boss will be with you in a moment." A minute later, a broad-shouldered African man in a well-cut tan suit ducked out from an office. He shook my hand.

"I wondered what became of you. Glad you made it," he said. "I'm Prince. Please come in." He asked his secretary to get me a cup of tea. He also asked her to hold his calls. I began to relax.

"So, tell me a little about yourself. I see you grew up nearby in Bethesda. You went to Bard College in New York? Attended the Sorbonne? What was it like to live in Paris?"

"I wasn't in love with Paris," I told him honestly, "but at least I can speak French fluently, now."

"You didn't love Paris? Everyone loves Paris."

"You don't when you're an American, living on her own in a city for the first time, and doing it all in French."

"But it must have made you strong, right? Figuring it out?"

"Who knows? It didn't kill me," I laughed. "Maybe it made me strong."

I wasn't sure this was the right answer and did my best to redirect the conversation.

"So, Prince," I said. "Tell me about you. Where are you from?"

"Me?" He smiled, not a bit taken aback by my presumption. "I'm from Cameroon. I only joined the Bank a month ago. I'm still finding it a bit of a maze."

I certainly agreed with him on that. "So, what do you think? Is it more than I can handle?" I asked.

"If you could figure things out for yourself in Paris in French at twenty, and if you can get the upper hand in conversations the way you do, I think you can probably find your way around the World Bank. Maybe not right away. I'm guessing you can talk yourself out of any scrape. Am I right?"

"I try," I said. Noting Prince glancing surreptitiously at his watch, I stood up to leave.

"Wait a minute." He picked up the phone and set up some interviews for me after lunch.

More interviews?

He handed me a paper with an office number written on it in bold letters. "You'll be fine," he said, shaking my hand.

After grabbing a sandwich at a crowded deli, I spent a distracted hour wandering around among the government workers, university professors, and businesspeople who owned the city at midday, then headed down Pennsylvania Avenue toward the World Bank again.

"You're back?" asked the guard in the lobby. "Well, that's got to be a good sign."

"Maybe." I flashed him a smile that I hoped was convincing.

This time, when I took the elevator behind the guard's desk to the seventh floor, I was relieved to find the office of Mr. El Darwish, Chief, Country Programs, Europe, Middle East, and North Africa Region directly in front of me. I knocked on the door, and a cheerful, pudgy, balding Egyptian in shirtsleeves ushered me into his office.

"*Fateh*," he said, inviting me to sit across from him at a desk piled high with reports and loose paper.

Mr. El Darwish was relaxed and friendly. An hour passed as he asked me about my studies, my family, my reason for wanting to work for the World Bank. I told him that, frankly, I'd always wanted to work for the United Nations, but since it was in New York and I wanted to live in Washington, at least for the time being, I thought the World Bank would be the next best thing.

"Oh, yes?" He laughed. "You may find plenty of people at the United Nations who wished they worked for the World Bank."

"Why's that?"

"The Bank's got more clout. We lend millions of dollars to developing countries all over the globe. To qualify for loans, the governments of these countries have to meet many conditions. The Bank makes the rules, and borrowing countries have to follow them. Mr. McNamara's vision for international development is huge," he said. "But you're frowning. Isn't this a place you'd like to work?"

"Well, sure," I said. "Staff from many countries, who speak many languages, who have had so many different experiences? That sounds like a place I'd like to work. But I'm not fluent in economics or finance. Does that matter?"

"I don't see why it would," he said. "No one will ask you to calculate rates of return or draw up loan documents. You'll work for a loan officer and a country economist. Type and file and answer the phone. I shouldn't think you'd have any trouble doing that, right? But maybe you're overqualified for the job."

"Certainly not," I was quick to say. "There aren't a lot of jobs out there for a French literature major with a BA. I'm a fast learner. This job would suit me fine." I decided not to get ahead of myself. Not mention how I didn't expect to type forever.

An hour after I had stepped into Mr. El Darwish's office, he was on the phone with Prince. "Your recruit should report for duty on Monday at nine," he said into the receiver.

Could that be right? Had I convinced them to recruit me? Damp and wrinkled as I was? This was very good news. A real job with benefits. Even if it meant typing for a living. It wouldn't be forever.

Back in the Recruitment Office, Prince shook my hand. "You must have passed the test," he said. "Be ready to fill out lots of forms and read lots of manuals. The Bank is nothing if not bureaucratic."

We shook hands again. "Come Monday, you'll have the World Bank all figured out."

I didn't have a clue.

The first day of my new job, I clicked down 19th Street in fashionable black leather pumps and another work outfit I couldn't afford. Again, I entered the double-glass doors and smiled at the security guard, who smiled back. Without asking directions this time, I took the elevator to the seventh floor, where a white-haired Lebanese administrative assistant named Laila waited to greet me. Laila was short and round, and looked a bit world-weary.

Her first task was to fill me in on such things as World Bank life insurance, health insurance, tax reimbursement for American staff, annual leave, sick leave, yearly physicals, working hours, lunch hour, and the dress code. Then she handed me a black binder, three-inches thick.

"You'll find anything else you need to know about the Bank's administrative procedures in here," she said, patting the binder. "Read it at your leisure."

I rolled my eyes, expecting at least a grin in return.

No grin.

Laila plodded on. "The World Bank was created in 1944 to rebuild Europe from the devastation of the Second World War. Once much of that work was done, it turned its attention to the less-developed countries of Africa, Asia, and Latin America. In its first thirty years as the largest and most powerful international lending institution in the world, the World Bank lent half a trillion dollars for more than three thousand development projects in two hundred twenty countries worldwide."

Clearly, Laila had said all this before, but it was all new to me. Like most Americans, I knew virtually nothing about the World Bank and what it did. The plethora of rules and regulations and detailed information was overwhelming. And not a little intimidating. But I was young and fast, I'd figure it out.

Briefing over, Laila was ready to introduce me around.

"Let's begin with the boss," she said. As we waited at his office door, the director scowled at a report. Laila coughed discreetly. He looked up as she nudged me forward for his inspection.

"Monsieur Bart, I want to present Jerri. Today is her first day."

"*Enchanté*," said Monsieur Bart, without conviction, then nodded to Laila and returned to his document.

As we backed away from Monsieur Bart's door, a large woman who looked twice my age, wearing a crimson jacket and too much lipstick, headed our way.

"Raquel," whispered Laila, "Monsieur Bart's secretary."

"Well, they keep hiring them younger and younger," said Raquel. After looking me up and down and sighing, she instructed Laila to introduce me to *the men*, which seemed to mean "the professionals." At the World Bank in 1974, the words were virtually synonymous.

Laila led me along the long corridor to the offices of Misters Gonella, Hadjadj, Faltas, Al-Bustany, and Rangachar. How was I ever supposed to remember so many odd names? Laila never failed to introduce me as "our new girl."

Once I had met all the men, she ushered me into a spacious office with four large desks. Sitting at one of them was a woman about my age with shoulder-length auburn hair and a warm smile. Laila introduced her as Ghislaine from Quebec. To my surprise, Ghislaine from Quebec jumped up and kissed me on both cheeks, then offered me *"le grand tour."*

"This is me," she said, pointing to a desk covered with black binders and reports, along with a bright red geranium. Pointing to the desk next to hers, with a push-button telephone, IBM Selectric typewriter, metal paper stand, and steno pad, she added, "And this is you." She moved the red geranium from her desk to mine.

"Think you'll like it here?" asked Ghislaine, warmly.

"Absolutely," I said, and meant it. I wasn't sure I'd be a terrific secretary, but working alongside Ghislaine, I knew I'd have fun.

A small Filipina woman in her late thirties, whom Ghislaine identified as our Division Chief Secretary, emerged from Mr. El Darwish's office. When she saw me, she said, "So, American?"

I nodded uncertainly.

"Oh, you're okay. Don't worry. We like Americans well enough."

I wondered about this as I made the rounds meeting my coworkers from Egypt, Italy, Iraq, France, Lebanon, Pakistan, Peru, The Philippines, and the UK. As far as I could see, I was the only American—except for one loan officer who was away on mission in Yemen. "On mission," I quickly learned, meant business travel in World Bank-speak.

Within a few weeks, I was getting the hang of my new job. I liked the subsidized cafeterias, where I could eat enough roast beef at lunch that cheese and crackers would suffice for dinner. I spent more than half my monthly salary on rent for my apartment in a slightly rundown building in a fashionable neighborhood north of Georgetown. Thanks to Bank cafeteria food, I made ends meet. Barely.

A week before I had arrived in town, my grandparents' elderly friend had died. Thanks to my stepmother Kate's resourcefulness, I assumed the lease of her studio apartment. When I moved in, the apartment was as she'd left it, completely furnished. She'd smoked, drank too much, and couldn't afford a cleaning person. All the teak furniture she'd left was badly marred with cigarette burns and watermarks, but it was still furniture. I had a place to sit and sleep, and a kitchen to cook in. I could see the Washington Monument, the Jefferson Memorial, the Tidal Basin, and the Potomac River through my picture window. It would be the perfect place to watch the national fireworks display on the Fourth of July.

I graced the walls of my new studio with professionally framed photographs my college boyfriend Larry had taken when we lived together in Paris. Larry was a cynical New Yorker whose approval I'd always sought. I'd given him up for a new job and a new life. I missed him a lot, but I was ready to make the most of what was ahead—like the handsome Tunisian professor I met soon after I arrived at the Bank. He didn't speak much English, but I was thrilled to be speaking French again, and enthralled with his description of Tunis. I'd never traveled anywhere but the US and Europe.

Maybe one day I'd travel to Tunis myself. Why not?

My first months at the World Bank were like a lovely dream, full of elegant men and beautiful women in colorful clothes, a multitude of different cultures and languages swirling around me. African masks, Chinese scrolls, Japanese kimonos behind glass, and expressionist paintings from Latin America filled the lobbies and halls. I liked the sparkling glass and the polished floors.

Most of all, though, I liked Ghislaine, who seemed to know everyone in the Bank and was happy for me to know them, too. Ghislaine planned brunches and parties at which recent recruits to the World Bank's young professional program danced energetically with Bank secretaries from Bolivia, Guatemala, Sweden, Switzerland, and France. I was American, had grown up in Washington, D.C., and spoke English as a first language. I didn't even have an accent. I towered over most of the European men I met. I liked to dance, but I liked intelligent conversation, too. It didn't take long to learn that World Bank secretaries weren't expected to make intelligent conversation; dancing was enough.

Dinner parties at Ghislaine's were lavish and usually featured a leg of lamb pierced with garlic and rosemary, potatoes *au gratin* creamy with cheese, and *Poire Belle Helene*—fresh pears steeped in raspberry syrup with vanilla ice cream. In the summer, Ghislaine offered brunches replete with baked brie, figs, and water crackers, Quiche Lorraine, and brown-sugar streusel coffee cake. There was always a hefty watermelon scooped out to look like a picnic basket, heaped with melon balls of cantaloupe and honeydew.

At work, Ghislaine never seemed to care or even notice when the men spoke down to her. She never objected to being called by her first name while always addressing her boss formally. Perhaps this was how women kept their jobs as secretaries at the World Bank. They put the men at ease. They didn't have an opinion, and they didn't argue. They answered the phone, took messages, screened calls, typed fast, ran errands, got coffee, and smiled.

My job was to type reports and memoranda, and for the most part I typed them without grumbling. The first time, at least. By the time they handed me the same thing to retype a third time, I started numbering the drafts. I knew filing was part of my job, and I dutifully filed documents in green hanging folders and three-inch black binders. On the other hand, I decided it was not my job to sharpen the men's pencils. I answered their phones, but I wouldn't screen their calls just to make them feel important.

I tried to show the men that I had other qualifications beyond my office skills. Since I was the only native English speaker on our team, I made a point of editing the men's drafts while typing them. Unfortunately, the men didn't like having their English corrected, especially by a young American secretary. I realized that the men didn't care how smart I was; they cared that I knew how smart they were.

I spent what seemed an enormous amount of time in the Bank's basement print shop waiting for reports to be copied and stapled. This gave me the chance to know the print shop supervisor, Dan Johnson. My lunches with Dan were always fun and enlightening. One of the first things he told me was never to trust a woman named Lacy Carter.

Dan began his career as an elevator operator, the only kind of job a Black man could get at the Bank. He and his Black American colleagues were trained to be seen and not heard. Do their jobs and no chit-chat. They could be fired for the smallest infraction, without a warning. The person who saw to it that they towed the line was, as Dan described her, a "little old British lady" named Lacy Carter.

As far as he knew, Lacy Carter had no professional credentials of any kind, but she served as *de facto* advisor to the director of personnel and arbiter of what was—and was not—appropriate behavior at the World Bank.

"I knew several secretaries Lacy Carter sent home to change because their skirts were too short," he told me. "I knew several elevator operators who were fired for speaking to secretaries on the elevator."

"But how does she get away with it?" I asked.

"Probably because she's willing to do things other people don't want to do, which puts them in her debt. When someone dies overseas, Lacy

Carter takes charge of the corpse. When someone gets sick on mission, Lacy arranges their evacuation."

"You wouldn't believe the kind of trouble these overpaid, overblown Bank types get themselves into—what you might call a 'lack of ethics.' Lacy Carter considers herself an expert on ethics. The Bank doesn't want scandal and Lacy sees to it things are kept quiet. But there's no doubt she knows the men's secrets, and they know she knows." I'd definitely keep an eye out for Lacy Carter.

I liked to get to the office before anyone else, but one day my division chief beat me to it.

"Good morning!" he chirped, getting up from his desk, holding a large, square envelope. "Perfect timing. The Arab executive director just called and asked me to have a secretary hand-carry this document to him for the Board meeting today. Could you?"

"Sure," I said, taking the envelope.

On the thirteenth floor, what we called the "celestial heights," each of the executive directors had two offices, one for himself and one for his secretary. The Arab executive director's secretary wasn't there yet, so I placed the envelope on her desk. As I was leaving, a rotund, elderly man with thinning hair and squinty eyes opened the door from his private office. He asked me to bring the envelope to him rather than leave it on his secretary's desk.

"Of course," I said. I walked into his office and handed him the envelope, then turned back to the door.

"What's your hurry?" he asked. Still standing, he walked around me, closed the door, and pulled up two chairs. He sat in one, patted the other, and told me to sit down.

"I'll be going now, sir," I said, moving toward the door again.

For a heavyset man, the executive director moved fast. Before I knew it, he'd flattened me against the door and was nuzzling my hair, trying to kiss me. Without a thought, I shoved my hands against his chest, got some distance between us, and lifted my knee fast and hard up between his legs. He yowled and grabbed his crotch. I ran for the stairs, then took them two at a time back to the seventh floor. At my desk again, I straightened my skirt, steadied my breath, and began typing.

What happened on the thirteenth floor wasn't supposed to happen. This wasn't what I'd imagined working internationally would mean. I knew it wasn't my fault. But I worried. I was a big, strong American woman. If he could try that with me, no Bank woman was safe, especially not foreign women on G-4 visas who would have to leave the United States were the Bank to let them go. In 1975, sexual harassment wasn't even whispered about at the World Bank, let alone reported. As employees of an international organization, we had no recourse, no ombudsman, no union, and no access to the US legal system. Our job was to put up and shut up. I'd never forget that man on the thirteenth floor. One day, I'd make it my business to stand up for World Bank women.

As a child, I'd spent some of my favorite times having lunch with my father at the Library of Congress, where he worked as a speechwriter. We usually ate in a dingy lunchroom with vending machines that offered sandwiches in plastic wrap, cold, grey hamburger patties, and Coca Cola with too much ice. Sometimes we'd have a piece of soggy cherry pie for dessert.

Now, it was my turn to invite my dad to join me for lunch at the Bank.

When I arrived to meet him in the D Building lobby, he was deep in conversation with the security guard. I interrupted to give him a kiss and sign him in. I led him up the marble stairs, through the glass doors, and into the cafeteria, redolent with the smell of curry, peanut stew, ginger rice, and veal Parmigiana.

We joined the line of men in turbans and pinstripes, women in saris and three-inch heels. An animated group of Senegalese ahead of us in line was speaking Wolof, while the young couple behind us spoke Urdu. I greeted several friends in French and introduced them to my dad. He shook hands but said little, probably afraid they might expect him to speak French, too.

My dad and I had always taken turns being proud of each other: he of me for twirling a baton and marching in parades, knowing how to keep the score at major league baseball games, and learning to play the clarinet. I was proud of him for writing a book about Abraham Lincoln and for being the only white member of the Black Employees of the Library of Congress. I learned a lot about racism from my father. As a civil war historian, he knew just how racist American society could be. "Everyone who's ever written about the Civil War or reconstruction has either misremembered or lied," he would say. Any time he'd see a confederate flag pasted to a pickup truck's back window, or waving in front of a house, he'd become so furious I was afraid he'd stop the car and make a citizen's arrest for treason.

My father didn't limit his concern about race to the US. Although he'd never traveled abroad, he knew plenty about apartheid in South Africa. As bad as racism was in the United States, he said, it was even worse in South Africa. I was horrified by the stories he told me about the way Black South Africans were treated by the white authorities, how brutally Nelson Mandela was treated in prison, where he'd been for years and years, with little chance of release. My father spoke so vehemently and cared so deeply about people like Abraham Lincoln and Nelson Mandela, they felt almost like family to me.

I was especially proud that my dad liked and respected women. He thought there was nothing that a girl like me couldn't do. Now that I was a college graduate, he was proud that I spoke French and worked in a place like the World Bank. Although his approval made me happy, I often thought my grandparents and parents would have preferred me to be a writer or a librarian like my mother and grandmother. Not a secretary at the World Bank. But I kept that to myself.

As we ate, my father had a hard time staying focused on what I was saying. His eyes kept darting left and right at my exotic colleagues from around the world. Toward the end of our lunch, he leaned across the table and whispered: "It looks like a Hollywood set!"

I laughed. "Yep."

The World Bank was full of people wearing expensive clothes and brimming with self-confidence. After four years at a small, artsy college, I didn't know how to fit into a place like this, and I was afraid I never would. That is, until I picked up the phone one evening at home to find a suave, sexy Frenchman on the other end of the line. To my astonishment, he asked me out on a date.

I'd never been on a date before.

In college, my friends with Willie Nelson braids and scruffy beards drank in a grungy bar down the road and smoked dope on the lawn. We coupled up, but never went out on dates; we certainly never dressed up. No one I knew in college had prepared me for World Bank men.

But now I was in my apartment waiting for the dashing Frenchman with a deep tan and sparkling blue eyes who'd written my phone number on the back of his hand during an elevator ride the week before. I couldn't imagine what a cosmopolitan, older man would see in a Bard girl like me, but I was eager to find out.

To my surprise, my date had left his perfectly formfitting suit at home and arrived at my door in jeans, sandals, and a Hawaiian shirt. He escorted me to his Plymouth Valiant that was as beat-up as my own.

"*Comme tu parles bien le francais,*" he said, complimenting me on my fluency in French as we drove together to Wolf Trap Farm Park. From then on, we spoke only in French. Maybe living in Paris for a year had been worth the effort, after all.

At Wolf Trap, we watched what seemed to me a modern, sophisticated, even shocking dance performance by a troupe called Pilobolus. Between the stage lighting and the dancers' leotards, the performers looked like they were dancing naked. I glanced at my date to see his reaction. He didn't seem even slightly shocked. But he was forty and French, so no wonder.

We spent much of the following evening in Georgetown at *Au Pied de Cochon*, his favorite French restaurant. After living on a shoestring, I found it the height of luxury to devour mussels steeped in garlic butter and drink glass after glass of cold champagne, while the Frenchman footed the bill.

My new boyfriend loved sailing on the Chesapeake Bay, and co-owned a boat with a World Bank personnel officer. After sailing several times alone with me, he suggested that we include his boat's co-owner, Jim Dyck, on our next weekend sail.

"*Mais attention,*" he said. "Don't forget Dyck is with Personnel, and you know what that means." No, I did not know what that meant.

"It means we must show discretion." He gave me a stern look.

"Hey, I can be discreet," I said, sidling up to him.

"*Serieusement*, you are a friendly and outspoken American. You have to be a bit careful about Personnel people. They don't need to know too much about you."

The following Saturday, I met Jim Dyck. The morning's sail was full of banter and comfortable conversation. By noon, we were munching sandwiches and downing gin and tonics.

"So, how do you like your new job at the Bank?" Jim Dyck asked. "You are a typist, yes?"

"I'm a secretary," I said, slightly put out.

"Okay, right. How do you like it?"

"It's not too bad," I said, "even if the men are a little silly and full of themselves."

"Oh?" Now it was Jim Dyck who seemed put out.

"You can't imagine how rude they can be. And dismissive. I'm not used to being dismissed."

"But as you said yourself, you are a secretary. What exactly do you expect from this job?" asked Dyck.

"To be treated with some respect, maybe?" I replied. "Seen as someone with potential? Able to do more than type, file, and answer the phone? But I'm okay with it for now. It's a foot in the door. Once I have more experience, I'll start moving ahead, don't you think?"

I gave him my warmest smile; he didn't smile back.

"So, you think you are too good for your job?" he asked.

"It's not that. But is there any reason I can't learn enough on the job to get a promotion?"

"But you are a secretary," he said, a little louder than I thought was necessary. "You think there's a chance you'll move up through the ranks to a professional World Bank position?"

I nodded. "Why not?" I didn't need to tell him about my plan to work at the UN. The principle was the same.

"This is the World Bank we're talking about. McNamara's best and brightest. It seems a bit unrealistic to expect you can compete with an internationally recruited young professional for a job, doesn't it?"

Out of the corner of my eye, I glimpsed my Frenchman frowning.

"Never mind," I said. "Let's talk about something else." Clearly, any expectations at all were, by definition, unrealistic.

For almost a year, I continued to view my first job at the Bank as a reasonable first step toward bigger things that would eventually land me the professional job at the UN I'd dreamt about since I was nine. Over time, however, I discovered that Jim Dyck was not alone in thinking that my expectations were unrealistic and that I was hopelessly naïve. Joining the Bank at twenty-three, there was so much I didn't know. About the Middle Eastern and North African countries, for example. I knew nothing about the impact that French colonialism had had on North Africa, or why the discovery of oil in Saudi Arabia, Kuwait, and Abu Dhabi would change the world economic order. I didn't know that the Yemen Arab Republic became part of the modern world only a few years before I joined the World Bank. I had to admit that all I knew about Egypt was pyramids and sphinxes and what I'd learned about Tutankhamun, Akhenaten and the Sun God at the Smithsonian. I'd seen *Lawrence of Arabia* with Peter

O'Toole and *Casablanca* with Humphrey Bogart. From conversations around the family dinner table, I knew Israel was small and unprotected, always under attack by the Arab states, who I firmly believed were always wrong.

Eventually, I would travel for the World Bank to Egypt, Yemen, Tunisia, Morocco, and Israel, but in 1974, I knew next to nothing at all, except that I'd do my damnedest to prove Dyck wrong.

The Men

At the end of my first year at the Bank, my personnel officer called to tell me I'd passed the probation period. I was now "regular staff," and eligible to receive salary increases and promotions. Congratulations.

I mulled over what this meant. World Bank professionals were recruited internationally from among the best in their field. World Bank secretaries, on the other hand, were recruited locally. No matter what college degree a secretary held or how many languages she spoke, it would be virtually impossible to move from an administrative to a professional position. The *men* and the *girls*. Would a decent salary and generous benefits compensate for remaining a girl forever? I was glad I'd managed to put aside enough money to make a deposit at Georgetown's School of Interpretation and Translation. I didn't plan to be a secretary forever.

One afternoon, as I was typing the seventh version of a President's Report written by my loan officer boss, Achour Hadjadj, I sensed someone large, heavy, and out of breath approaching my desk.

"Yes?" I asked Nabil Faltas, the Egyptian economist for whom I also worked, as I continued to type.

"What are you doing?" Faltas asked, waving a sheaf of papers in my face.

"Finishing Hadjadj's president's report," I said, head down, still typing.

"Why do you always work for Hadjadj and not for me?"

At the Bank, the rule was two professionals to one secretary. Men like Faltas didn't like this ratio; men like Faltas wanted a secretary to themselves. Since I didn't like Hadjadj any more than I liked Faltas, I didn't play favorites. Still, presidents' reports took priority over other work, no matter whose they were.

Faltas, always red-faced and flustered, was now furious.

"I'm sick of this," he said, slamming his hand on my desk. "I want my half of you."

The other secretaries stopped typing.

I took my hands off the keyboard, stood up, and closed the gap between us. Although I was about half as wide as Faltas, I was at least three inches taller. I looked down at him, my mouth tight.

"Please tell me, Mr. Faltas, which half of me do you want? My arms or my legs?"

He turned on his heel and stormed out the door without another word.

Once he'd left, I looked around at the other secretaries, assuming they'd show some sign of approval, appreciation for how I'd stood up for myself, stood up for all of us. But none was forthcoming. The women kept typing and didn't say a word. Until then, I don't think I realized how irritating I could be to the other secretaries. Not just irritating, perhaps, but insulting. By suggesting that the men didn't have the right to lord it over us, to diminish us with their words and their manner, I was suggesting something about them, too. That perhaps I held them in contempt for accepting the men as they were. While this certainly wasn't my intention, it's more than likely that this was the reason that the secretaries—with the exception of Ghislaine—tended to avoid me.

"No more Faltas," I said to our division chief, Sani El Darwish, after my encounter with his countryman.

As of the following Monday, I no longer worked for Nabil Faltas. Nchour Hadjadj now shared me with a Sudanese economist named Fareed Atabani.

Fareed was portly with a warm smile. He wore custom-tailored suits and starched white shirts. His face was the color of charcoal and the shape of a ripe pear. He was an avuncular former economics professor in his fifties. I liked him immediately, but what if he were yet another elitist economist?

At our first meeting, Fareed asked me to sit down, to make myself comfortable, and to please call him by his first name. He poured us each a cup of tea.

"So, what's all this business about you and Faltas?"

I told him how rude and dismissive Faltas was, and how offensive to secretaries in general, and me, in particular. Constantly annoyed and complaining, he brought out the worst in me. I resented his insistence that in his country I'd have taken his work more seriously, been less casual, shown him more respect. But we were in America, weren't we? My country. And didn't my culture matter at all? Finally, I described our last run-in where the man insisted on his "half of me."

"That was enough, more than enough," I said. "I wasn't raised to be treated this way. The men in my family respect women."

Fareed nodded, smiling a bit sadly. "I'm sorry that you had to go through that, but I'm not surprised. Let's not talk about the Egyptian anymore. Let's talk about you."

From that first meeting, I knew Fareed Atabani was no Achour Hadjadj, Nabil Faltas, or Jim Dyck. As long as we worked together, I spent as much time sitting with him, just talking, as I did at my desk typing his reports. No matter how sexist his fellow economists, how unfriendly my fellow secretaries or how confusing my love life, conversations with Fareed always soothed me. We talked about his teaching career in Cambridge, his travels around the world, his children, and his wife, Bodour.

"My wife is a brilliant woman," he said once. "And modern." I may have looked a little surprised. I'd met her a couple of times in passing. She spoke softly, purred her words. She dressed conservatively, wrapped from head to toe in her traditional Sudanese *thawb*. As if reading my mind, Fareed laughed.

"Don't be fooled by her *thawb*. Or that she stays home with the kids. Bodour always does what suits her. She likes to wear a *thawb*, so she does. Once the kids are older, she'll go back to school, get a PhD."

Perhaps Bodour was the reason Fareed respected women, why he respected and encouraged me. It seemed likely. All the feminist men I knew—or would know in the future—had a profound respect for the women in their lives: mothers, wives, and daughters.

Every weekday morning at ten-thirty, I joined Fareed for coffee with four of his economist colleagues—a German, an Indian, an Iraqi, and a Pakistani. I'm not sure how the men around the table would have treated me had I not been there with Fareed, but they didn't seem to object to my presence. I laughed and listened intently to what they said about their work and the world. Their conversations filled in many gaps in the project documents and economic reports I'd been typing.

The men joked about the World Bank President Robert McNamara's American idealism. They made fun of his huge new programs, groaned about budget cuts and his latest unfunded mandate, and how his focus was always shifting. They wondered aloud what his priority would be that week: highways, health, the rural poor, the urban poor?

"What the hell isn't a priority?" asked the Pakistani.

"Pretty soon we'll have to give up fieldwork and appraise our projects at our desks in D.C.," said the Indian.

In many of these conversations over coffee, I was unnerved by the economists' cynicism, and their obvious dislike of Robert McNamara. But, of course, they weren't the only ones to dislike the man.

In the early 1960s, my parents loved Jack Kennedy and thought highly of all the brilliant young men who surrounded him, people like his secretary of defense, Robert McNamara. Although a pacifist in principle, my father bought into the domino theory—that if one country in a region came under the influence of communism, then surrounding countries would follow—and supported McNamara's war in Viet Nam. But as a pro-Robert Kennedy anti-war demonstrator in 1968, I was furious with him. For my friends and me, McNamara was the ultimate bad guy.

By the time I got to the Bank in 1974, however, McNamara was no longer secretary of defense. He'd been president of the World Bank for six years already. During those years, I hadn't heard much about him. I had known nothing about this international organization and certainly didn't know that he was shaking things up at the World Bank.

From my conversations with the economists, it was clear that McNamara was still making enemies. As he did at the Pentagon, he strode the halls of power with confidence. He was a technocrat with a genius for numbers. He was autocratic and lacked much in the way of diplomacy. Bigger was always better, and money was no object. He had a new mission at the World Bank, but the same personality and way of doing things as he'd always done.

"At least he's trying to make things better in the world, isn't he?" I asked, looking at the faces around the table. "Maybe he wants to redeem himself?"

"For how wrong he was about the war? For the thousands of people who died for no good reason?" asked the Iraqi.

The Pakistani looked at me in mock sorrow, shook his head. "Ah *Jerroise*, you are so young. Such an idealist. So American."

It was true. I was young and idealistic, but the men around the table liked me, anyway. I was at least ten years younger and several pay grades lower than them, but they didn't seem to hold it against me. They treated me with respect, enjoying my company and my conversation.

After a year of Faltas and Hadjadj, it felt like a miracle to be one of the boys, however cynical they were. Thanks to Fareed, I felt appreciated. I learned to hold my own. I joined in, though always under Fareed's watch-ful eye.

Fareed was fatherly in a way my dad wasn't. While my dad and I talked and laughed together like old college friends, Fareed treated me like a daughter who needed encouragement and a little looking after.

One afternoon with Fareed, I began my familiar rant: what's wrong with the men at the Bank? This time, he had an idea for me.

"Why not join the staff association?" he asked. "It's as close to a union as an international organization can have, and they have a working group on the status of women in the Bank. Why not put your outrage to good use?"

I wasted no time finding where and when the staff association's status of women working group (SWWG) met. Less than a week after my talk with Fareed, I was sitting in a stuffy, windowless conference room, eating lunch with a group of none-too-happy World Bank women. Being a third-generation working woman whose grandparents had fought for women's suffrage and whose parents had fought for women's reproductive rights, I joined the Bank thinking—erroneously—that the battle for women's rights had already been won. A couple of years at the World Bank had taught me otherwise. Still, I was a little put off by the women gathered for the SWWG meeting: a small, unsmiling British young woman, wearing a braid, who looked at me suspiciously from behind her cheese sandwich; an unnaturally thin, angular, blonde American who whined constantly; another intense American, who seemed perpetually furious; and a third, older woman of indeterminate nationality, who seemed sad all the time. The only optimistic one at the table was the SWWG chairperson, Diana, who did what she could to keep everyone's spirits up.

"We publish the SWWG report once a year, and no matter the statis-tics, nothing changes," said the angry American. "You can't convince World Bank men about anything."

"True enough," said Diana, with a laugh. "No man but Cliff!"

All the women around the table nodded their agreement. As the meeting continued, several of the women mentioned Cliff, and some good thing he'd said or done. "He is a rare find at the World Bank," one of the women observed. "A feminist man."

After the meeting broke up, Diana took me aside, asked what I thought of SWWG, and whether I'd like to join. Not yet sure how I felt about being part of this somewhat-unfriendly group, I muttered something noncommittal. Then I asked her about this guy, Cliff, they kept mentioning.

"You don't know Cliff?" she said. "The Patron Saint of the Liberated Woman? Wait here. I'll call him." She left me standing while she made a quick call.

"Done!" she said as she hung up the phone. "He said to tell you he'll be waiting for you tomorrow at noon at the park next to the Old Senate Office Building. He said to tell you he'll be the one with a rose in his teeth!"

The next day, I met Cliff Senf at the park for a picnic lunch. To my delight, he had a rose in his teeth. A feminist with a sense of humor. I loved it. That he was gorgeous didn't hurt, either.

We sat on a bench near a duck pond within view of the Washington Monument. For three hours, we munched sandwiches and swapped stories. He described running young men from New York to Canada to avoid the draft during the Viet Nam war. I told him about living in D.C. during the riots in 1968 after Martin Luther King's assassination. He described his tenant association's fight with the slum landlord. I told him about my father and the Black Employees of the Library of Congress. He told me about his divorce and his three-year-old son, who lived in New York with his ex-wife.

Cliff had joined the Bank after leaving a job teaching economics at American University, while studying for his PhD. He never finished his dissertation, realizing he could make more money as a researcher at the World Bank than he could as a university professor. A poor boy from a factory town, he was the first in his family to graduate from college. Even as a research assistant, he was already making more than his father had at the height of his career as a factory foreman. Cliff considered himself a Marxist, which may have had something to do with his progressive views about hierarchy and gender at the Bank. He reminded me a bit of the Dell men who raised me.

We walked around the duck pond in the sun and learned more about each other. When we got to the light at the corner, I didn't want to go back to work. I wanted to stand there and talk to him forever—this Marxist in Frye Boots with his big beard and deep-throated laugh.

We'd taken much too long a lunch "hour." We reluctantly said goodbye at the Bank flag entrance; he went on to the C building, and I to the E. It felt like the start of something new and exciting—almost too good to be true. I couldn't wait for him to call me.

He didn't call.

A week or so after my lunch with Cliff, I rushed through Fareed's office door without knocking, as was my habit, and dropped into the chair across from him.

"So, what's up?" he asked.

"I just passed Nabil Faltas in the hall. He acted like he didn't see me, like I wasn't there."

"You mean the Egyptian who wanted 'his half' of you?"

"Exactly," I said, starting to pace. "What is it about these Bank men? Why are they all such jerks?"

"All?" Fareed grinned.

"Well, almost all. What kind of place allows arrogance like this?"

Fareed stood up from his desk and removed a grey box labeled "The World Bank Versus Development" from the top shelf of his bookcase. He handed it to me.

"Take a look. I think you'll find you aren't the only casualty of arrogance running amok."

I pulled several envelopes from the box. Among them, I found a collection of newspaper articles and a packet of memoranda. I read the headlines and skimmed the memos. Each article told some of the Bank's story. The disaster of the Narmada Dam in India. Millions of dollars to governments that went missing with nothing to show for the money. Relocation schemes that trampled the rights of indigenous people. Bread riots in Cairo. And then, memos authorizing first-class travel for World Bank officials.

"Though management doesn't want to believe it, the Bank gets a lot of things wrong. Things you'll read about in those papers. I keep them to remind me what not to do, how not to be," said Fareed.

One afternoon, Fareed asked me, as he regularly did, for an update on how things were going.

"Okay, I guess," I said. "But sometimes the other secretaries drive me crazy. They kowtow to the men. Don't seem to have any self-respect at all."

"Not like you, then," said Fareed, drily.

"Of course not," I said, pulling my chair up closer to his desk. "What's more, it feels like they can't stand me. Whenever I try to start a conversation, they find something else to do. File papers. Answer the phone. Anything."

"But, my dear, aren't they simply doing their jobs?" Fareed was trying for lighthearted, but I ignored it.

"If I'm going to work here, I have to fit in. I need the women out there to like me. Right?"

"Has it occurred to you that you may never fit in? That you know this, and that they know it, too?"

I considered this. Maybe I was more comfortable with the men than the women. Ghislaine was the exception. But Ghislaine got along with everyone; she wasn't easily angered or even annoyed. Once I asked her if she thought I came across as arrogant. She looked confused. Why would they think that? But I think they did. I may well have come across to them as the Bank men came across to me. Maybe their hostility toward me made perfect sense. I hated to think so, but maybe.

"My advice?" said Fareed. "Be diplomatic. You won't be here forever."

I nodded. I had just made my deposit at Georgetown University, after all.

"In the meantime, if you want to talk to someone, talk to me."

Fareed and I discussed his work in Turkey, Cyprus, and Malta. He talked about how much he enjoyed getting out of the capital cities, traveling in the field, spending as much time away from government offices as possible, visiting villagers and farmers and listening to them. His passion for the field work was inspiring. I imagined what it might feel like to talk to people whose lives were so different from mine. To experience those villages.

"Economic growth in developing countries isn't enough. Not without social justice. But the Bank doesn't always see it this way," he said.

"No kidding," I said. This sounded like talk I was used to hearing in my family.

"When people like me draft reports that suggest different ways of working, our suggestions rarely see the light of day. By the time my draft goes through many layers of management review, it isn't remotely like the same report I wrote. It's enough to make a person cynical."

"Exactly," I said. "How can you stand it? Just talking about it gives me a stomachache."

Fareed laughed. "Hold on. I'm far enough along in my career to be cynical. You're at the beginning of yours. You still have enough time to change the Bank."

He had to be joking.

"Being smart isn't enough; you need the Bank to take you seriously. You need a plan," said Fareed. "And don't get a graduate degree in economics. You'd hate it. I can't even imagine you sitting behind a closed door, writing country economic reports. Get an MBA. It will give you all kinds of flexibility in what you can do later."

From the few economics classes I'd taken, I knew he was right about that part. But an MBA?

"I already have a plan," I said. I told Fareed about my visit to the United Nations at nine that inspired me to study French, go the university in Paris, become fluent in the French language, get a certificate in interpretation and translation at Georgetown, move to New York City, and become an interpreter for the UN.

"You decided this all at nine?" Fareed looked a little skeptical.

"Well, not every detail. But that's where it all began. I made up the plan as I learned more about how these kinds of things work. After I left Bard, I got a job here so I could afford to take classes at Georgetown. In fact," I confided, "I've just made my deposit to register for classes there."

Fareed let me talk.

"Then, a while after getting here, I realized I didn't have the vocabulary in English I'd need to translate from French to English for an international organization. I took a couple of economics courses and learned that I would probably never have the vocabulary."

"Well, this isn't the UN," said Fareed, finally, "but if working for an international organization was what you wanted, the World Bank ought to suffice. Don't you think? And you are already here. Why not let the World Bank work for you? Let it pay for you to get a graduate degree?"

"And maybe think about changing your plan," he continued. "Maybe what sounded exciting when you were nine years old isn't really exciting now that you're an adult. Why would you want to translate somebody else's words? Wouldn't that be a lot like typing somebody else's words? Maybe translating would be no more satisfying than typing."

Within a week of our conversation, I withdrew my registration. It hurt to forfeit the deposit, but I knew it was time for another plan. Instead, I enrolled in the MBA program at George Washington University. And the World Bank paid for my education.

Alone

Shortly after Christmas 1976, Ghislaine proposed we go to Quebec to visit her sister and to ski. While Ghislaine talked about renting skis and teaching me whatever I needed to know, I imagined myself tumbling headlong into trees, breaking both my legs in several places. She had no idea that as brave as I seemed to be when it came to speaking up, I had never been on skis, and the idea terrified me.

In Quebec City, Ghislaine's older sister kissed us warmly on both cheeks, asked about our lives in Washington and treated us to a delicious *tourtiere* meat pie. After three hours and more than enough wine, we collapsed on our air mattresses. Ghislaine fell asleep at once; I lay wide awake, imagining ski slopes and broken limbs. When her sister knocked on the door, Ghislaine woke instantly, refreshed and eager to start her day. I was a zombie.

"*Je suis desolée*," she said. "Things aren't looking good for today. It's ten degrees below zero—too cold and windy to ski the mountain. They've closed the lift."

Ghislaine groaned her disappointment. As for me, I could not have been happier.

The next night, after a frigid day of sightseeing, I slept for about three hours, then woke up sobbing from a terrible dream. My grandmother, B. Marie, was in her bed, fighting for breath, and losing the fight. I tried to make her stop flailing but couldn't get hold of her hand.

My father's mother, B. Marie, was the woman I always imagined I'd grow up to be. A free spirit, she was a young socialist from the Midwest who graduated from the University of Wisconsin. After a few years doing social work in New York City, she met my grandfather, Floyd Dell, managing editor of the *Masses* magazine in Greenwich Village. Together my grandparents marched down Fifth Avenue waving banners and shouting, "votes for women!"

While Floyd wrote and published a dozen novels, B. Marie worked for Near East Relief and raised their two sons. In the 1930s, the Dells moved to Washington, D.C., where Floyd worked for the Federal Writers Project of the Works Progress Administration (WPA), an agency of FDR's New Deal, and B. Marie went to work for the D.C. public library as a children's librarian. Twenty years later, my young parents left Goddard College in Vermont, where I was born, to live in Washington, D.C., where they both worked to save enough money to buy a small house. Until I started school, I spent as much time with B. Marie and Floyd as I did with my parents.

Like B. Marie, I loved to read and tell stories. Thanks to B. Marie, I stood up straight. She paid for ballet lessons. "Tall girls like us must learn good posture," she said. She even encouraged me to twirl a baton, to march in parades as a majorette. "Eyes up, shoulders back," she said. "That's it!" she encouraged me as I practiced my routines. B. Marie taught me how lucky I was and taught me to care about people who weren't so lucky. I was B. Marie's biggest fan, and she was mine.

But as I slept in Canada, B. Marie was dying in Washington, D.C. I saw her in my dream. I knew it without being told. Our connection was too strong for her to die without my knowing. Ghislaine knew something was wrong, but when she asked why I woke up crying, I couldn't tell her about the dream. I didn't want to reveal my sixth sense about B. Marie. I told her instead that I had had a dream about getting old and losing the people I loved.

"Don't worry." Ghislaine said, trying to cheer me up. "We won't get old. Even if we do, we'll be together, running wheelchair races in the corridors of our nursing home. It'll be fun!" Sometimes I wished I could see the world the carefree way Ghislaine did.

After breakfast, I called my mother and asked about B. Marie. She let out a long breath and told me what I knew already: B. Marie was gone.

The spring after my grandmother died, I spent my annual leave at her summer house in Richmond, New Hampshire. I loved everything about the house in New Hampshire on Whipple Hill Road, with its front door on the side that nobody used, and the side door at the front that nobody locked. It was a quirky old house with no right angles. B. Marie's kitchen was lemon yellow, her chairs were painted orange, and the doors were navy blue. Her prized Mexican plates were badly chipped and none of them matched. Off the kitchen was the dining room, where we'd eat at a narrow wooden table Floyd had built himself, a living room with Adirondack chairs and a faded mural of a tree in autumn, and B. Marie's sitting room, with its old woodstove, worn-out easy chair, and painting by Bror Nordfeldt of four nudes bathing in a waterfall. Upstairs was a rabbit warren of rooms for sleeping, sitting, and studying.

It felt good to be back on Whipple Hill. Although I was alone in the house, the place was crowded with ghosts from my grandparents' past: the artists and writers who visited them there in the 1930s and '40s; the poet Edna St. Vincent Millay; photographers; painters. Their guests included the famous and the not-so-famous, who sometimes stayed at the house for months during the Great Depression. Those who couldn't afford to pay for room or board often left paintings or sculptures as payment instead. The ghosts included the farmers who stopped in to deliver eggs and stayed to chat, and the itinerant carpenters and handymen who showed up regularly when they were hungry and needed to make a bit of money.

By the time I was born, B. Marie and Floyd had fewer guests, and I was on my own to find friends. The only person my age was Marie, pretty and slight, who lived with her parents and three brothers across the road in a weather-beaten cabin with a big stone chimney. When my grandmother gave us pails to go berry picking, Marie knew just where to take me. She knew the fields and forests much better than I did, and where the blueberry bushes were. Sometimes I was jealous that Marie had brothers and I didn't, that she was free to roam the countryside all year long.

"No cause to be jealous," said B. Marie. "Little Marie's life isn't so easy. Her mother was only fifteen when she married old Dad Shinn. She had four babies by the time she was twenty. No chance for an education, she had to take in laundry and look after those kids by herself. Dad Shinn is at least seventy-five now and hasn't had a job as long as I can remember."

I promised my grandmother I'd try not to be jealous.

Marie always came to our house to see me, never the other way around. She liked following me from room to room as I played tour guide, telling her authoritatively what a good artist Nordfeldt was, pointing to his paintings of naked ladies on our walls, which made Marie blush. On rainy days, I brought Marie to our tall toy closet, stood on the stepladder and took out board games. She could never believe how many toys I had. I tried to give some to her, but she said no, she'd better not. B. Marie told me later that Marie's mother was too proud to let her accept gifts. Charity. When I insisted it wasn't charity, because Marie was my friend and I was just sharing, B. Marie agreed, but said, "It doesn't matter what we think. What matters is what Marie and her family think." I learned a lot about poverty, kindness, and pride on Whipple Hill.

Back in the house decades later, B. Marie and all those memories lived on. For two weeks that summer, I scrubbed floors, washed windows, and beat rugs. I made gingham curtains for all the windows. Since my father had inherited the house, it would be up to him to decide what to do with it. I hoped I could make it too beautiful for him to give it up. I couldn't bear to lose B. Marie and her house, too.

I returned to work. Months passed. I kept typing and filing and answering phones. I took night classes toward my MBA. I struggled with statistics and learned about a new IBM mainframe computer—the wave of the future. I spent vacations with Ghislaine in California and in Canada and danced at her parties.

A year-and-a-half after my grandmother died, I returned to the house on Whipple Hill again. My father and stepmother Kate still hadn't sold it, and I harbored the hope they never would, however unlikely that was. Kate didn't like the mountains. She wanted a cottage by the sea, and my dad was inclined to give Kate what she wanted.

"Don't you remember?" I had said to my father a few months back, on the verge of tears. "B. Marie always said this house would stay in the family forever."

He shook his head. "No, she always said her children should do with their inheritance whatever they wanted. She believed parents didn't have the right to make that decision for them."

"When she said that, she must have meant the money she left as your inheritance. Not our house."

"It's my house," my father reminded me. "If I choose to sell it, that's my decision."

For once, my pleas had no effect at all. It was the only serious disagreement my father and I ever had. So, on this second solitary visit to the house, nothing seemed quite right. Having made it beautiful the year before, there was little to do. Other than to reconnect with B. Marie, I wasn't sure why I was there. I couldn't put the fight with my father out of my mind. Still, I loved being there, remembering B. Marie and my friends on Whipple Hill, most of whom—other than Marie Shinn—were what B. Marie called "your old ladies."

When I was seven, one of those friends was a retired doctor, Marion Freeman. Marion had steel-grey hair and wore tan trousers, short-sleeved white shirts, and sensible shoes. She was a serious person who talked about medicine, science, and the law, while I did my best to follow along. I was honored when she asked my opinion on important matters, and when she listened intently as I offered them at length. Her shelves were lined with books that my grandfather Floyd had written, which made me proud.

During one of our visits, as I ate oatmeal cookies, drank orange juice, and asked Marion questions, we were interrupted by a knock on the door. Marion got up and stood on the stoop, talking to a girl I didn't know. The girl mumbled something and left. Marion slammed the door behind her. Replying to a question I hadn't asked, Marion said, "That's the urchin who cleans for me," and glared at the door. I'd never seen Marion this way.

I didn't know what an urchin was, but I didn't ask Marion to explain. Instead, I asked what the girl did to make her so mad.

"Yesterday, my silver candy dish went missing," she replied. "I told the girl to go to Skunk Hollow and find out who took it. That was her back to tell me no one in Skunk Hollow knew anything about it."

"Where's Skunk Hollow?" I asked.

"Oh, you know where it is? Down below your grandparents' place, where all the good-for-nothing Tullocks live in their burnt-out cars, drinking beer and getting girls in trouble."

I was shocked to learn about a place like that so close to us. If Skunk Hollow was as bad as all that, I was surprised B. Marie had never told me about it. After saying goodbye to Marion, I ran all the way down the gravel road to our house where B. Marie was shucking corn. When she asked about my visit to the "old ladies," I told her they were fine, then blurted: "Why didn't you ever tell me about Skunk Hollow? You know, down the road where the Tullocks live."

B. Marie stopped shucking corn and looked at me hard.

"I don't know what you mean," she said. "Yes, the Tullock family lives down the road. I know nothing about a Skunk Hollow."

I protested, "It's just that—"

She stopped me. "Don't tell me any more about this," she said. "You know young John Tullock, don't you? Is he a skunk? Does he stink?"

I thought about the tall, shy, sixteen-year-old boy with strong shoulders and only one arm who'd been up at the farm yesterday, looking for work. B. Marie hired him to lay some new linoleum in the kitchen. I felt my body crumple.

"But I never said John stunk. I didn't mean anything by calling it Skunk Hollow."

"You may not have meant it, but to call the Tullock's place 'Skunk Hollow' is ignorant and mean." B. Marie taught me a lot about not being mean.

After a quiet week of mopping, dusting, and missing my grandmother, I got ready to leave for Washington. After packing the car, I grabbed my camera and walked from room to room, upstairs and down, taking pictures. B. Marie's house would always be my house, too.

On my drive home, I stopped in North Adams, Massachusetts, to visit a weaver who worked at an arts co-op in an old riverfront factory building. She greeted me warmly and made us a pot of tea. While we drank it, she described the co-op—how it started, how it was organized, and the craftspeople who worked there. She talked about the community of young people who made these beautiful objects. We talked about their communal meals and meetings to discuss how to earn a living without "going corporate." She described the work involved in turning the old mill into art studio space and the process by which artists were chosen to share that space. It wasn't just their artistic skill that counted, she explained, it was their philosophy of life—cooperation rather than competition. I longed for more of that in my own life.

When she asked me how I happened to be in New England, I explained about my Bohemian grandparents and their house on Whipple Hill. And all the reasons I loved it so much. I described the artists and craftspeople I knew in New Hampshire and those I'd known in New York, when I was still a student. How I'd been an art major, but switched over to French literature, and wasn't sure I'd made the right choice. I never told her I worked for the World Bank. I assumed that like most Americans, she knew nothing about my employer. Or if she did, didn't like what she knew. I knew I'd have to defend it against attack, which was the last thing I was thinking about while on vacation in New England.

It was peaceful at the co-op by the river. I realized I was tired of working for a vast international bureaucracy all day and studying international finance at night. I was tired of living in a self-important, buttoned-down city. I remembered B. Marie's stories about being young in Greenwich Village and imagined how much she'd love this place where weavers wore Birkenstocks. Two hours went by, then another. I realized it was getting late. I had a long drive home and had to be at work in the morning. As I finally stood up to leave, my new friend said: "It gets cold here in the winter and the pay isn't much, but would you like to stay here and manage our shop for us?"

God, yes. I thought how much I'd love to manage this shop, live with these weavers by the river. I already had a job in Washington, though, and while there was plenty about the Bank I didn't like, I wasn't ready to leave it behind. Not yet. I'd think it over, I told her, and call her when I got back to D.C.

As I drove home, I thought about the crafts co-op, the work I was doing in the World Bank, how much I wanted Kate not to sell the house on Whipple Hill. I imagined moving to the Berkshires, forgetting the MBA, advocating for craftswomen like the young weaver I'd just met. Maybe I'd learn to weave myself, or throw pots, or paint. Why not? I ramped up the volume on my radio. A favorite rock song blared its refrain: "Burn, baby, burn." I bounced in my seat, drummed the heels of my hands on the steering wheel, sang along to the radio at the top of my lungs.

"Burn, baby, burn."

Oddly, I began to sweat. I smelled smoke. It had to be my imagination. The power of suggestion. The song on the radio. The car got hotter, and the smell of smoke didn't disappear. I turned into the next rest stop and parked. The heat and smell of smoke subsided, but when I closed my eyes, I saw a house consumed by flame.

When I entered my apartment a few hours later, the phone was ringing. On the other end of the line, my father told me to sit down. Then he said, "A few hours ago, B. Marie's house caught fire. The fire truck couldn't get up the hill fast enough to save it. It burned to the ground." I gasped, shut my eyes, and saw the house in flames again.

"Floyd used to say that B. Marie had special powers," said my father. "He said she was a psychic. Maybe she hated our argument and burned the house down to put an end to it."

I needed my father more than the house. Maybe B. Marie was right to burn it down.

Two months after the fire, the ringing of the phone brought me bad news again. This time it was Bodour, Fareed's wife, on the other end. "Fareed's had a heart attack. We are at Suburban Hospital in Bethesda. Come quickly."

I grabbed my keys and ran for the car. I could hardly breathe. At hospital reception, I was directed to the intensive care unit, but there I was told that only family was allowed to visit the patient. I told the nurse that I was a member of the family. She looked dubious but gave me the room number, anyway.

I met Bodour outside the door of Fareed's room. We hugged tightly. Usually sturdy and sparkling, Fareed's wife suddenly seemed frail. She was wrapped, as always, from head to ankle in a soft white *thawb* that covered her tunic and skirt. Greeting me in a whisper, she told me to go into the room and see Fareed. I explained that only family was allowed in the room. She instantly removed her *thawb,* wrapped it around me, and pushed me gently through the door.

Fareed lay on the bed, his face ashen, eyes half-closed, arms connected to tubes attached to machines. I took his hand. He blinked twice, and his eyes fluttered open.

He said in a muffled voice, "You're here."

I patted his hand and told him to rest, but he was already asleep again. I went out to the hall to join Bodour.

"The doctor tells me he will live, *In shallah*," she said.

We hugged again. I unwrapped the *thawb* from around me and returned it to Bodour. I could barely speak. The tears didn't come in a torrent until I got in the car. A combination of grief and rage. How could my Fareed do this? How could he let the World Bank almost kill him?

The heart attack didn't kill Fareed. But he resigned from the Bank, and he and Bodour moved back to Sudan.

I was on my own.

Without Fareed, I did the best I could. But it never seemed to be enough. I continued to attend the SWWG meetings. I had come to appreciate the group, even if the women were often angry, irritable, and self-righteous. They had a right to be. SWWG women seemed to be the only ones at the World Bank who drew attention to gender discrimination and talked about feminism in political terms. In the beginning, I hoped working with SWWG would make me feel better about being at the Bank. I was getting my credentials to make up for all I hadn't learned as an undergraduate. I'd passed probation and had a permanent World Bank position. I'd gotten three pay increases in two years. I was working toward an MBA. I should be feeling proud of myself. Then why did my stomach hurt all the time?

Maybe Jim Dyck had been right. Despite the progress I'd made, maybe it was unrealistic to think I could make anything of myself at the World Bank. I was not World Bank material. My grandparents were Greenwich Village socialists, writers, librarians, and teachers. I didn't belong in the world of international finance and all the highfliers from "fancy" families from around the world. I knew nothing about economics or finance. I didn't go to Stanford or the University of Chicago. I hadn't competed with the "best and the brightest" to enter the Bank through the young professional program. Why was I still pursuing a path that was clearly wrong for me? Maybe my chronic stomachaches were telling me something.

Several months after I had started working for Fareed, a young Pakistani economist, Arshad Zaman, had joined the division, and became my second boss. Arshad was closer to my age than to Fareed's. His thick blue-black hair was stylishly long, and he dressed in well-tailored, pinstriped suits. He wore glasses meant to be clear when he was indoors and dark when he went outside. They remained, however, permanently dark, which lent him an air of mystery. Much to his delight, I began to refer to him as the "Prince of Darkness." He began to call me *Jerroise*, adopting Fareed's other Pakistani friend's joking reference to my fluency in French, whenever I had joined Fareed and his economist friends for coffee in the morning.

Like many of Fareed's friends, Arshad was cynical about working for the World Bank. "It looks good on a résumé," he said. "But that's about it. The longer I work here, the less confident I am that I have anything to offer."

According to Arshad, once a young professional had spent a few years in the Bank, he was good for nothing else. He lost his identity and became part of the bureaucratic Bank machine. Arshad never expected to make a career at the Bank. He was there to learn how it did business, then use this knowledge when he returned to Pakistan. He was serious about development, but cynical about the Bank.

This was not what I wanted to hear. I wanted to believe I could do some good, even if I did work for the World Bank.

After I'd worked with Arshad for a year it was time for him to complete my annual performance report (APR). Staff members were expected to complete part one of the APR, in which we elaborated on what we had achieved in the past year. The supervisors completed part two, which was their assessment of our performance.

Unfortunately for me, Arshad viewed the process differently. He wanted me to fill in both my parts and his. Filling out his part was a misery. When I finished, I gave the completed APR to Arshad. He told me to sit down while he read it. Clasping my hands in my lap, I watched him. He stopped smiling; I clasped tighter. By the time he finished reading, I was in a state. Arshad put the paper on his desk and looked at me curiously.

"Why are you so hard on yourself? You did a perfectly good job last year, and yet here you are pointing out only the ways you think you let me down. You give yourself no credit at all. Is it me? Do you think I'd write these things about you?"

"Well, maybe. I've never been quite sure what you thought," I said.

"But why would I say such negative things?"

"Let's face it, Arshad. I'm a pretty lousy secretary. There's always a big pile of paper I haven't filed. I type fast, but I'm inaccurate. I'm terrible with detail."

"Okay, that's all true. But so what? You are articulate and smart. You work fast and never refuse to do the work I give you, and you're great company."

"I'm paid to be a secretary, though, not to be great company."

"Okay. Maybe it's time for you to start applying for a different kind of job. I'll miss you, but it's time to get you out of here."

Fareed had passed the baton to Arshad, and he'd accepted it. Arshad believed in me, and he was kind enough to say so.

Growing up, I had taken for granted that men expected women to take the lead. It came as a shock to me when they didn't. It wasn't until World Bank sexism hit me broadside that I began to understand how rare my upbringing had been. Bank culture reflected the greatest common denominator of sexism worldwide: European, British, Latin American, Arab, Asian, and American. Even worse than Bank sexism was Bank elitism. It wasn't enough to be a college graduate, one must have studied economics or finance, graduated with a doctorate from one of the world's most prestigious universities. While the Bank claimed a diverse staff, the fact was that, irrespective of nationality, most of its staff were graduates of

Harvard, Stanford, University of Chicago, Wharton Business School, or the London School of Economics.

I wasn't an Ivy Leaguer, but had been lucky enough to go to Bard College as a scholarship student, and with some help from B. Marie, thanks to money she'd inherited from a wealthy friend. In the '60s and '70s, Bard had been a hippie school. During my years there, it offered one course in economics and nothing in business or finance. The literature, philosophy, and art classes I took were of little help to me at the World Bank. The classes I'd taken at George Washington University for my MBA in international finance had been, to my mind, a "necessary evil."

I graduated from George Washington in August 1977. Fareed would have been proud, but Fareed was in Sudan and I wasn't sure exactly why I'd bothered to get an MBA or why I was still working for the World Bank. I prepared my résumé, sent it out, and got quite a few calls back. Two interviews later, though, I knew I didn't want to do the work my graduate degree had prepared me for. I didn't want to work for an American corporation. After three years at an international organization, Americans seemed ordinary, bland, and boring. I loved the variety among World Bank staff.

Even when the Bank infuriated me, it was still the devil I knew.

In addition to interviewing for outside jobs, I kept an eye on the Bank's vacancy posting system. After a couple of months, I applied for a new position as operations assistant in the agriculture division in the Bank's Middle East and North Africa region. It wasn't a professional position, but it required an MBA and offered an office with a door that closed. Within a week of applying, I was working for a Canadian water resources engineer responsible for something called the Egypt Water Master Plan.

The Master Plan project was financed by the United Nations Development Programme (UNDP) and executed by the World Bank. Long- and short-term consultants did all the work in Cairo. At headquarters in Washington, D.C., my new boss, Dick Heiges, and I coordinated everything within the Bank, taking care of the things that the consultants couldn't handle in Cairo. Dick was a water engineer, frustrated with how unimportant he was in this job. He liked being the boss when he was with the consultants in Cairo—even when he knew much less than they did. In Washington, he liked being my boss, too.

That was all right with me. At least I wasn't typing or filing for him. Since I had more work as his administrator than he had as my supervisor, I was busy and happy most of the time.

Dick went to Cairo several times a year and inevitably reported how well things were going to our division chief, Peter Naylor, a gentle soul from the south of England who had no reason to doubt anything he said. I, however, regularly received calls from the consultants in Cairo saying that things were not going well at all. Whenever I raised their issues with him, Dick shook his head and called them "whiners" and "babies." He made it clear that he didn't want to hear about anything they said. He wanted to be left alone to do his "real" job. If supporting the expatriates in the field wasn't his real job, though, I wasn't sure what was.

But who was I to judge? I knew nothing about water resource management, irrigation engineering, agricultural economics, or fisheries. I had been hired to help Dick Heiges. Nothing more than that. I'd gotten a promotion, for which I was grateful. What difference did it make how stuffy and self-satisfied he was?

The calls from Cairo kept coming. Shipments were delayed—if they arrived at all. Housing was inadequate. There didn't seem to be anyone around to fix anything that needed fixing. Dick said he'd follow up, but he never did. The expatriates and their wives were fed up with the Bank and they didn't hesitate to tell me about it, since telling him did no good at all.

Dick complained to me about the expatriates in Cairo. So needy. The expats complained to me about Dick. So bossy. So unhelpful. Every week there was a harder edge to the conversations I overheard through the wall between Dick and the team leader in Cairo. It got to the point where Dick slammed the phone down whenever he finished talking with any of the expats.

I offered to intermediate. I managed to get the expats paid on time, followed up on shipments, and scurried around doing the work Dick thought was beneath him. The men in the field came to think of me as the one in charge in Washington. One afternoon, through the wall that separated us, I overheard Dick tell someone on the phone that "his girl would handle it." Four years at the World Bank and an MBA, I was still some man's girl.

No matter how hard I worked, I was going nowhere. I even remembered with fondness my days as Fareed Atabani's and Arshad Zaman's secretary. At least he believed in me, and treated me with respect.

One evening in November, the fourth in a row that I was working late in the office, I was feeling particularly down. I was halfway through my annual performance report, but didn't have the heart to finish. I started a letter to Fareed, but didn't get past the first paragraph. I tried listing international organizations where I might apply for another job. I was tired of Dick Heiges. Disappointed in myself. What was I doing here?

Work wasn't much fun, but there wasn't a lot to look forward to at home, either. I no longer had to study for school. Ghislaine spent most evenings with her new heartthrob. My father and Kate had moved to Florida. My mother, who lived nearby, was too busy to talk. I sat in my windowless office, staring dully at the closed door. In two years, I'd lost B. Marie, then her house in New Hampshire, then Fareed. An MBA and a new job, even an office with a door that closed, didn't begin to make up for all those losses. I hadn't slept well for weeks. I crossed my arms on my desk and put my head down, willing myself to sleep.

A knock on my office door jolted me back to life. Lifting my head, I tried to think who'd still be at the office this late. Another knock. The door opened slowly to reveal the tall, bearded Marxist in Frye boots: Cliff Senf, the Patron Saint of the Liberated Woman, the man who had never called back.

"May I come in?" he asked, smiling.

Home

Our first evening together, Cliff Senf greeted me at the door of his house in a red-and-white striped apron, a dish towel flung over his shoulder.

"Love the look," I said, nodding at his midsection.

"Yeah?" He lifted the apron's bottom edge, turned once, and curtsied. The sight of this bearded, bear-like man doing a pirouette made me giggle. I was glad I had accepted his dinner invitation.

Cliff gave me a glass of Chardonnay and led me to his tiny kitchen. Pot roast, potatoes, and carrots simmered deliciously. At the table, we tore off pieces of crusty French bread, devoured the roast, and sipped red wine. We talked about Niagara Falls, the factory town where he grew up. We talked about my childhood in Washington, D.C., my summers in New Hampshire, my socialist grandparents, my speechwriter father. I talked about poetry; he talked about opera. He made fun of his little box of a house, but I loved it: the round oak table set for two; the floor-to-ceiling bookshelves on either side of the brick fireplace; the rust-and-orange Danish rug.

While I washed the dinner dishes, Cliff pulled apple dumplings from the oven, sugar syrup bubbling in the pan. He served us each a dumpling with a scoop of vanilla ice cream. We kept on talking. He told me about his father who died young, a factory foreman, the wisest of four brothers, the one they all turned to for advice.

After dessert, fully sated, I stretched out on the rug; Cliff brought us a second bottle of red wine.

"I've got something I want you to hear," he said. "Do you know the composer Ralph Vaughn Williams?"

I shook my head.

"Listen." He placed the needle gently on the record and joined me on the rug in front of the fire. We closed our eyes.

A solo violinist. A bird circling, soaring. Wistful. Sad. Suspended in time until flute, oboe, horns amplified the sound. A triangle trilled. The violin alone, again. The bird alone, again, its song filling the sky. Beyond joyful. Pure. Such exquisite sweetness. Then, silence. I opened my eyes and looked at Cliff. How could I not love a man who loved this music?

A week later, I began thinking more practically about Cliff. Was it possible he wasn't like the other men who'd come and gone from my life since I joined the Bank? Men from Tunisia, France, Turkey, Australia? Men who found me sexy, and occasionally noticed I was smart, as well? Could this man be as passionate as he seemed about music and politics and me?

By Thanksgiving, we'd spent three weekends together, lying in front of the fire, drinking wine, sharing our life stories. He told me about the winter he was working in construction and his glove froze to the back of a Mack truck. He couldn't pull his hand out in time to save it from being crushed. He lost a finger and spent a year on disability. He spent the next year reading whatever the library had to offer. Disability insurance paid his college tuition. It allowed him—the son of a factory foreman—to escape Niagara Falls and eventually teach economics at Clarkson College. His missing finger also kept him out of Viet Nam.

Cliff spent Thanksgiving in Potsdam, New York, with his son, Christian. I spent mine with a dozen Dells, none of whom I told about this older man, a political radical who loved opera. It was too soon to know where this relationship might lead. I also remembered how he had never called after our first wonderful lunch together. To my relief, this time he called as soon as he returned from New York, and invited me to another dinner at his place. As we ate, we continued the conversation as if we'd never been apart. He talked about Potsdam, the son he adored, and his ex-wife, Ellie. He told me they'd moved to Virginia as a family to allow him to teach economics at American University.

"Soon after we got here, I fell for someone else. A student. I moved out to live with her," he explained. He described the poor neighborhood where he and his girlfriend had lived in D.C. and the long bus rides he took to and from Arlington to spend time with Christian. Then his ex-wife, Ellie, had moved back to Potsdam with Christian. Cliff returned to the house he'd lost in the divorce, the house we were in now, renting it from Ellie.

That night, we listened to Mahler's Resurrection Symphony. I knew nothing about Mahler, but Cliff loved him. I wondered about this fondness for such moody, sometimes morose, music, with the lower strings dominating, the orchestra almost shrieking. I watched as he sat, eyes closed, conducting the orchestra, slicing the air with an invisible baton, absolutely absorbed. Was he elevated by, or identifying with, Mahler's grandeur, power, excess?

Cliff spent Christmas with Christian in Potsdam. I was disappointed and a little jealous that I wouldn't be spending the holiday with him, but I understood. He made it home for New Year's Eve.

When Cliff asked what I'd like for dinner to celebrate the new year, I didn't hesitate. I wanted escargots, lobster, *salade vinaigrette*, and strawberry tart—the same meal I'd eaten with my boyfriend Larry on New Year's Eve in Paris in 1970, a memory I treasured. So Cliff made me a beautiful lobster dinner. We drank Prosecco. I regaled him with stories about my year as a student in Paris. How hard it was to get an education there as the students tried to recreate the revolutionary days of 1968, the worker-student uprising. *Anarchistes. Marxistes. Trotskyists.* Political tracts flying.

Ferocious policemen in riot gear appearing at the university. Kids shouting, threatening to jump out of windows. "It was all a little much," I told him. "So, I spent many afternoons reading Stendhal, Flaubert, and Balzac in the café across the street from the university."

After dinner, my eyes began to itch. My face swelled, then my eyes almost disappeared. My head throbbed. Sometime since that meal in Paris, it appeared, I'd become allergic to shellfish.

Cliff gave me Benadryl, covered my face with a cold, wet washcloth, lay me gently on his bed, spoke in soothing tones, and told me funny stories. Gradually, the swelling went down, my eyes reappeared, and I was ready to welcome 1978. Lying on Cliff's large bed in his small bedroom on the second floor of his little house, we watched the revelers in Times Square celebrate the start of the new year.

Earlier that year, Cliff invited me to attend a staff development committee (SDC) meeting he chaired. The director of personnel would be there, he said, and I could get a sense of what the man was like, since I might have to deal with Personnel myself if I continued to work with SWWG. The subject of the meeting was the print shop staff. Cliff had spent a lot of time talking with my old friend, Dan Johnson, the print supervisor, about his team. Virtually none of the print shop operators spoke English. When he tried to get English-language training for them, Personnel told him that it wasn't a priority. When he tried to reward high-performing staff with salary increases or promotions, Personnel refused, explaining that print shop operators couldn't speak English, lacked education and training, and the opportunity to do anything else. I was familiar with these issues; we'd talked many times about the struggles the operators faced. I was very curious to see how Cliff would mediate this seemingly unresolvable conflict.

That day's SDC meeting—like all my SWWG meetings—took place in a windowless conference room. Unlike our SWWG meetings, however, this room was packed. Cliff liked a challenge, wasn't afraid of Management, and got things done. People loved watching him work.

By the time I sat down, Cliff was already kidding around with the director of personnel and the chief of the staff training division, as if they'd been friends for years. They hadn't, but Cliff was good at putting them at ease. He knew that in order to be taken seriously he had to use logic and make a strong argument—and avoid offending anyone. For an hour, Cliff and the senior managers went back and forth, making their points, asking and answering questions. Cliff invited others in the room to make their positions known. By the time the meeting was over, the personnel director had agreed to offer print-shop staff as much English-language and other job-related training as they needed, and to make the issue of grade and salary increases for the staff a priority of the upcoming support staff development review. After the personnel men left, people crowded around Cliff, full of thanks. He was their hero. Mine, too.

I watched Cliff perform feats like this, again and again. He wasn't loud, but he was insistent. His broad shoulders, his beard, his way of leaning in to confide the truth to a whole room of people—all that combined to make him a compelling presence. Convincing Personnel to invest time and effort in support staff—whether print-shop workers or messengers, clerk-typists or administrative secretaries—was something he taught me to do, too.

Even better, he was a feminist in the spirit of my father and grandfather. He believed in me and encouraged me. Cliff helped me get over the loss of my grandmother, her house in New Hampshire, and my mentor Fareed Atabani. He was happy for my successes and glad to be the man behind the successful woman. He truly was the Patron Saint of the Liberated Woman.

Meanwhile, I still worked for Dick Heiges, ran interference for the expatriates in Cairo, attended meetings of the staff association, visited my parents, and spent time with Ghislaine. But with Cliff in my life, everything else seemed like a distraction. My biggest worry was how cautious Cliff seemed about getting too close. We were always together on the weekends, but what about the rest of the week? I didn't want to make a big deal about it. What liberated woman would expect—or even want—to spend seven days a week with her boyfriend? Still, it bothered me, and the only thing I could think was that his marriage scared him off too much intimacy. No matter how trustworthy I was, he was unlikely to trust another woman again for some time. Fair enough, weekends were fine.

Two of my closest friends in college, Penelope and Jamie, had been a couple since our sophomore year and were living together in New York City. Penelope and I shared a late-March birthday, which we decided to share with Jamie and Cliff in Arlington.

We were a perfect foursome and the weekend was wonderful: we drank wine; Cliff cooked; Penelope, Jamie, and I sang. When it was time for them to leave, I drove them to Union Station to catch their train for New York.

On the way, I stopped at a light and began fiddling with the radio dial. Penelope batted my hand away. "No radio," she said. "Tell me . . . what's the deal with Cliff? Why don't you live together?"

"Haven't a clue," I said.

After dropping them off, I headed to my apartment in Georgetown, thinking about how I hadn't had an answer for Penelope. I parked, slammed the car door shut behind me, and sped into the building and through the lobby. I hammered the button for the elevator and took it to the seventh floor. In my apartment, I heaped clothes, cosmetics, and a hairbrush, plus some books and papers, into two large suitcases, picked up the bags, flipped the light switch off, and stumbled out the door. Twenty minutes later, I was standing on the front porch of Cliff's house, holding two suitcases. My knees trembled, and my heart beat way too fast. I rang the bell. Cliff opened the door, looked at me, then down at my bags.

"I'm here," I said. "To stay."

Cliff reached down, picked up the bags, and held the door open for me. "Welcome home."

By spring 1978, with Cliff cheering me on, I continued to attend the SWWG meetings, but was growing ever more frustrated with how powerless the women felt. After joining us at one of these meetings, Cliff sat me down with a glass of wine before dinner.

"I hate to say it, but SWWG's a disaster," he said. "Unless you shake it up, nothing will change. The only way to do that is to get yourself elected chair of the group."

I wasn't sure I had the confidence to manage that group, but I agreed that things probably wouldn't change if I didn't. Perhaps at Cliff's suggestion, Diana invited me to lunch and told me she'd be stepping down. She thought I'd be the perfect one to replace her, and she'd lobby for me to get the job. She must have been very convincing, as I was elected chair by acclamation. Now it was up to me to try to turn things around. Diana wished me luck.

As long as I'd belonged to SWWG, we'd been polling World Bank staff at least once a year to determine the demand for on-site childcare. Every six months, we circulated a questionnaire, and every six months, we wrote a report summarizing our conclusions.

The arguments were pretty obvious. Lack of adequate childcare was creating problems not just for mothers but also for their colleagues and bosses. Not everyone could have someone at home to take care of the children. The Bank was losing good secretaries once they had babies, and an on-site childcare center would help reduce that. If they could count on care for their children and be able to see them at lunchtime, they would be more likely to continue working after they gave birth. If they didn't have to worry about missing work when a babysitter fell sick or just didn't show up, it would be better for everyone. But Lacy Carter, the little old British lady whom my friend, the print shop supervisor, had warned me about, didn't think so.

"The World Bank isn't a babysitter," said Lacy Carter. "It just isn't in the ethos of the World Bank to have little children running around in our halls."

Hard as it was to get the men in management to see why this would be an excellent use of Bank money—and to the Bank's advantage, it seemed one of our biggest enemies at the Bank was a woman. Lacy Carter whispered her views of women in the workplace into the ear of the director of personnel and any other senior manager who would listen.

But Lacy Carter wasn't the only woman who didn't see the point of on-site childcare. At Thanksgiving dinner with my family, I recounted my conversation with Lacy Carter.

"It's not in the ethos of the World Bank!" I repeated. "Can you believe that?"

My mother's mother Florence, who had worked in New York City as a secretary and an editor throughout my mother's childhood, looked puzzled, then said, "Do you really think the men at the World Bank should be interested in childcare? When I was a working mother, we had to figure it out for ourselves."

I looked at Mom, who grimaced. I knew all too well how my mother felt about her mother, how much she resented being left with a housekeeper, ignored by her mother.

Mom said with a laugh, "And we know how that turned out, don't we?"

Florence was not to be deterred. "When I was in Geneva, I made Mother and Daddy keep you in Philadelphia. When your sister Jo was little, Irish Mamie took care of you both."

"Exactly!" said Mom. "It was the servants who took care of us. We aren't all wealthy enough to have servants to replace us at home. I didn't when my girls were small. Luckily, I had B. Marie and Floyd nearby. And Jerri wouldn't be able to have any help at home. She's absolutely right to fight for onsite childcare."

Florence still looked puzzled.

As SWWG Chair, I was happy to have more influence with Bank management where women were concerned, but it was a lot of work. Not only did we have to publish and distribute that year's annual report, but when I took over, I found several complaints of sexual discrimination waiting for me.

One complaint was filed by a female economist, who years later would become a director and special advisor to the World Bank president. She was five months pregnant and had been informed that the Bank considered it too risky for a pregnant woman to travel on mission, given the possibility of a miscarriage. It was a liability issue, said Lacy Carter. her travel would be curtailed until after the baby was born.

"This isn't any of Lacy Carter's business," the economist said, furious, not only for herself, but for all Bank women. "My decision whether to travel or not should be up to me, not Lacy Carter."

It was a matter of principle. Any woman could be pregnant at any time, whether she knew for sure or not. Lacy's Bank liability issue argued that no potentially pregnant Bank woman should be allowed to travel— which was a large percentage of all Bank women. International travel was critical to Bank work. Not traveling meant not having a World Bank career. It was already hard enough for the Bank to recruit highly qualified professional women. A restriction on traveling while pregnant would make it even harder. Lacy Carter was the vestige of another time, a time when women weren't traveling around the world. At the economist's request, I wrote a letter to Bank management in support of the economist's complaint. She won; Lacy lost.

I took a lot of pleasure in taking up the gauntlet for one of the Bank's professional women. Not just because it was the right and fair thing, but because it allowed me a chance to thwart the mysteriously powerful Lacy Carter.

Cairo

One day in April, the Egyptian minister of irrigation called from Cairo to let me know he was on his way to Washington. He asked me to join him for lunch at the World Bank executive dining room. Although I didn't understand why he was inviting me to lunch, I said it would be a pleasure. A week later, we were in the dining room enjoying our filet mignon, medium-rare.

The minister was a large, imposing man—someone the Egyptians would have called "prosperous" and Americans might call fat. Like many Egyptians I knew at the Bank, he was flirtatious, friendly, and keen to talk. Taking a forkful of salad, the minister began asking questions—about the Bank, my family, and my life. I was more than happy to tell him whatever he wanted to know, then asked him in turn about himself, his ministry, and Cairo. By dessert, we were almost friends.

"You know, my dear, we Egyptian men love our women. We must protect and care for them. They are fragile. The weaker sex, you know?"

"Hah," I said, moving the plates to the side, pushing up my sleeve and putting my elbow on the table.

"Want to arm wrestle?" I asked, grinning.

He raised an eyebrow, then smiled, pushed up his sleeve, and put his elbow on the table next to mine.

"Okay. Let's go," the Minister said.

We both pushed hard, but I got the edge—no doubt with some help from him—and flattened his fist with mine.

"Okay, *Madame*," he said, laughing. "You win!"

Seeing that that it was now safe to clear the dishes, our server did so, then brought us espresso. As we sipped, I asked the minister why he'd asked me to lunch, suggesting that it probably wasn't to arm wrestle.

"No, indeed," he replied. "Actually, it was the Canadian, Fred Durrant's idea, that we should talk. When I told him I'd be in Washington, he said I'd better talk to you if I wanted the real story."

"What do you mean, the real story?"

"The Dick Heiges story," he said. "Something strange is going on, and we don't understand it. It seems that whenever he comes to my country, he gets in the way, complicates things, and insults somebody. Is he with the CIA?"

I wasn't crazy about Dick, but I hadn't expected this. I placed my cup carefully back on the saucer. "No, your excellency, I don't think he's a spy. I hate to say this about my boss, but I think he's incompetent."

"Good—that is, if you are sure." I was glad the minister was prepared to give me the benefit of the doubt. "But doesn't the man have a boss? Can't you talk to him, make sure he doesn't keep coming to Cairo?"

I loved that the minister thought I had enough influence to keep Dick Heiges off a plane.

"*Madame*, you insist American women aren't weak. Your consultants say you are the one who gets things done. Come to Cairo yourself and leave Heiges at home."

Before taking the elevator to the twelfth floor to see Robert McNamara, the minister extended his hand to shake mine. "Don't forget," he said, "you must come to Cairo." Ten minutes later, I was with my division chief, Peter Naylor, telling him about the lunch.

"You arm-wrestled with the minister of irrigation?" he laughed. "And you won?"

"Not only did I win," I said, "but I got myself an invitation to go to Cairo to get you a second opinion on what's going on there. What do you say?"

Peter hesitated for a moment.

I went on. "I'm the ideal person to do this errand for you. Men talk to me differently than they talk to other men. From what I can tell, Egyptian men aren't like American men. They won't feel threatened; they'll want to impress me by telling me things. We need information and I can get it."

Two weeks later, I was on my way to Cairo. I'd typed enough statements of expenses to know that World Bank professionals always traveled first class. Although a luxury, this made some sense. Bank staff traveled halfway across the world several times a year. Mission travel was exhausting and staff needed to rest so they could begin to work as soon as the plane landed. I would be taking two long flights—the first from Washington, D.C., to Rome, the second from Rome to Cairo. I needed to be alert and ready to work when I got to Egypt. Still, on my first World Bank mission, I was startled to find myself sitting in the front of the plane.

Every time the polite steward tapped my shoulder, I expected him to tell me there'd been a mistake. That my seat was several rows back . . . in economy class. Some part of me was sure that the steward on this British Airways flight knew perfectly well that I'd been raised by socialists, that flying overseas, even in economy class, was a luxury my family could never afford. Three years as a secretary gave me no reason to expect to travel first class at the Bank's expense. But whenever the steward tapped my shoulder it was only to offer more champagne and caviar.

Something else I had learned as a secretary was that the Bank covered the cost of fancy hotel rooms for staff on stopovers in Europe on their way to their mission destination. For my stopover in Rome, I had a room at the five-star Hotel Hassler, located at the top of the Spanish steps, near St. Peter's Basilica, the Coliseum, and the Trevi Fountain. I'd heard about this hotel, where each room was different, one more elegant than the next. I'd heard about the hotel's priceless art and antiques, ornate mirrors framed in gold-leaf, meticulously carved four-poster beds. But by the time I got to Rome, I was too tired to luxuriate in the grandeur of the Hotel Hassler. After requesting a wake-up call from reception, I pulled the heavy burgundy velvet drapes closed, and collapsed.

When I awoke, the room was dark. Still groggy in the grip of jet lag, I stared at the clock: 10:30 a.m. My plane had already left Rome for Cairo at nine. The heavy drapes had kept out the morning light, and there had been no wake-up call. I tried not to panic as I raced to shower and dress. I grabbed my bag and headed for the lobby, cursing myself for letting this happen.

At the airport, I dashed from one airline to another in search of a flight to Cairo. The only one available would arrive at 5 p.m., several hours after I was scheduled to get there. I had no way to contact the Canadian couple, Fred Durrant and his wife, Marj, who were to meet me to alert them to the delay.

I was on my way to Egypt to help the expatriate consultants with their organization, and I couldn't even organize myself to get to Cairo on time. For the duration of the flight, I fretted about making such a poor first impression and embarrassing myself on my first trip for the Bank. I wondered if anyone would be willing to meet me at the airport.

When I arrived though, the Durrants were there, waiting and waving. I apologized for being late, and thanked them for not giving up on me. Marj shrugged. "Nothing to worry about," she said, as Fred picked up my bag. "Welcome to Cairo."

The ministry driver, Mohammed, was in the hotel lobby to meet me at eight o'clock the next morning. I could hardly believe that I, a twenty-seven-year-old operations assistant, was in Egypt, on my own, being met by a driver in the lobby of a fancy hotel.

I stepped into the blistering Cairo heat and Mohammed opened the back door of the car for me. I hadn't been sure I belonged in the front of the airplane and now I wasn't sure I belonged in the back seat of the ministry car. I slid in, anyway.

In the car with Mohammed, I experienced for the first time the chaos that was Cairo. The noise of the traffic was deafening. Mohammed kept the heel of his hand permanently pressed on the car horn. "I am here!" shouted the horn. "I am here in the street in my car making noise. Do you hear me? I am here!"

Motorbikes zigzagged at top speed among the cars, while sauntering camels and plodding donkey carts slowed everything down. The air was rife with black exhaust. The two-mile journey from the hotel to the ministry office took more than an hour. Mohammed looked back at me and shrugged. "That's Cairo."

On a shady street, away from the worst of the traffic, Mohammed parked in front of a large, grey, concrete building, opened the door for me, and announced we had arrived at the ministry of irrigation. "The elevator is out of service, *Madame*, there is some climbing."

I was young enough that climbing shouldn't have been a problem, but it was dark, and the stairs were uneven and crumbling. Mohammed led me safely up the three flights to the boss. Engineer Sarwat, director of the Egypt water master plan project, was a diminutive man in a safari suit with a neat mustache and doleful expression.

"Please be seated," he said politely, showing me to a chair upholstered in an unappealing olive-green brocade. In no time, a tea boy was there to take my order. Sarwat assured me I'd love the Egyptian coffee. To please him, I ordered it. What I received was unlike any coffee I'd ever seen: black and thick as mud. It was dreadful, but I sipped it as politely as I could.

After a few pleasantries, Sarwat invited me to join him at the large window, through which we could see the traffic below and the river Nile beyond.

"Impressive, yes?' he asked.

I nodded dutifully, recalling how it felt to be stuck in that traffic. We returned to our chairs. Sarwat ordered more coffee.

Making conversation, I asked Sarwat about the four telephones on his desk and why he needed more than one.

"All directors have many phones," he said, "but they don't work well."

"Not even one?" I asked with a half-smile.

"None," said Sarwat, all seriousness. "We have telephones, but if we wish to get a message to someone, we must send our drivers."

Surveying Sarwat's office a bit more, I was surprised to see an unplugged computer console on a side table, underneath a large, potted plant.

"You use a computer?" I asked, pointing to the plant.

"That young Englishman you hired is here to teach my staff to use computers. Perhaps, one day, I will learn, too," said Sarwat, solemnly. A director with a spacious corner office, four non-working telephones, and a computer used as a plant stand.

Sarwat rarely smiled, but I worked hard to get him to lighten up a little. From that day on, I always greeted him with a kiss on both cheeks. This usually made him blush, but he didn't seem offended. Had I not been an American woman in my twenties, he might have taken exception to my informality, but I took it as a good sign that my friendly assertiveness didn't seem to bother him. This behavior came naturally to me. I may have been uncomfortable sitting in first class on a plane or in the back seat of a chauffeured car, but I was not intimidated by powerful people.

I spent most mornings with the reticent Sarwat and most afternoons with the frustrated, but generally cheerful, expatriates: our team leader, a buttoned-down Canadian with a military haircut, a quirky Dutch economist, and a young British information technology wizard.

At the time, the World Bank did not have a resident mission in Cairo to help anyone with anything. I smoothed the way between the expatriates and the ministry of irrigation, and between the ministry and Bank staff in Washington. As a generalist with an MBA degree, I didn't compete with, or second-guess, staff in the field. I made myself useful, created contacts for them, and listened to them. I was the runner and go-between. The one who kept feathers unruffled. I saw trouble coming and headed it off. I also showed a more human side of the World Bank. Its reputation as powerful and arrogant didn't always serve us well. I wasn't big, powerful, or intimidating. I was more eager than egocentric. I was the right person for the job.

Some evenings I ate with the expats and their garrulous wives. During these dinners, I learned more about how difficult it was to work as a World Bank consultant in Egypt. Each expatriate couple gave me a laundry list of problems to solve once I got home. I accepted their lists with pleasure. Traveling first class made me nervous, but I was an expert in getting things done in Washington. After three years of learning chapter and verse of the administrative, operational, and organizational manuals, I was in a position to help the people in Cairo understand what was going on in Washington.

Among Cairo's many icons—the mosques, temples, pyramids, and sphinxes—the one I came to love most was the Khan el-Khalili, Cairo's ancient central market. I went to the market for the first time looking for a gold *cartouche* necklace for my stepmother Kate.

Although I would come to know the market well over the next few years, on that first visit I had no idea what to expect. When I hopped into a taxi and instructed the driver to take me to the central market, I had no idea how many goldsmiths did business in the Khan el-Khalili, or how many cups of mint tea I'd need to drink before negotiating a good price. I didn't realize how many hours it would take for the taxi to get from one end of the market to the other, while tourists and Egyptians alike— women in black burkas and men in white caftans—joined in the confusion of trucks, scooters, Mercedes-Benzes, bicycles, and the odd camel.

On that first trip, I watched Egyptian life from the back seat of the taxi: gazing at half-open shuttered windows, looking down a labyrinth of alleyways where merchants stood in their doorways offering Bedouin dresses, perfume, radio-cassette players, semiprecious stones, plastic laundry baskets, gold and silver jewelry, hookahs, spices, olives, dates, limes, textiles, and carpets. I saw dark, round men with mustaches and water pipes pouring the sludge coffee into cups, and mint tea into small glasses. I took in the noise, the smoke, the smell of mint, the shisha.

The driver got as close to the market stalls as he could, pulled the taxi to a stop and looked back at me for instructions. I told him to drive back to the hotel. "*Malesh*," I said. Never mind, I'd return to the bazaar when I was ready, and feeling brave.

Family

In June 1978, Cliff drove his five-year-old son down from Potsdam to live with us for the summer. The day they arrived in D.C., I watched the tall, dark man I loved walk hand-in-hand with a little blonde boy down Pennsylvania Avenue to the parking lot where we'd agreed to meet. As we drove over the Roosevelt Bridge together to Virginia, Christian and I imagined aloud all the stuff that we might find in the river below—fish, boats, kayaks, maybe some big old boots. By the time we got home, the two of us were laughing and already great friends. After dinner, Christian asked if I could sleep over.

"You'll have to ask your Dad," I said.

"Daddy says it's fine," said Christian.

This was good, since two of Cliff's closets were full of my clothes.

The three of us spent as much of the summer together as we could. Cliff and I alternated who took annual leave so we could take Christian to the playground, watch him climb trees, and splash in the community pool. Christian helped Cliff make bread and weed the garden. Christian and I curled up together before bed and read books. By the end of August, I was in love with Cliff's little boy and dreading his departure.

When the appointed day arrived, we made the ten-hour drive to Potsdam in Cliff's Volkswagen bus, then set up camp on the outskirts of town. I wasn't much of a camper, but Christian loved sleeping outdoors. Lucky for me, Cliff knew how to raise a tent. We joined some campsite neighbors for a makeshift dinner, then played ball with Christian and a few friends he'd already made. The three of us fell asleep, our two sleeping bags zipped together as one.

The next morning, I met Christian's mother, Ellie, for the first time. She gave Christian a quick kiss, shook my hand briskly, then got down to business. She needed Cliff to help her develop a business plan for her new wine-and-cheese shop, set up her stereo, and fix her sink. Ellie and Cliff had been divorced for several years by then, but the dynamic between them hadn't changed. More often than not, their conversations ended in argument.

Leaving Christian in Potsdam was heartbreaking. As Cliff pulled the bus out of the drive, I looked out the back window at our little boy. Ellie held one of his hands in hers. He used the other to wave goodbye, tears running down his cheeks.

My second trip to Cairo began with a great flurry of birds. As it happened, my arrival there in September 1978 coincided with the triumphant return of Egyptian President Anwar Sadat from Washington, D.C., where he and Israeli Prime Minister Menachem Begin had signed the Middle East peace accords with Jimmy Carter at Camp David.

As I set foot in the arrivals hall, a flock of doves appeared from the vicinity of the ceiling, wings flapping wildly. I asked an Egyptian security guard what on earth was happening. Why the birds? He moved closer and said softly, almost whispering, "These are Doves of Peace. A Hero's Welcome."

Lest I be found loitering or waiting for Sadat to arrive, airport security whisked me quickly away from the main hall and into the care of my friendly driver Mohammed.

"How about that?" I laughed with Mohammed. "To think I'd be given a hero's welcome in Cairo. Greeted with all those doves!"

On this trip, I was lucky enough to be working with Soheir Habib, a United Nations Development Programme (UNDP) officer. She was a whirlwind of ideas and enthusiasm. She knew everyone. Eleven years my senior, Soheir had come up through the ranks and had to work twice as hard as the men to get half the credit. She had gone to good schools; her father expected big things from her. At twenty-nine, she had married a television celebrity, who admired her intelligence, industriousness, and independent spirit. Still, he made it clear he wished she'd spend a little less time working for the UN, and a little more time at home with their daughter.

Small and slender, Soheir was a powerhouse. She was charming when she needed to be, but preferred solving problems to making small talk. No matter how smartly dressed Soheir was when she arrived at work, by midday, her elegant silk blouse was usually untucked, the result of speeding from one place to another, getting things done. To her credit, Soheir was more concerned with her causes than with her clothes.

During that visit, and subsequent ones, to Cairo, Soheir and I talked for hours in her office, sitting at a desk piled high with books, papers, and reports. We commiserated about what it was like to work in the UN system, how dismissive the internationally recruited men were of the locally recruited women. No matter how much we talked, there was always more to say. We continued our conversations at lunch in Soheir's high-ceilinged apartment in the fashionable district of Zamalek, where she lived with her husband and daughter. On Sundays, she organized picnics for us at the foot of the Great Sphinx of Giza. During one of these lunches, Soheir described what it was like to be a young wife and mother in Cairo.

"Once I married Tarek," she said, "people told me to give up my job and enjoy life. At first, I was tempted. I was tired of having to fight so hard to accomplish anything. But there was much to be done. As a woman, I needed to show others what a woman could do."

I knew what she meant.

Soheir talked to me about women in Egypt. She shared my concern about the young environmentalist Amal Sabri who was not given her due at the ministry of irrigation. We talked about the ways her organization and mine were alike. Our conversations about women and water got me thinking about ways in which Bank staff were finally paying attention to Women in Development, whether or not they were benefitting from Bank projects. Or whether their needs or potential contributions were taken into consideration in Bank project design. Although my job as the administrator of the Egypt Water Master Plan project did not focus on the impact water planning might have on women or how women might contribute to conserving water, I was always finding women to work with—identifying with them and intervening on their behalf.

Soheir and I had both learned about sexism firsthand. When I told her how powerless I sometimes felt at the World Bank, she pointed out that working at the Bank gave me more influence than I knew.

"You must join forces with the women in countries like Egypt," she counseled me. "They need you on their side."

Back in Virginia, a week before Halloween, Cliff and I got a call from his ex-wife. She needed surgery. Her health insurance only covered costs incurred in D.C., so she would have to have it down here. She didn't have anyone to take Christian or a place in D.C. to recuperate.

"Tell her we'll keep Christian, of course," I said. "And she can stay here until she gets better."

Cliff raised an eyebrow, but gave her the message.

A week later, I was sitting on a chair next to a groggy Ellie, prepped for surgery at GWU hospital. Struggling to focus, she reached for my hand.

"Promise me that if anything happens, you'll take care of Christian?"

"Nothing will happen," I assured her. "But if you want me to, I promise."

Ellie drifted off, and I returned to work. Her surgery went smoothly, and a few days later the hospital released her to our care.

After four weeks, with some prodding from me, Ellie left for Potsdam. Without Christian.

A week later, Christian and I sat on the sofa, snuggling and singing "Green Grow the Rushes O," a song my mother sang to me when I was small. I sang:

I'll sing you three O Green grow the rushes, O / What is your three-O?

Christian sang back:

Three, three, for Daddy, Jerri, and me."

Christian and I sang together:

Two, two for your two pretty eyes / Looking at the wide world O

One is one and all alone, and never more shall be so.

At home with Cliff and Christian, I felt that I belonged at last. I'd come into my own. I'd found useful things to do at the World Bank. So much travel wasn't easy, but it was worthwhile. I got my old self-confidence back.

My trips to Egypt were proving helpful to the project in several ways. Making things easier for the expatriates administratively was a good beginning. This allowed them to do the work they were hired to do and spend less time struggling to settle in. I also helped communication between the Egyptians and the expatriates on the team. I never tried to second-guess anyone, and I got along with everyone. With all the money pouring into Egypt as a result of Jimmy Carter's peace talks at Camp David, there was plenty of friction among the many players. I did my best to keep everybody talking to each other, with some success.

The more I traveled to Egypt, the more at ease I felt with the Egyptians and expatriates alike. I had a lot to learn about water resources, though. I studied up on riparian water rights, hydro-politics, and the socioeconomics of fish farming. Neither my degree in French literature nor my MBA had prepared me for the mysteries of water resource development. But I needed to understand what the project staff was doing. Since I had promised Sarwat to help create a water resources library for the ministry of irrigation, becoming knowledgeable about the subject was a must.

I attended ministry staff meetings and nodded sagely as Sarwat repeated *ad infinitum* that planning was a continuous process. Every once in a while, the deputy minister would lament that the ancient Egyptians hadn't needed feasibility studies to build the pyramids, why should modern Egyptians need them?

After my fourth trip to Cairo, Cliff asked me to marry him. "If you're going to keep spending so many nights on mission in Egypt, it's time for me to start accruing spouse points, don't you think?"

Although this was a joke, and hardly a reason to marry, Cliff did have a point. Married staff members who traveled on mission were able to accrue one point toward spouse travel for each night they spent away from home. Once the staff member accrued enough points, the Bank would cover the expense of a trip for the spouse.

Spouse points aside, I couldn't think of a single reason not to marry Cliff.

I said yes.

Cliff and I didn't have a lot of money. I borrowed a wedding dress and asked my sister Katie to make the three-tier wedding cake. For the reception, we planned to serve finger-food instead of dinner, and dance to music on a boom box instead of a band.

On our wedding day, fifty people filled the chapel of the Unitarian church that I had attended as a child. Since Cliff's sister was the only member of his immediate family still alive and able to attend the wedding, both sides of the chapel were reserved for me.

In the hall with my father, waiting to walk down the aisle, I watched so many people I loved filling the chapel, waiting for me. Still, I couldn't help but think about the people who weren't there. Ghislaine had returned to Montreal to attend graduate school; she didn't come. Arshad's wife was giving birth to their first child, so he had to bow out. Fareed, of course, was back in Sudan. My mother's mother, Florence, was in Peru, watching the sunrise at the Inca ruins of Machu Pichu. When she'd declined my invitation to the wedding, she explained: "There is an energy that is conducive to great spiritual transformation. The Earth's chakras are constantly changing. Like Tibet." She seemed to think this would convince me to change my wedding date. It didn't. Florence was dismayed by my insensitivity. Later, she would remark how unfortunate it was that my wedding fell on such an auspicious day—one on which she had no choice but to watch the sunrise at Machu Pichu.

Of course, the person I missed most at my wedding had already been gone three years: my grandmother B. Marie.

When the organist began the wedding march, I took my father's arm. Together, we walked down the short aisle, me as resplendent as I'd ever been in white satin and lace, a crown of baby's breath, clasping a bouquet of ivy and white roses. At the front of the chapel, tall, bearded Cliff and small, tow-headed Christian, in matching navy-blue suits and striped ties, waited for me, beaming.

At the reception, my mother recited a wedding poem she'd written for us and my father delighted us with his toast: "You know how annoying it is—night after night coming home from work and tripping over your daughter's bicycle on your way to the front porch?" The crowd nodded. "Yes, well, it is annoying until one day there is no bicycle to trip over anymore. That is not a good day. Your daughter no longer rides a bicycle because she's gone away to college, where who knows who she'll take up with? Drug dealers, ax murderers. Then, no sooner does she leave college, she lands a job for the World Bank, where everybody speaks fluent Economics and French, neither of which her father can speak.

"Yet . . . here we are. The daughter isn't marrying an ax murderer after all. And this new son-in-law of mine—to my colossal relief—actually speaks English!"

As Cliff and I drank from the loving cup, I thought back on the ceremony and the pastor's words: "Jerri tells me she comes from three generations of divorce, and this is Cliff's second marriage. For them, this wedding is the triumph of optimism over experience." Yes. Optimism was my stock in trade.

Although the wedding was in October, I was too busy at work to take a proper honeymoon right away. Instead, I organized for Ellie to look after Christian for a week while Cliff and I honeymooned in Egypt at the end of my next Bank mission. We'd spend Thanksgiving in the shadow of the Pyramids.

Honeymooning in Egypt was a big deal for Cliff, a boy from a factory town, and he was nervous. I was nervous, too. I was good at compartmentalizing my two lives—the one with Cliff and Christian, the other with the master plan project. I had friends, colleagues, and plenty of independence in Cairo. I was liked and respected for who I was. Suddenly I wasn't sure I wanted my husband there. Maybe he wouldn't fit in, or worse, maybe he would, and I'd become just some man's wife Still, I knew I had to make more room for him. He needed to know what I did when I was away.

Cliff arrived in Cairo rumpled and a bit haggard, having learned that the airline lost his luggage. Mohammed tried, unsuccessfully, to locate the bags. But I was grateful that he was there to handle the formalities of getting Cliff into the country, shepherding him through the airport security and passport control and out to the government car while other travelers stood in endless lines for hours. Then he took us from the airport straight to the office, explaining to Cliff that everyone wanted to meet *Madame* Jerri's new husband.

At the Ministry, Sarwat stood at his office door, waiting. The diminutive project director was dwarfed by my large, bearded husband. Still, he smiled up at him and extended his hand. "Hello, Mr. Cliff, welcome. *Mabrouk* on your marriage. We have all been wondering what kind of man our Jerri would marry."

"A brave man, Sarwat!" said Cliff, "It takes a very brave man to marry your Jerri!"

Everything about Cairo that had surprised and worried me on my first trip now surprised and worried my husband. In a taxi, Cliff held my hand, knuckles white, as the taxi-man drove up the ramp to the Corniche, found it too crowded to continue and backed down again, almost slamming into a dozen cars on the way.

The minister of irrigation invited us to visit, greeting us warmly. "We are delighted you've chosen Egypt for your wedding trip. You will want to see the Aswan Dam, of course. A marvel of engineering. And the Valley of the Kings in Luxor, and Abu Simbel. We will arrange it. A small plane will take you to Aswan tomorrow. You will stay in the ministry guest house there, and a private car will take you to Luxor. One of our own ministry tour guides will accompany you. You don't need a guidebook. You'll have a most knowledgeable guide with you all the time."

We followed the ministry's itinerary to the letter. As advertised, the Aswan Dam was a marvel of engineering. As the resident engineer droned on, my eyes glazed over. I loved my work with the people on the master plan, but I had yet to find anything fascinating about irrigation systems. I came quickly back to life, however, when we stopped at a bazaar. This was my chance to show Cliff how Egyptian I'd become. I bargained with a caftan vendor, and eventually got eight caftans for the price he'd initially proposed for one.

From Aswan, we went to the Valley of the Kings in Luxor. Cliff scampered around the ruins with his camera, showing no signs of slowing down. As I wound down, he revved up. I reassured myself, this was my sixth time in Egypt, and it was Cliff's first. It was fitting that it be Cliff who leaped over rubble to take pictures of hieroglyphics and wall paintings, while I tried to cool off in the shade of an umbrella.

On our return to Cairo from Luxor, Soheir Habib and her husband had a surprise waiting for us. The director of American Express for the Middle East, Soheir's husband, Tarek, had secured us the honeymoon suite at the Mena House Oberoi that faced the pyramids. We spent the morning at the pool; the Habibs joined us. That night we stood on our balcony and watched the sun set over Cheops, the Great Pyramid of Giza.

Over the years, Bank friends would comment on how lucky I was to be married to someone who knew so much about my work. Of course, Cliff had spent many years at the World Bank, so he understood the environment I worked in. But that trip to Egypt gave him a close look at what I did when I was away, and the relationships with the people I worked with. Being part of that world with me kept Cliff from feeling left out or threatened. He couldn't have been happier to have been in Egypt with me and I couldn't have been more relieved to see him happy. I needed his support. Now I had that, too.

We were a team.

The President

By 1979, our SWWG committee was crunching numbers for our seventh annual report. As usual, the percentage of total World Bank professionals who were women was woefully small. In 1975—the year I joined the group—women made up only 8.3 percent of all Bank professionals. Four years later, it was 10.5 percent. Pathetic.

By 1979, I had a platform that allowed me to support women in two ways: one, by focusing the ministry of irrigation's attention on the valuable work women were doing on the Egypt Water Master Plan project—the work the Bank paid me to do; and two, by chairing SWWG and the work I did during lunch hours, evenings, and weekends, for which I wasn't paid.

While the SWWG annual report exposed the many ways the World Bank discriminated against women, it was clear that people either didn't read the report or didn't care what was in it. There was only one obvious way forward.

"Who makes all the decisions at the World Bank?" I asked at our monthly SWWG meeting in November.

"Mr. McNamara," everybody answered as one.

It was no secret that leadership at the World Bank was top-down. This was "McNamara's Bank."

"Well, then," I continued. "Let's get McNamara to read the report, discuss it with us and act on it. Isn't that better than complaining that nobody cares?"

Not waiting for a reply, I found a routing slip, clipped it to the SWWG report, then wrote in large letters: "Mr. McNamara: Can we discuss?"

"But . . ." the British woman with the braid started what I knew would be a torrent of reasons I shouldn't do this.

I carried the report to the twelfth floor, handed it to McNamara's secretary, and asked her to pass it on to the president for comment.

"Well, this is unusual," she said, glancing down at the report's cover page. "But I'll make sure he gets it." She gave me a wink.

The following morning, she called me, "Mr. McNamara would like to meet you to discuss your report at 2 p.m. on December 10. How does that sound?" I could hear the smile in her voice. We had an ally.

Earlier that year, I had written an article about feminism for the Bank staff newsletter, in which I quoted the British philosopher and self-proclaimed feminist John Stewart Mill and my grandfather Floyd Dell, who had written a book back in 1913 entitled *Women as World Builders*. My article had gotten people's attention, and had been an opportunity to claim my feminist credentials as the granddaughter of an early twentieth-century suffragist—who, nearly sixty years after women got the right to vote, was now fighting for the rights of women at the World Bank.

I wasn't sure whether Robert McNamara had read the article, but this first meeting with him would be an opportunity for me to share the concerns I had laid out in it. In preparation for the meeting, I wrote my presentation on note cards and practiced in front of the mirror. I knew that McNamara made people nervous. He was smart, opinionated, abrupt, and impatient. I wanted to be ready.

On December 10, flanked by the chairman of the staff association on one side and three SWWG members on the other, I waited for the president's assistant to announce us. When we entered McNamara's spacious office, I noticed three yellow pads on the polished mahogany table. The other SWWG members must have noticed them, too, as they eyed the row of chairs a few feet away from the table, apparently meant for them.

After a few minutes, the office door flew open and a tall man with wire-rimmed glasses wearing a dark, slightly rumpled suit and striped tie loped into the room. A shorter and skinnier man in a brown suit—a man who made me think of a hungry chicken—followed close behind.

"Hello, hello," said Robert McNamara heartily, shaking each of our hands. "I'm sure you know Martijn Paijmans, our vice president of administration? I've brought him along to hear what you have to say and to answer your questions if I can't. Please be seated. Ms. Dell, why don't you come here to the table."

I did so.

"So," said McNamara, facing me. "What have you got for me?"

Glancing briefly at my note cards, I took a deep breath. "It's bad news, Mr. McNamara." For more than twenty minutes, I made our case. I began by quoting the report's statistics, although I suspected he already had them in his head. He was reputed to have a phenomenal, almost photographic, memory for numbers. I talked about meetings with Bank managers, most of whom thought of women as a "special interest" group. I compared the Bank's performance in recruiting and promoting women with that of other international organizations. I outlined the elements of a more successful approach: affirmative action policy for women, the option of part-time employment, on-site childcare.

"Mr. McNamara," I concluded, "I recently read an article in the *Washington Post* where you are reported to have said that the situation of women in the World Bank is 'ghastly.' We couldn't agree more."

Without a word, he stood up from the table, took off his suit jacket, put it on the back of his chair, rolled up his sleeves, sat down again, lifted his elbows on the table, leaned toward me.

"Now, enough speeches, tell me: what should we do about all this?"

Suddenly I was looking at my father's round face, hearing his booming voice. My father never scared me. Robert McNamara didn't scare me, either. I stood up, put my jacket on the back of my chair, sat down again. I lifted my elbows on the table and leaned toward him.

"Well, sir," I said. "Here's what I think."

McNamara ended our two-hour meeting with a warm smile for me and stern instructions for the VP to come up with a recruitment plan for bringing more women on board. He proposed that the personnel department bring in consultants to find out why the Bank wasn't recruiting more women into its ranks, promoting more women within the Bank, and why it was paying women less than men for the same work.

Convincing McNamara that something needed to be done to improve the status of women at the Bank wasn't hard. He had no quarrel with SWWG; his quarrel was with the managers who reported to him. Arguing the case for women with the Bank's president was pushing an open door.

The second time I met with McNamara was in the spring of 1980. This time he had both the vice president and the director of personnel in tow.

McNamara wasted no time. "Martijn, what do you have to tell us?"

Rather than answer the president's question himself, the VP introduced his personnel director, an Austrian with thinning white-blonde hair, a ruddy, round face, and a nervous tic that made him blink.

"Hans, what do you have to tell us?"

After blinking several times, the personnel director pressed his hands against the table as if this might give him strength. "Mr. McNamara," he began. "Women do indeed make up only a small percent of Bank professional staff. But recruiting women poses a big problem for us. You must consider the talent we need at the Bank. We need sanitary engineers, for example. There aren't many trained female sanitary engineers out there. We can't recruit them if they aren't there."

McNamara turned back to the VP. "So, please tell me we aren't just recruiting sanitary engineers. What about economists? Can't you find any university-trained women economists, Martijn? Can't you find any university-trained women lawyers, architects, or urban planners, Martijn?"

The vice president gave his director a dark look. The director sputtered. "But Mr. McNamara, we can't recruit women because they are women. We need highly qualified professionals. We can't lower our standards."

McNamara raised his voice by several decibels, and gave the vice president a piercing stare. "Is your director of personnel saying that to recruit a woman, we must lower our standards? What crap is that?"

Riveted by this exchange, I said nothing. Abruptly, McNamara turned to me.

"It appears that my personnel department can't figure this out. I guess it'll be up to you to do it."

He turned back to his vice president and said, "I want you to find someone in your shop to help Ms. Dell write an equal opportunity policy for women in the Bank."

The vice president stiffened.

"I know, I know. Everybody hates 'affirmative action.' That's too damn bad."

I had no experience writing personnel policy. How was I supposed to write an equal opportunity policy for women?

"I want that equal opportunity policy on my desk in one month, no later," boomed McNamara to his senior personnel managers. Although I was flattered the president thought I could do the job, I wished he hadn't embarrassed the vice president of personnel by assigning it to me.

One day, I'd pay.

An unexpected outcome of my first meeting with McNamara was getting to know personnel policy officer Lee Roberts. Unlike so many personnel people, Lee was unpretentious and fun to be with. Over the course of drafting the Bank's equal opportunity policy for women, I learned quite a bit about Lee, a white South African who refused to live under apartheid. Although I'd never been to Africa myself, I remembered what my father told me about Nelson Mandela and the African National Congress, the brutal treatment of Black South Africans. Lee called South Africa's system of apartheid a blot on humanity. I was reminded of my father's remark that slavery, segregation, and racism constituted America's "original sin." I liked Lee.

While I was traveling back and forth to Egypt, managing SWWG, and co-authoring an equal opportunity policy for women at the Bank, McNamara hired Gloria Scott, an affable, middle-aged Jamaican woman, to serve as the Bank's women in development (WID) advisor. This was the first time that Bank management had showed any particular interest in gender as a development concern. Gloria's first task was to review the Bank's lending operations and see how well women were taken into account, either as contributors to or as beneficiaries of development. Gloria's report—"Invisible Women in Development"—was aptly titled. Once I read it, I knew that my next meeting with the president would be about more than the status of women at the Bank.

When my two SWWG colleagues and I arrived on the twelfth floor for the third time, McNamara and Martijn Paijmans were there to greet us, the president a bit more enthusiastically than his vice president. McNamara asked how I wanted to proceed. After thanking him for seeing us again, I explained that while we usually talked SWWG statistics, this time I wanted to offer him a new argument for increasing the ranks of professional women in the Bank.

"I read Gloria Scott's report, and I see a direct link between the number of female Bank professionals and the Bank's ability to reduce poverty."

I was sure this would provoke a strong reaction. The idea of linking women working in the Bank with the women in development had few enthusiasts.

"Wait a minute," said McNamara. "Are you saying that women are the only ones qualified to deal with women in developing countries?"

"Not at all," I said. "Nor do I think that Bank men neglect women on purpose."

"Well, that's a relief." McNamara relaxed back in his chair.

"Here's the problem. In many of our borrowing countries, women aren't permitted to speak to men they don't know. When an all-male Bank mission shows up, it holds discussions with men only. How can the appraisal report reflect women's concerns if no one talks to the women?"

McNamara looked interested.

"Something else. If the Bank fields men-only missions, this sends the message that either there are too few female professional staff members to send, or that the Bank doesn't take women seriously enough to send them."

"Makes sense to me," said McNamara, turning to his VP. "What about you?"

"I suppose," said the VP, unconvincingly.

McNamara looked thoughtful. "Isn't there a big UN women's conference coming up in Copenhagen soon? Are you going?"

I told him I wasn't.

"Well, you should be." Turning from me to the VP, he told him to speak to Gloria and make sure I would be part of the Bank's delegation to the women's conference in Copenhagen.

He turned back to me. "Go get the word out . . . The World Bank is hiring women . . . and tell them why."

I was more than happy to join Gloria at the conference. I'd always wanted to go to Denmark. I knew several Danes and they seemed cheerful, uncomplicated, and politically progressive. I was enthusiastic enough about the trip to want Cliff to join me there once the conference was over. By then, Ellie had moved from Potsdam to live a few blocks away from us and could look after Christian while we were gone.

This would be my first UN conference and I wasn't sure what to expect. I spent most of the night flight to Copenhagen studying. I learned that the conference was intended to assess the progress made in implementing the World Plan of Action agreed upon at the first UN

Conference on Women in Nairobi in 1975, including what countries were doing to improve women's control of property and their rights to inheritance and child custody. I learned that the Commission on the Status of Women at the UN had existed for more than twenty-five years, but it wasn't until the 1970s that women's issues had moved to center stage.

The evening before the conference began, Gloria asked me to meet her in the hotel lobby, where Lucille Mair, the Secretary-General of the conference, would join us. I was honored that she had made time to meet me. She joined us at the table, ordered tea, and gave me her full attention.

"Gloria told me this morning that Mr. McNamara suggested you join the Bank's delegation to our conference. More than one person on the Bank delegation to discuss women in development. That's a nice change."

When she asked what I hoped to take away from the conference, I explained that I was there both for education about women in development and to generate interest among conference participants in the World Bank as a place to work.

"Interest?" said Lucille. "I expect women will clamor to hear about the World Bank's interest in women. I warn you, though, they aren't likely to believe it. They won't trust in the Bank's willingness to change. Still, it's worth a try." She left our meeting to take charge of what would later be described as "the world's largest consciousness-raising group about and by women."

I spent the first morning in the opening plenary, trying not to feel intimidated. Such formal proceedings. Such a packed agenda. So many "points of order." Passionate speeches. Enthusiastic applause. Resounding boos. Major disagreements emerged right away: North-South feminism; socialism versus capitalism; the Israelis and the Palestinians.

Next door, ten thousand women had gathered for a forum of nongovernmental organizations, where the debate was just as intense. One thing was clear: there was an enormous diversity of both perspectives and needs among all of these women. I focused on what I could learn from these women and took copious notes wherever I went.

By lunch the first day, I realized that Gloria was there primarily to catch up with friends. An old UN hand, she had very low expectations of UN conferences. She left me to explore on my own and to do as I wished. During coffee and tea breaks, I mingled with the crowd, discreetly checking people's name tags to learn who they were and where they worked. I eavesdropped on conversations and invited myself to lunch with staff from an alphabet soup of UN agencies: United Nations Development Programme (UNDP), International Labor Office (ILO) UNICEF, World Trade Organization (WTO), International Fund for Agricultural Development (IFAD), Food and Agriculture Organization (FAO), and many more.

I managed to avoid many of the speeches made in the plenary. There were too many, and they went on too long. Still, I looked forward to hearing what the leader of the Egyptian delegation, First Lady Jehan Sadat, had to say. Having worked in the Bank's Middle East department, I knew her reputation: President Sadat's well-educated and progressive wife cared deeply about the lives of Egyptian women, especially the poor.

In her speech, Mrs. Sadat spoke forcefully about girls' education. She described women and girls as the "most precious capital any country could have" and insisted that investing in this capital was the best way for any nation to achieve lasting economic, social, and political equality. She also spoke specifically about Egypt's Personal Status laws that had for decades kept women from reaching their political and social potential and denied them the right to participate fully in public life. She was pleased to announce that during the previous year, the Egyptian Parliament had passed legislation to reform these laws, which opened the doors to women as never before. I was glad I stayed to hear this speech.

When McNamara sent me to the women's conference in Copenhagen, he'd invested in my education. Until then, I only had my conviction that women mattered in developing countries, as they did in the World Bank. And I was convinced more needed to be done to address this. After attending the conference, I understood Women in Development (WID) in a different and more comprehensive way. I would always have a lot for which to thank Robert McNamara.

When the conference was over, I looked forward to Cliff's joining me in Copenhagen. The room I'd been occupying during the event was much too small for two people. So, the day before he got there, I went looking for a place for us to stay. I located a spacious apartment near a canal: two bedrooms, a living room, and a kitchen. Once Cliff arrived, we ventured out to see something of the city.

We walked for blocks and blocks, taking in the casual way the Danes went about their lives—such a contrast to the structured formality and pressure of the conference. We loved the Tivoli Gardens—a park with benches for the elderly, and a playground, Ferris wheel, and carousel for children. We were particularly taken by the family of ducks swimming in a large pond at the center of the gardens.

"You know how our esteemed director of personnel always tells us we need to get our ducks in a row?" said Cliff. I nodded. "Look at all these ducks. Not one of them in a row."

"Let's not tell him," I said, and took Cliff's hand.

Continuing to stroll around the pond, we saw a group of three little boys, all with white-blonde hair in a bowl cut, just like our Christian's.

"Christian!" called one of the mothers nearby. Two of the three boys looked up. So many tow-headed Christians in Denmark.

After our tour of the apartment and our visit to the Tivoli Gardens, Cliff said, "Maybe we should forget about D.C. and move here."

I knew he was joking but it was awfully tempting. As was the idea of more little tow-headed boys. It got us both thinking about babies.

The Palace

Egypt was such a different culture for me, such a complicated place. I learned something new every day in Cairo: I learned about tenacity, loyalty, and spunk from Soheir; about an enthusiastic sense of adventure from our team leader's wife, Marj; gentleness and devotion to people and place from Mewaheb el-Khatib, an intelligent, soft-spoken, shy, clerk-typist. I also learned something about women in Egypt—women who had a voice, like Jehan Sadat and Soheir, and women like Mewaheb, who did not.

Amal Sabri, the project's young environmentalist, became a good friend. Unlike the male engineers, each of whom had his own office, a desk, and a large window, Amal and her sister, a sociologist, shared space with six administrative staff. They never sought me out, but as I made it my business to know what the local staff were doing, I invited them to speak with me. The more we talked, the more impressed I was with the Sabri sisters. They were both college graduates about my age. They were smart about their subjects and full of insight about their culture. Amal, in particular, spoke up about women in Egypt, the way they were perceived, the way they were dismissed as nonentities.

"Women are of little consequence," she said. "We just have to go on our way, help each other when we can, do what we can do. Some of us are lucky enough to have parents who believe in us and send us to university. Most do not."

One afternoon, I joined Sarwat Fahmy in his office for coffee. I was actually getting used to the black sludge in the tiny cup. After chatting a while, I asked him to come with me on a little "walkabout" in his ministry office. He seemed surprised, but happy enough to follow my lead. In the senior Egyptian irrigation engineer's office, the man's jacket was hanging neatly on the back of his chair, his briefcase under his desk, but the engineer himself was not there. We went to the office shared by two agricultural economists, both of whom were at their desks, absorbed in reading the morning newspaper. In the room Amal and her sister occupied, both young women were so busy writing they didn't hear us come in.

Sarwat and I returned to his office. I asked what he'd seen on our tour. The question confused him. "People working?" he said, as if hoping it was the right answer.

"Yes, but who is working?" I asked.

Sarwat was flummoxed.

"The women, Sarwat. The women are working. Amal, the social scientist; Aisha, the environmentalist; Mewaheb, the librarian; your secretary, Magda. These are the hardest working people in your operation. It is good to know. Yes? If you want it done right, hire a woman." I grinned at him.

Ever serious, Sarwat repeated after me slowly, tentatively, "Hire a woman. Hire a woman."

The evening after my walkabout with Sarwat, I knocked on Amal's door and asked if she'd like to go with me to the Khan el-Khalili. As we got out of the taxi, I thought of my first experience of the Khan el-Khalili, when I was too nervous to get out of the taxi and of the many times after that when I went with Marj and she introduced me to all of her favorite vendors. Then again, I remembered when I was there with Cliff on our honeymoon. By now, I had had a lot of practice drinking endless cups of mint tea and negotiating good prices for items, however long it took. I was no longer surprised by the women dressed in black from head-to-toe, by the water pipes and shisha or the camels sauntering among the trucks and scooters.

At the café, Amal and I shared a basket of warm pita and a plate of garlicky hummus, while I told her about taking Sarwat on a tour of the ministry.

"You did what?" she asked.

"I took Sarwat around to show him what his staff was up to."

"Why didn't you come see me? I would have been happy to show Engineer Sarwat what I do."

"We did come see you, but you didn't hear us. You were too busy working."

We both laughed.

"Do you think he noticed?"

"He didn't at first, but I think he did after I pointed it out to him. I also brought to his attention all the men who weren't working. Who knows if it will do any good? But I had to try."

Later, with Sarwat's blessing, I would get Amal training as an environmentalist in Colorado, and her colleague, Mewaheb, training in library science in Washington, D.C. But at that moment, she was dubious. Sarwat was so conservative. A traditional Egyptian man. He was kind, yes. But she wondered if it was naïve of me to believe he might also be open-minded. Amal may have been skeptical, but she appreciated what I was trying to do.

As she and I talked, I noticed a small group of men standing close together, whispering. I asked Amal what she thought they were up to.

"Things are not okay with Egyptians these days. There's too much poverty in my country. The men over there are part of the Muslim Brotherhood. It's gaining ground. People can only bear a great burden for so long. One day, everything will explode."

Twenty-one years later, on September 11, 2001, I'd remember Amal's words.

The morning after my conversation with Amal at the Khan el-Khalili, I got a call from First Lady Jehan Sadat's secretary, who invited me to meet with the first lady the following afternoon at the presidential palace. I was never sure exactly how this invitation came about, but I was very pleased by it.

The first lady's secretary greeted me on the palace steps and led me into a massive front hall. It took me a moment to take it all in—the ornate architecture, columns and clerestory, paintings, sculpture, and gold-coated clocks. I'd once heard the palace described as one of the most sumptuous in the world. The secretary and I walked together down a long corridor. Our heels clicked on the marble floors. On the wall above Mrs. Sadat's huge desk hung a portrait of her husband in his military uniform. Fresh cut flowers overflowed alabaster vases. Two velvet-upholstered armchairs faced a long sofa.

Waiting for Mrs. Sadat, I considered what I already knew about her. Daughter of an Egyptian surgeon and a British music teacher, she had attended the best Christian girls' school in Egypt, but was raised a Muslim. At fifteen, she married Anwar Sadat, a thirty-one-year-old revolutionary, a peasant from a poor village who'd spent three years in prison. In 1971, twenty-two years after their marriage, he was elected president of Egypt.

Jehan Sadat was a role model for women everywhere, especially in the Arab world. This had become clear the evening I heard her speak in Copenhagen at the UN women's conference.

Deep in thought, I never heard the door open, and almost jumped from my seat when the first lady tapped me on the shoulder and extended her hand in welcome.

"No need to stand," she laughed. "I'll join you. We'll have tea."

Jehan Sadat had a warm smile, expressive eyes, and evident curiosity that put me at ease. At forty-seven, she was my mother's age. She was also my mother's height, about six inches shorter than me. Yes, Egypt's first lady was sophisticated and elegant in a way that my mother wasn't, but both women read poetry, were well-spoken, and liked to laugh. I immediately felt at home.

Sipping tea from gold-rimmed, bone-china cups, Mrs. Sadat asked me about the World Bank. What did Mr. McNamara think about discrimination against women in developing countries? Was he prepared to do anything about it? What were my impressions of the UN conference in Copenhagen? Did I think the UN's commitment to women in development was real or was it window-dressing?

As usual, I had a few things to say. There wasn't enough opportunity for women at the Bank. Not enough attention to gender issues in World Bank projects. Not enough action. As for Copenhagen, we'd have to see. "I want to be optimistic," I said. "But . . ."

"I know. It's hard, even when you have the 'man at the top' on your side. Even if Mr. McNamara wants to improve things for women, and even with my husband, who is generally sympathetic to the women's cause, serving as president of our country, what will change?"

I asked her to tell me more about the situation of Egyptian women. For an hour, we talked about her projects: the Talla Society, a Nile Delta cooperative helping women to be self-sufficient, and the S.O.S. Children's Villages, a way for orphans to receive care in a family setting. She also told me about several laws approved by their parliament to improve rights for women that included rights associated with alimony and custody of children. "They call them 'Jehan's laws.'"

Over time, we moved from our work to education and our love of books. I mentioned my studies in French literature as an undergraduate. She explained how she'd gone back to university at forty-two years old to study Arabic literature. "I did my master's thesis on the influence Shelley had on Arabic poetry. Can you believe it?" she asked.

"Shelley was one of my grandfather's favorite poets," I said, and launched into a story about my grandfather Floyd Dell. A favorite subject of mine.

"You must be proud of him, proud to be his granddaughter," she said. I blushed. Why was I accepting compliments for my grandfather's accomplishments decades ago from this woman of such influence in the world today?

For more than an hour, Mrs. Sadat gave me her full attention and listened respectfully to what I—a twenty-nine-year-old American woman—had to say. Although I was amazed to find myself in the presidential palace and awed to be sipping tea with Egypt's first lady, I must have exuded confidence, as she treated me as a kindred spirit and asked nothing about my job at the Bank. We agreed about the status of women in the world—my world in Washington, her world in Cairo. Heartened, I realized that if Jehan Sadat had confidence in me, it was time for Bank men to do the same.

As I stood to leave, Mrs. Sadat patted my arm. "You will do good things in your life. Women need champions. I believe you will be a champion for women."

I hoped she was right.

Early in 1981, we learned that McNamara would be stepping down and A.W. Clausen, president of the Bank of America, would become the World Bank's new president. This was not good news for Bank women. We were losing our most powerful advocate. In his place would be a man against whom a sexual discrimination class-action suit was pending in California.

On McNamara's last day at the Bank, his secretary called to ask me if I had time to drop in and say goodbye to him. Ten minutes later, I was in the president's office.

"Good to see you," McNamara said, awkwardly extending his left hand to shake mine. His right arm was in a sling.

"Forgive me," he said, nodding down at his clothes. "I've developed tennis elbow. My arm's out of commission. I can't get myself into a suit and tie."

I laughed with this man who, in his casual clothes, looked and seemed even more like my father than ever. "Don't worry. You look fine to me,"

I said. "The only thing that isn't fine is that today's your last day at the Bank."

"Now, now," he said, motioning me to the sofa. He leaned against the chair next to me.

"Let's talk about you and the work you're doing. You probably know I've had my differences with the staff association over the years. Especially when it's about staff compensation or travel policy. Hell, Bank staff make plenty of money. And as for travel, if I can travel business class, why do staff need to fly first class? I don't get it."

I agreed with him, but said nothing.

"Never mind," he continued. "What your group is doing is something else. Getting more women to run things makes us more productive. You're doing us a favor. Fighting for childcare is another good idea. It won't help mothers only, will it? It'll help the men, right? On-site childcare makes it easier for women to keep working when their babies are born, and less likely to take emergency leave when a babysitter doesn't show up. Yes?"

Listening to him, I was sorrier than ever that he was leaving. "The men I grew up with believed in women," I told him. "They encouraged and respected us. When I joined the Bank, I was shocked by how dismissive men were of women. You aren't like that, though. Why is that?"

"Like the men in your family," he said, "I've been surrounded by smart women. My wife, Margaret, doesn't let me forget the problems men create for women. My daughter had a baby recently, and she's been filling me in on what it's like not to have good childcare when she she's at work."

I nodded. Here was a man who was willing to learn from the women he loved.

"Our problem here is that Bank men don't want anything to change, and they ignore the problem. They stonewall."

I loved hearing McNamara argue my case for me. Stepping briskly to an expanse of empty desk, he removed a rubber band from a long roll of paper, then smoothed the paper out on the desk.

"Come, take a look at this," he said, pointing to the paper.

I joined him at the desk.

"These are blueprints for the new Bank building going up next year. See this? It's your childcare center. On the ground floor. A separate street entrance. Enough room for babies and toddlers galore."

I stared at the blueprints in disbelief.

"Once I'm gone, you've got to keep fighting for the women and children. The men won't like you for it. But you've got to do it."

"Thank you," I said, giving Robert McNamara an awkward hug.

"It's not easy hugging around a sling," he laughed.

On my way to the elevator, I stopped at the secretary's desk and stared back at the president's closed door.

"He's a good man," I said.

"He is," she agreed. "No matter what some people say."

I would miss Robert McNamara terribly. His leaving meant my conversations with World Bank presidents were over. I had no confidence in the future of women at the Bank without McNamara. Perhaps it was time for me to do something new.

I was ready to have a baby.

I was nearly through the first trimester of my pregnancy when, on October 6, Egyptian President Anwar Sadat was assassinated by members of the Egyptian Islamic Jihad, a militant group dedicated to overthrowing the Egyptian government and replacing it with an Islamic state.

I was horrified and grief-stricken for Jehan Sadat, for her personal loss and for the Egyptian women she'd cared so much about. Would all her work on their behalf come to dust? Had Amal been right that the Islamic Brotherhood was eager to take charge? Would Americans give up on peace in the Middle East? I knew nothing about Hosni Mubarak, but I wondered if as an American I'd still be welcome in Egypt? Would I still have a job?

Less than a week after Sadat's assassination, I was back in Cairo. The threat of continued violence there was real, but it never occurred to me not to go. This time my trip coincided with a visit by my division chief, Peter Naylor.

"I know you're used to being in Cairo on your own," Peter said one day, soon after I'd arrived. "But I thought I'd join you for the afternoon, before I head off to supervise our fruit-and-vegetable project in Crete."

"Ah yes, those out-of-control fruits and vegetables. They need a lot of supervision, they do." Teasing Bank managers was one of my favorite sports.

"No, really. Just because you were the first Bank person to show up in Cairo after the assassination—a pregnant woman, no less—doesn't mean you get to have all the fun. We old men want to see the pyramids, too. And the Sphinx. And the Egyptian Museum. Speaking of which, have you been to the museum yet?"

No, I admitted, I hadn't. For all the times I'd been to Cairo, I'd never made it to the museum.

"Let's go now," said Peter, offering me his arm, ever the English gentleman.

In the midst of chaotic downtown Cairo stood the majestic Egyptian Museum, a great domed neoclassical vision in salmon pink.

"Extraordinary," said Peter, opening the door, nodding at the guard, and following me in.

I was struck by how dark the place was. And musty. I'd seen Egyptian artifacts before in the British Museum and the Smithsonian, but this was one of the most magnificent collections of Egyptian antiquities in the world. The exhibits, though, were uninspired, to say the least. The lighting was terrible. The display cases were so old and dark we could barely see some of the objects. Dust danced in the light descending from the skylights in the central atrium. Unopened wooden crates looked like they'd sat there for at least one hundred years. Signage was vague or nonexistent. Case after case of ancient marvels begged to be pored over, but with little-to-no information on offer, they blended into an indecipherable whole.

Peter and I walked quietly from one room to the other, looking at the collection of treasures from the days of the pharaohs and their mummified remains. The place was packed with grave goods, jewelry, eating bowls, toys—more than a hundred thousand objects in fifteen thousand square meters of space.

"I hate to say it, but doesn't it feel a bit like a glorified storeroom?" Peter whispered, echoing my thoughts.

Still, it was a welcome respite from everything outside—the vendors shouting in the Khan el-Khalili and the young boys with machine guns over their shoulders on every corner. I was grateful to Peter for suggesting the visit.

We continued to walk from mummy to sphinx to statuette to necklace to stoneware. As we headed towards the front hall to leave, I was drawn to a friendly statue of a blue hippo standing in a small display case. A card stood next to it with an English translation of the Arabic, identifying it as: "Taweret, the goddess of fertility. The fierce protector of small children." Of all the museum's glittering treasures, this was my favorite.

"Peter, look!" I said, and pointed at the hippo.

"What a lovely creature," said Peter. "Such a kind smile."

Later that week, I ducked out of my work in the ministry to join a Bank agricultural economist friend to visit a Bank-funded sites and services project in Manshiyat Naser, a slum settlement on the outskirts of Cairo. Nearly every space of this village was covered in garbage, including streets and rooftops. The municipal government had no garbage collecting to speak of, so the Zabbaleen, or "garbage people," filled the gap, by collecting the garbage of Cairo's residents for a small fee, then transporting it via donkey carts or pickup trucks to their homes in Manshiyat Naser. Once home, they sorted the garbage for recyclable materials. Men collected the trash, and women and children sorted.

I was amazed at the Zabbaleen resourcefulness and the pride they took in their work and their "city of garbage." I was also pleased to know the Bank was there to help improve conditions, build on what was there already, not destroy it or relocate anyone. In Manshiyat Naser, I saw a different kind of Bank project, one that spoke more directly to my heart. I had always identified more with small non-governmental organization (NGO)-type projects like this one, direct action with a community, than with multi-million-dollar highway projects. Perhaps, I thought, there was more I could do at the Bank than I'd believed. My visit to Manshiyat Naser gave me hope, and would serve me well later.

My last night in Cairo, I had dinner with a British-Egyptian couple and their cheerful, gregarious ten-year-old son, Adam. Clearly at ease with adults, Adam had a story to tell.

"There was a big military parade last week, where President Sadat was going to review the troops. My friend, his dad, and I went to the parade and sat on the platform with the president.

"We were so excited; we couldn't sit down. We watched the planes do acrobatics in the air. We watched the paratroopers. We cheered as the soldiers drove their tanks down the street to where we were sitting on the platform. Once they got there, the troops turned to face us. Well, to face President Sadat," he admitted. "Then, there was a huge noise and commotion on the platform. People started screaming. Chairs toppled over. Soldiers from one of the tanks were shooting at the president!

"It sounds funny, but right away, I thought *"Malesh"* [never mind], like it must be a joke. Only, suddenly, I knew it wasn't a joke. I watched my friend jump on a chair to try to take a picture. When I shouted, 'Get down!' he was already out of sight. I got down on the ground, pulled a chair over my head, and stayed there until a policeman came and took me home," Adam finished.

"Eleven people died from bullet wounds," added Adam's mother. "Miraculously, Adam's friend and his father also lived through it. We're so proud of Adam for quickly realizing he had to duck for cover. He saved his own life."

I looked at Adam, tears in my eyes. If my baby was a boy, I'd name him Adam. A prayer that whatever came, my son would survive.

New Mother

My water broke before dinner on April 2, 1982. Knowing it would be a long night, Cliff headed upstairs to take a nap while Christian and I watched Warren Beatty's movie, *Reds*, about the Greenwich Village socialist Jack Reed, who was famous for writing an eyewitness account of the Russian Revolution. The role of my grandfather Floyd—a close friend of Reed's and editor of the radical *Masses* magazine—was played by an unknown actor. It was a small part, but Floyd was there, nonetheless. Watching *Reds* was a good distraction for me. By the time the movie ended, Christian had fallen asleep and Cliff had woken up. My contractions were seven minutes apart.

Cliff set me up in our ugly recliner in the living room. I and my huge belly stretched out and got as comfortable as possible. Cliff put on some soothing classical music, sat on a stool, and massaged my swollen feet. As my contractions came faster, he called my obstetrician.

"Wait," said the doctor. "Your wife is better off at home than in the hospital. More comfortable. Tell her to wait."

We waited. Cliff was bright and alert, funny, excited, and definitely in charge, ready at a moment's notice to help me into the car and head for the hospital.

At 5 a.m., Cliff called the doctor again, and convinced him to meet us at the hospital. We roused Christian and took him to Ellie's nearby home.

In the early-morning darkness, we arrived at the hospital. While Cliff was parking the car, I chatted with the staff at the front desk. A nurse brought me a wheelchair, which I thought was odd. I was pregnant, not sick or disabled. When she insisted, I sat in the chair, continuing to chat and laugh with Cliff while he filled out the paperwork.

"You are probably the most cheerful couple I've ever seen on its way to the labor room," said the nurse. If I'd thought about it, this comment might have taken me aback. But I didn't; I was proud and glad for us. I loved Cliff and this baby-to-be. The waiting was almost over, why shouldn't we laugh?

By noon, I was definitely not laughing. I'd been having contractions for almost twenty hours. They were coming harder and closer together. But each time the doctor checked, he found me no more dilated than before. A large clock on the wall ticked in slow motion. The contractions became blinding. My failure to dilate seemed to go on forever. I was doing a terrible job. I hadn't prepared well enough. I was letting all of us down—myself, Cliff, and the new baby. The pain quintupled. Nothing of me was left but helpless gasps.

After twenty-four hours of labor, my contractions began to slow down. I was frantic.

"The doctor is here," soothed Cliff. And he was, hooking me up to a fetal monitor, attaching an IV, sending Pitocin into my bloodstream. In childbirth preparation class, I'd learned Pitocin would bring about block contractions. Instead of the gradual building-up and releasing of pain, there were likely to be long periods of intense pain.

Intense pain was right.

"Okay, Doctor, I see the head. Baby's coming," said the labor nurse. "Let's get her to the delivery room." They wheeled me out the door into the impossibly bright, fluorescently lit hallway.

"I've got the front, you grab the back," the doctor called to Cliff, as they careened down the hall, looking for a delivery room. Suddenly I was on a table, surrounded by people in green clothes wearing masks. Cliff was wearing a mask, too, and a hospital gown over his clothes. Someone spread my legs far too wide, splitting me in half. Someone was swabbing me with an iodine disinfectant.

"Push, push!" shouted the nurse.

Why had I chosen natural childbirth? Why had I refused painkillers? I couldn't remember. Why had I insisted on feeling all of this?

I closed my eyes tight as the room spun and pain engulfed me.

I was sure that my insides were exploding when I heard Cliff shout, "Sweetie, look! It's a boy! It's a boy!"

As I promised myself I would in Cairo, we named him Adam.

The World Bank was a good employer when it came to mothers with new babies: three months' paid maternity leave and an additional one month of annual leave, if we wanted it. I took all four months.

When Adam was one week old, I was at the soccer field, baby strapped to my chest, to cheer on his brother Christian. A week later, I stood on the dining room table to attach balloons to a chandelier, having organized a big party for Cliff's forty-third birthday. I even had a few reports to edit while the baby was sleeping. I saw no reason a baby should slow me down. I was third-generation working mother. My mother and both my grandmothers raised their children while working full time. Surely I could do the same, just add a baby on to everything else.

Cliff was not a young father. Much as he loved the baby, he had less energy than he had ten years earlier, when Christian was born. He wasn't getting much more sleep than I was. He suffered one serious sinus infection after another, and underwent surgery for a deviated septum. The dentist he had seen as a kid in Niagara Falls was a fraud, and the year Adam was born, Cliff needed implants to replace all his teeth. All this, and a baby, too. The Bank was much less generous to new fathers than new mothers. In the early 1980s, the idea of paternity leave had not even entered the public discussion. Sleepy and in pain, Cliff went back to work a week after Adam was born.

Sometimes, though, I resented Cliff's freedom to go off to work at the Bank every day. For eight years, the World Bank had been my life. I saw and talked to dozens of people constantly—in the offices, the cafeterias, the corridors, and the elevators. Now I was home alone with a baby all the time. Maternity leave was an extrovert's nightmare. It didn't help that my baby was prone to painful ear infections, which could only be treated by antibiotics. This meant many trips to the pharmacy for pink medicine. He was also plagued with terrible digestion. Perhaps he was allergic to my breast milk? This meant many trips out for goat's milk. Between his ear infections and digestive problems, it felt like Adam was constantly crying, and inconsolable. When I asked the pediatrician for a diagnosis, he said "colic." When I asked what colic was, he said "unexplained crying."

That wasn't much help.

During those difficult months, I spent my happiest moments with another mother with whom I'd attended my childbirth preparation class, and her baby. Whenever I knocked on her door, she would greet me with a cheerful, "Welcome to the Land of Chaos!"

Nothing about being home with a baby full-time came naturally to me. My grandmother Florence had been only nineteen when my mother was born. When my mother was still a toddler, Florence left her with her parents in Philadelphia, while she flew off to Geneva to work unencumbered at the League of Nations. I don't think my mother ever forgave her mother for this. My mother had been only eighteen when I was born. She left college in her sophomore year to take care of me, and I wasn't sure if she ever forgave me, either. These days, my mother and her mother, both single, were busy with jobs, friends, and going out with men. Neither of them had much interest in babies or babysitting.

Meanwhile, I couldn't wait to get back to work. Dealing with office politics and World Bank bureaucracy, traveling to and from Egypt, writing reports, and advocating for women's rights seemed easy compared to being home with a baby full-time.

When Adam was two months old, I took him to the office. At the end of a long line of well-wishers stood my division chief, Peter Naylor. When his turn to meet Adam came, Peter placed on my desk a box the size of a small loaf of bread, tied with twine.

"A baby gift," he said.

I handed Adam to him, untied the twine and removed a piece of soft cotton cloth. There lay a bright blue ceramic hippo with a round belly, a funny face, and four stubby legs, smiling at me.

"Taweret," said Peter. "Remember? We saw her that day we spent together in the Cairo Museum when you were first pregnant. All those priceless artifacts in that dusty, miserably lit, first-floor gallery . . . you gravitated straight to the hippo. Am I right about that?"

"Oh, yes!" In my enthusiasm, I gave Peter a hug that almost crushed the baby snuggling against him.

"Taweret—she who is great, the goddess of fertility and childbirth, the fierce protector of children. I thought it fit," said Peter, smiling. "The perfect mother."

I wondered about that. I'd waited a long time to have a baby—thirteen years longer than my mother did. Surely I was old enough, competent and confident enough, to take care of a newborn. So why did I feel so overwhelmed and inadequate toward the task? Why did my confidence desert me every time my baby cried with an earache or stomach pain? In the years to come, I'd look to the blue hippo and what she represented for comfort and courage.

I loved my new baby with a passion I could never have imagined, but I felt like a mother without a map. Meanwhile, my husband Cliff, for all his feminism, clearly resented the time I devoted to our baby instead of him. Like me, he found that a baby with colic was exhausting, and made worse by the baby's mother who thought she could do it all, and when she couldn't, became anxious and unhappy.

Despite my best efforts, the Bank still didn't have a childcare center. The week Tom Clausen replaced McNamara as president, he'd removed the on-site childcare center from the blueprints for the new building. In order to return to work, I'd need to figure out my own childcare solution.

Veronique, a friend of mine from the Bank, had given birth a few weeks before I did. She was French and—as an employee of an international organization—held a G-4 visa. This visa permitted her to hire non-American, live-in, domestic help on a G-5 visa. Since she and I lived only four blocks apart, we decided to share the services of a live-in babysitter on a G-5 visa. It seemed like a great idea, but then Veronique and her husband decided their house was too small to accommodate a live-in babysitter. We needed a different solution.

I started making calls. I lucked out when I reached the social services department for Arlington County, and a polite, soft-spoken man named King answered the phone. King was a social worker from Laos who'd emigrated to the US several years earlier. He had many connections in the Lao community and thought he could help us identify someone suitable to look after the little boys. Less than twenty-four hours later, King was at the house, introducing us to a gentle young woman named Bé, also polite, also soft-spoken, and also from Laos. We hired her on the spot.

Although Cliff had always been a drinker, I'd not worried too much about it. Once we had a baby, however, he started to drink more. And more. The more he drank, the more his anger erupted. If I called him on the drinking, he'd tell me this was my, not his, problem. My lovely, agreeable husband seemed to have vanished. Added to that, Christian's mother had begun to pressure us to let Christian live with her. It often felt like more than I could manage.

After four months of maternity leave, I was eager to get back to the office, where I'd be more myself and less the frantic new mother of a baby with colic. I wanted to have adult conversations about Egypt and water resources and job classifications. I wanted to wear dresses, pantyhose, pumps, and makeup again. I wanted to be the woman I would recognize as me.

My first day back to work, my boss, Peter Naylor, greeted me warmly. When he asked to see baby pictures, I brought out the inevitable images of a chubby, bald baby. As we flipped through the photos, Peter asked how I had liked being home with a baby.

"Fine," I said, a little too quickly, "But I'm glad to be back. *Really* glad."

Peter raised an eyebrow. "Bad as that, eh?"

I shrugged. "So, what's been happening here?" I asked, quickly changing the subject.

"There's some news I think you're going to like. Your promotion from "I" to "J" was approved, and the salary that goes with it, retroactive for two years."

"That's fantastic!"

"Wait, there's some other—less fantastic—news," said Peter. "While you were gone, the director decided not to renew the agreement with the UN to execute the Egypt Water Master Plan."

"What?" I was baffled. "You mean that I'm out of a job?"

"I'm afraid so," said Peter.

"You mean they've promoted me, graded me at a professional level, given me a salary increase, *and* they've eliminated my job?"

"That's about it," said Peter. "Nothing much we can do. It's up to the director whether or not to renew the contract with UNDP. I know it doesn't make any sense."

In terms of my director's perspective, however, it made plenty of sense. The job grading team had obviously concluded I was an assistant doing professional-level work, which might make it appear he had been exploiting a female staff member for two years. Rather than be called out for sexism and poor management, he abolished my job, and hoped to be done with me. Only it didn't happen quite the way he'd hoped.

I was furious. Not with Peter, of course. He had taken a risk by giving me my first chance to succeed at the World Bank. When things were going poorly in Cairo, and Peter sent me to give him a second opinion about what was going on, Dick stomped off, and got a different job. I took over as project coordinator for the Egypt Water Master Plan. But I was furious with my director, whose sexism was not a secret in the department, and whose ego was as big as a house.

I'd always known that the director of personnel would never forgive me for witnessing his embarrassment in McNamara's office. I was sure that, like my department director, he might have thought that eliminating my job meant getting rid of me.

But both men were wrong. My work on the Egypt Water Master Plan was fixed-term, but I'd been permanent regular staff for seven years. The Bank couldn't fire me unless I did something wrong. And I'd done nothing wrong. Unless being a woman and having a baby was wrong.

When I got back to my office, I made the first of many calls to Personnel. The telephone pressed hard against my ear, I said into the receiver: "This is Jerri Dell, back from maternity leave. We have a problem—a big problem."

Over the next weeks, I spent countless hours writing up my grievance, explaining in detail what had happened. I described the work I did, attached several glowing performance reports and letters of appreciation from the Cairo Office and the ministry of irrigation, and finally the results of the job regrading exercise. I was perfect for the job, I told them.

"But that's the problem," said my personnel officer. "There is no job."

"I understand that, but that's because the director chose not to extend the contract. There was no reason not to extend the contract."

"Yes, but . . ."

"What this means is that I've gone from being a productive World Bank employee to a troublesome personnel problem."

"Wait a minute," said the personnel officer. "The Water Master Plan isn't even a World Bank project. You were hired to coordinate a fixed-term project, which means the director is free to let you go."

"Wrong," I said. "The project was fixed-term, but not me. I am 'regular staff.' Check it out. I've been regular staff for seven years. The Bank can't fire me without cause."

Silence. "I don't think the director knows this. Let me get back to you."

For a week, I heard nothing more from Personnel. I arrived every morning at the Bank at eight and returned home at six. I filed papers, wrote goodbye notes to my friends in Cairo, lunched with friends in the cafeteria, and got angrier by the minute. It may have been the anger with the Bank that helped me get over what I had come to realize was post-partum depression.

At last, I got the call from my personnel officer. "We've read your grievance letter and reviewed your case. We agree that the Bank must respect its commitment to you as regular staff. No one can force you out of the Bank. But you can't force the director to keep your project in the department against his will, either. Since you two are at a stalemate, I've told the director he must hire you to work with him directly at your new grade and salary."

I was horrified. How could I be expected to work in such proximity to the man who had just tried to fire me? A director who was as furious with me as I was with him.

"That's all we have to offer," said the personnel officer. "Take it or leave it."

I took it.

My first meeting with the director as my immediate supervisor did not begin well.

"So, what are you going to do with me?" I asked. "I'd rather not spend my days erasing white paper. Have you got a plan?"

He gave me a pained expression, "You aren't going to make this easy for me, are you?"

"Not at all," I said, and stared at him without blinking.

This was the tenor of all our conversations. Finally, he chose a job for me: writing speeches for him to deliver.

"I have to give a speech about the transportation sector in Yugoslavia. The Bank has financed a lot of highway projects there. I want you to write a speech about highways in Yugoslavia for me to give at the Cosmos Club in a few months. Do you think you can do that?"

I sensed a smirk lurking there somewhere.

"I can write. Yes, I can do that," I said. I turned on my heel and walked back to my office, where I sat and thought more about my new assignment. "Highways in Yugoslavia," for crying out loud.

In 1982, with no internet, learning something new took quite a while. The World Bank financed many highway projects in Yugoslavia, and there were dozens of extraordinarily dull reports written about them: appraisal reports, loan agreements, supervision, and evaluation reports. One was more tedious than the next. To understand what was involved in Yugoslavia as a country, and as far as highways were concerned, in particular, was a dreary business.

Once I'd written up my notes on the Bank's work in Yugoslavia, I tried to find some way to engage an audience, the hardest part of the assignment. Over and over, I wrote what I thought the director wanted to say. Once a week, he called me into his office to update him on my progress. Once I'd summarized what I'd done, he'd snort.

"What? That's all you've done? What good is that? And, no, that's not what I want to say at all!"

"So, what do you want to say?"

Often I felt like he was holding a playing card in his hand and asking me to guess what the card was. When I'd guess "5," he'd say, "Wrong!" A week later, I'd say "3." He'd say, "Wrong!"

One step forward in research and writing and two steps back each time he changed his mind about what he wanted. It was like trying to hit a moving target.

When we'd finally run out of time, and he was due to give the speech in a week, he called me in and told me to leave my draft on his desk by close of business. I liked the final draft of my speech, and was relieved to hand it over. The day before I submitted the draft, I mailed a copy to my father. I was interested in his opinion as a professional speechwriter at the Library of Congress.

As soon as I arrived at work on Monday morning, the director called me into his office. When I walked in, he was standing, back to me, staring out the window.

"Sit down," he said, without turning around.

I sat in one of the two guest chairs across from his large desk. He continued to stand silently, his back to me, for some time. At last, he turned around, walked toward me, and said:

"Do you expect me to give this speech you wrote?"

"Why not?"

"Because it's worthless, that's why not. You've heard nothing I've said. You don't know the first thing about the World Bank. This document of yours proves what I've known all along. You are not professional material. Whatever you've told the job grading team is as worthless as this speech."

"Excuse me?" I said, heat rising from my chest to my neck and face. "My speech is worthless and I'm worthless, too?" Now we were both standing, with only a desk between us.

"Sit down," he said, emphasizing "down."

"I'll sit down when you do," I shot back.

We sat.

"You know what your problem is?" He didn't wait for a reply. "You haven't suffered enough."

"I see," I answered. "A new school of management, perhaps? Management-by-suffering?"

He gave me a nasty look. "You can go now. I'll write the damn speech myself."

That night my father called. "It's an excellent speech," he said. "Well done. It's hard to believe you could captivate an audience with highways in Yugoslavia, but you seem to have done it."

"Oh yeah?" I asked, then recounted my conversation with my director. Not only was the speech terrible, but I barely deserved to live for having written it.

"Sweetie," he said. "Get out of there, fast. It's not the speech."

I followed my father's advice, and told the director he'd have to find me another job immediately. Although he glared at me—who the hell was I, telling him what to do?—he quickly found me a new job in one of his divisions.

After losing a job I loved, and working for a man who couldn't stand me, it was a relief to have something else to do. Anything else. It wouldn't be Egypt, but whatever it was, I'd give it a try. It felt strange to have been promoted to a higher grade, and to be earning a higher salary than ever, and yet to feel less significant than I'd ever felt.

In my new job, I worked with Noel, an Irish public sector specialist who'd taken a leave of absence from the Irish government to work at the Bank in the technical assistance division of the Middle East and North Africa department. Noel and I were both a little unsure of exactly what we were doing for the division, but we tried to make the most of our assignments.

Noel was short, trim, and eager. He wore polyester suits, brown oxford shoes, and wide ties in unfortunate prints. He had pale Irish skin and a shiny scalp. His forehead shimmered. Noel was easygoing unless someone crossed him. Like my former boss, on the Egypt Water Master Plan, he may have felt undervalued, his experience and talent wasted at the Bank. Unlike Heiges, however, he was friendly and appreciated the work I did.

After I'd been on the job a few months, Noel asked me to join a technical assistance mission he was leading in Yemen. The purpose of the mission was to identify a technical-assistance component of a Bank loan to strengthen the ministry of planning in the Yemen Arab Republic. I didn't see much of a role for myself on this team, which already was comprised of the Bank's loan officer for Yemen, a T.A. officer, and Noel. But Cliff encouraged me to go. He reminded me that when young professionals take on their first assignment, they are almost always sent on mission right away. Usually, the job was no more than to shadow the guy in charge, carry his briefcase, observe how he worked. Traveling together also gave the mission leader a chance to observe how the YP held up in the field, and to determine whether this young person could be trusted to be diplomatic or convincing enough in the field, to connect well with government people and project staff. Cliff saw this opportunity as a chance for me to prove myself. I decided to go.

I had usually traveled alone to Egypt. Within a short time, I had plenty of friends in Cairo to look after me. But the Yemen mission would be different. Noel wanted someone to carry his bag, take notes, and be the mission secretary. Nothing more.

We took a flight from Dulles to Rome and then from Rome to Yemen the next morning. The airport in Rome was chaotic; we had trouble finding the gate for our connecting flight. When we finally learned the number, we raced there without a thought about our luggage.

After landing in Sana'a, we waited at the carousel for what seemed an eternity. No luggage. While I had stuffed a change of clothes and a novel to read on the plane into my carry-on, all my mission documents—briefing papers, reports, terms of reference, background papers, a list of people to see—were in my luggage. The luggage was still in Rome. There was only one flight a week from Rome to Sana'a.

Noel was more than a little unhappy. "Don't you know you can never check anything important on the plane? There is always the possibility luggage will be lost. You must always assume it will be lost and act accordingly." For a moment, I imagined how Fareed Atabani, my mentor during my early days at the Bank, might have just let it go. Not humiliate me.

I had been to Cairo back-and-forth six times by then and my luggage had never been lost. I had no reason to assume it would be. I began to seethe. Why was I the only one carrying documents for the mission? I was angry with Noel but I was also angry with myself, and was glad when both of us realized that being angry wasn't helping. I also realized there was nothing I could do about the lost luggage. I'd have to wash my clothes in the sink, and wait at least seven days to get the documents.

It was 1985 and Yemen had only been a member of the World Bank for a few years. By then, Yemen was two separate countries: the Yemen Arab Republic (North Yemen)—where we were—and the People's Democratic Republic of Yemen (South Yemen). Conversations over dinner enlightened me about the politically volatile situation in the country, which may have been why it felt so dangerous, as if another civil war were inevitable. While the government officials were well-mannered and polite to us, I always had the feeling they were far from forthcoming.

Yemen was rougher than Egypt. I could tell by the glint in the eyes of the Yemeni men. And by the daggers most of them wore tucked into the belts around their waists. They looked like accessories rather than weapons. And yet, the Yemenis assured me the knives in their sheaths were always kept sharp, just in case. As I walked through the city, those daggers did nothing to put my mind at ease.

Cairo had been hot, but it didn't come close to the heat in Yemen. As Muslims, the Yemenis didn't drink, but this rule did not apply to foreigners. Although I rarely drank beer at home, in Sana'a I discovered the pleasure of a bottle of ice-cold beer at the end of the day.

Other than drinking beer, I did my best to respect Yemen's conservative Moslem culture. I wore long sleeves and long skirts. Except with my colleagues on the mission at the end of the day, I was quiet and reserved. I restrained myself. The only women I'd seen since I arrived were mysterious, eerie-looking figures swathed in layers of black fabric from head-to-toe. A window of fine black mesh allowed a woman to see out without being seen. Women were anonymous objects without shapes or features. They reminded me of stagehands dressed in black so an audience wouldn't notice them changing sets on the dark stage between acts.

Yemen was a mystery. In the three weeks I was there, I didn't learn much about the inner workings of the place. I did learn, however, that I was done going on mission for a while—especially on missions where I felt useless and redundant. I'd wait until Adam was older, and I had the opportunity to do work that was worthwhile—worth leaving Adam for.

It was bad enough that I felt inadequate as a mother, but I was losing my confidence as a professional as well. I could barely advocate for myself, let alone other women. I had to learn the hard way that at the Bank, men still had the power to put me down, stop me in my tracks, refuse me opportunities to succeed.

Ten years at the Bank and it felt like I still didn't belong. I was still learning firsthand what our staff association status of women working group reports had been documenting for years: The World Bank was not a welcoming workplace for women. Losing my job in Egypt made me miserably unhappy. I was furious with my director and outraged with the Bank. But it was more than that. I was disappointed in myself. Why didn't I have the courage to leave the Bank's "golden cage"? Did I stay because no other employer would offer the same benefits? I hoped not.

When I returned from Yemen, I wanted a project of my own. Something that would teach me more about Bank operations, perhaps. Noel didn't object and suggested I develop a technical assistance database for the department.

I'd identify the type of technical assistance the World Bank financed—technical advisory (TA) services, foreign experts helicoptered into government ministries to solve problems, or institutional T.A., foreign experts working alongside national staff to teach them do this work themselves. I'd use the information to determine the strengths and weaknesses of technical assistance, and suggest how it might be improved upon in the future.

For the two years I worked on the database project, I learned a lot about Bank financing in the Arab States—the extent to which they were (or were not) building national staff capacity to do the work itself. I discovered how little was actually being done when it came to capacity building. Although the Bank included T.A. and training in many projects, it was done in a perfunctory way, focused more on technical advice. And no attention was paid to women or gender issues in development at all. This mattered to me. I wanted to see if there was something I could do about it. Meanwhile, I'd keep adding to the database and start looking for another job.

Meanwhile, our babysitter Bé left us to marry King, the soft-spoken social worker from Laos who first introduced her to us, and to resume her studies. We were happy for her, of course. But we knew we'd never be able to replace her, and we'd have to do the best we could with the childcare center nearest to where we lived.

Every morning when I dropped Adam off at the center, he clung to me. He was sick all the time. I spent hours at work every day worrying about him. How often I thought of the SWWG childcare questionnaire we'd sent out year after year, long before I'd ever considered having a baby myself. Now I knew firsthand how important it was to have reliable, good childcare. But on-site Bank childcare had been off the table for five years; I harbored little hope of this changing any time soon. We'd just have to make do.

Respect

In spring 1986, one of my fellow childcare advocates called on the phone.

"You're not going to believe this. The vice president and director of personnel want to talk about childcare."

"What do they want to talk about?"

"How to set up a childcare center at the Bank," she said, sounding as skeptical as I felt.

When I contacted the VP's office, I learned that our new President, Barber Conable, thought on-site childcare might be good for staff morale. He had asked to be briefed, and recalled that SWWG had a childcare working group that would probably know something about what should be done to get a center up-and-running. Maybe we could put the briefing paper together for him. I jumped at this new opportunity to advocate for our longtime cause.

As I entered the waiting room outside the VP's office, I was surprised to find my old nemesis, Lacy Carter, the old colonialist in sensible shoes, advisor to the director of personnel, and self-appointed "conscience of the World Bank" sitting there. I'd barely seen her in the eight years since she told me that The World Bank was not a babysitter. That it wasn't in the ethos of the Bank to have little children running around, that the men would never agree.

In 1981, though, one man had agreed: Robert McNamara. He agreed enough to include a childcare site in the blueprints for the new Bank building. Then, his successor had taken it out. But now, it seemed, President Barber Conable agreed with McNamara about this important issue.

"Well, Miss Carter," I asked. "What brings you here?"

"It seems the Bank's management has decided to ignore my advice," she said stiffly, "and wants to give you a place for all those babies. Right here in the Bank building."

"So I understand," I said.

The vice president opened the door. He was the same skinny, birdlike Dutchman I'd first met with McNamara in 1979 about the status of women in the Bank. The Austrian personnel director was there as well: a few pounds heavier, his hair now whiter than blonde. The VP sat at the table with me to his left, the director to his right, and Lacy Carter next to him.

The VP didn't waste time. What does a childcare center look like? How much space will it need? Who will run it? What will it cost? Drawing from all we'd learned about childcare several years before, I gave rapidfire answers to his rapid-fire questions. The personnel director offered a few dull remarks, all obsequiousness to the VP. He said nothing about how many years ago we'd first given him this information, asked him questions, and hoped for answers that never came. The VP's head bobbed up and down as he scribbled notes on a yellow pad. The director followed his lead, scribbling furiously. In between scribbles, their eyes were on me.

Lacy Carter was not asked her opinion.

There was a lot involved in putting the World Bank Children's Center together. We had to create a parents' co-op, write articles of incorporation and bylaws, elect a board of directors, determine which age-groups to include, along with the center's educational objectives and a fee structure that would ensure equity and access to staff at different salary levels, coordinate with the Bank's architect on building design and with its general services department on construction oversight, write job descriptions for the director and staff, interview candidates, select a director, solicit applications from staff, and handle enrollment.

The details seemed endless; the effort, enormous. I knew we couldn't help all the women who needed care for their children to keep working. But we could help some. And then some more, year after year for decades. It was a worthy cause and a good investment. I knew it would be time well spent, even though it would mean I'd be busier at work than ever. But Adam would be in the center's first "graduating class," which meant this was something I could do for Adam and the World Bank at the same time.

Somehow, by September 1986, the World Bank Children's Center was ready to open. I was invited to speak at the opening ceremony and it was tempting to focus on the struggles of our past and all the abortive attempts we'd made to get Bank management to help us with childcare. Instead, I focused on our great achievement: the beautiful childcare center that would open its doors in a few days. I thanked Mr. and Mrs. Conable, our new director, and her highly qualified staff. I even thanked both the VP and the director of personnel, whom I'd seen earlier shaking hands with parents, smiling proudly.

Among the many parents there for the occasion, I was especially glad to see my old friend Veronique with her four-year-old Nathan, the little boy who spent the first two years of his life with Adam and our beloved Bé. She and Nathan stood talking with Cliff and Adam.

After my speech, Conable took a pair of small, blunt-edged scissors and cut through the brightly colored ribbon that stretched across the wooden jungle gym and playhouse. The crowd cheered. Adam and Nathan were the first to claim the center as they ran at top speed through the playhouse and slid down the slide. "I love it, Mommy. I love it!" shouted Adam above the din of the party.

After working so hard to get the center started, I was thrilled to see Adam's reaction. And Nathan's, Veronique's, and of course, Cliff's. This was a very good thing we'd done. Something that would benefit children and their parents for years to come. Something of which we could be proud.

The day after Conable officially opened our new childcare center for business, I attended a luncheon organized by a professional women's association. The keynote topic was "Women in the Board Room." The keynote speaker was Robert McNamara.

From my seat, I watched the former president of the World Bank walk slowly to the front of the room. This Mr. McNamara was old and stooped, almost small. Most of his hair was gone. He wasn't wearing his round metal glasses. He was hardly recognizable as himself—until he began to speak. I'd heard him give many speeches over the years, but this one was better than ever. If things continued taking their "normal course," he said, there would never be more than a few women in the boardroom. And with that, this old man became Robert McNamara again. Strong and impressive as ever.

"You've got to have affirmative action programs. You've got to establish targets. Quotas. Yes, I know company presidents and board chairmen hate this kind of thing. But it's either that or nothing changes. At least, not in my lifetime.

"When I worked at the World Bank, I learned this the hard way. It was a fight to convince my male colleagues to hire more women, to make the Bank a more appealing workplace for women, to offer part-time work and childcare. I never felt we accomplished as much as we should have. But the men at the World Bank didn't want to hear it, wouldn't even try."

It was good to hear his voice again.

During the question-and-answer session, I stood to speak at the microphone. "I've worked at the World Bank for twelve years. Everything Mr. McNamara says is true. Until he stood up for us, we didn't stand a chance. Support from the top made all the difference." I sat down.

Mr. McNamara replied, "Well, here's the woman who chaired the group that kept me honest, insisted that I improve things for women. Let me tell you, it's not only the man at the top who matters; it's the women agitating from the ranks as well. We can't do it without you!"

I returned to the microphone. "Mr. McNamara, when you left the Bank five years ago, your successor erased the childcare center from the plans for the new building. Your parting gift for us. Overnight, it was gone."

The room was quiet.

"But here's the rest. Five surveys and two presidents later, what do you know? The VP for administration asked us to help them create a childcare center for the World Bank. Yesterday afternoon, Mr. Conable cut the ribbon to open the center for business. We won."

Once the applause died down, Mr. McNamara turned to me and bowed.

New Manager

A few months after we opened the childcare center, I had lunch with my old friend and fellow feminist, Lee Roberts, the personnel policy officer with whom I'd authored the Bank's equal opportunity policy for women. Lee had moved from personnel to the Bank's Economic Development Institute, UNEDIL—a joint agency management training program for a dozen African management development institutes. At lunch he asked me if I had ever thought of working for the Bank's training institute.

I described an interview I'd had with a training officer ten years earlier, just after getting my MBA. But MBA or not, a twenty-five-year-old secretary without any operational or training experience had been deemed unqualified for the job. A few months later, I'd gotten the job working on the Egypt Water Master Plan and had put the training institute out of my mind.

"But that was ten years ago," said Lee. "Since then, you've managed to get McNamara and the Egyptian minister of irrigation to listen to you. You've put together a Bank-financed training database for the Middle East. Your group has a new childcare center up and running at the Bank."

"Don't forget the part about how I leap tall buildings with a single bound," I laughed.

But Lee was serious. An attitude survey had recently brought to light widespread dissatisfaction with the Institute as an organization. As a result, the director had hired a team of consultants to propose changes for bringing about improvement. These changes included a reorganization, a new divisional structure, and new job descriptions.

"A vacancy is coming up this week. A managerial position," said Lee. Now he had my attention.

"The director needs someone to manage a group of administrative officers, streamline training administration, and improve morale. According to the survey, the women in this unit have felt undervalued for years."

"Of course. It's the Bank, right?"

"Apply for the job. Make things better."

I followed Lee's advice.

My interview at the Institute went well. I was confident they'd offer me the job, and thrilled when they did. When I learned who'd be working for me, though, I wasn't so sure about taking it. Of the six administrative officers I'd be managing, I knew three: Laila, Annie, and Mona.

Laila was the same administrative assistant who'd shown me around my first day at the World Bank in 1974. If I accepted the job at the Institute, Laila would be working for me. Annie was the participant administrator who organized the Institute receptions, back when course participants were all men. I was one of the young women Annie had counted on to attend these receptions and entertain the participants. If I accepted this job, I'd be Annie's new boss.

I didn't know Mona very well, but what I did know worried me a little. We'd both been recruited as secretaries and had occasion to be together socially from time to time. Like my friend from the early days at the Bank, Ghislaine, Mona was from Quebec and both had joined the Bank about the same time. Whenever Mona was near me, she seemed edgy, almost as if she had a grudge against me. I always felt as though she had a grudge against me, though I didn't understand why. Maybe she resented my close friendship with Ghislaine? Whatever it was, I knew that being Mona's boss would be no easy feat. The other three women, whom I didn't know, were considerably older than me. Knowing I had joined the Bank as a secretary and risen through the ranks would not make it easy for them to accept me as their manager.

Confounded by all this, I called my father for advice. I explained the reasons I was nervous and told him I was reluctant to take the job.

"Do you think one of these women you'd be managing has a chance at the job?"

"No, not likely."

"If not, would whoever else they hire be likely to do a better job than you would?" My dad persevered.

"Probably not," I admitted.

"Take the job. The women will be lucky to have you." Of course, my father thought I'd do a good job; he was my father, after all. But maybe he was right. In spite of my reluctance, I accepted the job.

My first day at the Institute was not auspicious. Annie and Laila came to my office to greet me. Although they seemed ready to give me a chance, they warned me not to be hurt if my other staff members were less than friendly.

"They've been doing their jobs a long time. Your job is to make changes. They don't want to change. At all."

Prior to the reorganization, there were two separate positions—admissions officers and participant relations assistants. The admissions officers sent out course announcements to governments in developing countries, then selected the participants from among those countries' ministry officials. The participant relations assistants then organized the travel, hotels, per diem payments, and other administrative details. Courses usually lasted about two months and were held in Washington, D.C. Male trainers designed and delivered the courses; women administrators handled everything else.

More often than not, the trainers were late getting their courses ready in time for the admissions officers to announce the courses and select participants. This meant that the participant relations assistants didn't have the time they needed to make the best travel arrangements possible. Inevitably, the women had to compensate for the men's lack of planning. As a result, they worked long hours, usually had to put in a lot of overtime (without extra pay), and were always under stress.

Still, stress or no stress, the women seemed happier with the trainers than they were with me. When I proposed to impose deadlines on the trainers, they squirmed. When I insisted they take their annual leave and stop working so much unpaid overtime, they balked. From my perspective, they were martyring themselves to the institution. It took me a while to understand that they defined their worth by the sacrifices they were prepared to make for their male bosses.

As the Institute's most senior administrative assistant, Angela made it especially clear how insulted she was by my proposals. When I tried to get her to talk, she just stared, her mouth a thin line. She answered as few questions as possible. Mona's dismissive and often hostile behavior towards me made no secret of her point of view. I had no business managing the unit, much less managing her.

It didn't take more than six weeks before Angela, announced her retirement. Not surprisingly, she refused a farewell party.

Angela's departure created a vacancy, which I filled with Laurence Sage, a bright, young French woman. Laurence was open, warm, and cheerful. Best of all, she was more than happy to work for me. A born mediator, she would be key to the women's transition from the old practices to the new ones.

The Bank's management consultants made several recommendations, the first of which was to combine the tasks previously undertaken separately by admissions officers and the participation relations assistants into one new administrative officer position. From my staff's perspective, this meant a promotion for the administrative assistants and a demotion for the admissions officers. The consultants' solution seemed, at first, to solve very little. In fact, it seemed to have made everybody miserable.

In 1987, the Institute wasn't the only World Bank department to reorganize. Things were in a state of flux, Bank-wide. A goal of all the reorganization was to streamline the Bank's operation by reducing the number of staff. Consultants recommended that management offer "golden handshakes" to accomplish this goal. Cliff was one of the first to accept. He was thrilled that the Bank was ready to pay him to retire early. He disliked the Bank's hierarchy, in which he had to answer to multiple bosses. As an independent management consultant, he'd be free of that. As soon as he retired, he opened his own consulting firm, and became my personal guru again.

As a management consultant, Cliff knew things I needed to know—new approaches to human relations, how to motivate staff to do their best work, how to increase staff participation in the planning process, how to make meetings more interesting and productive. Not only was his guidance helpful to me as a unit manager, but it also helped me in my work as facilitator of departmental retreats and other large events. Cliff was a good teacher and I was grateful.

Even before Mona's death, though, over time, my staff began to realize they could do their new jobs, and do them well. As they gained confidence in themselves, they saw me less as a stumbling block and more as an advocate. Lee Roberts was the first to notice how much more efficient and productive the unit had become.

"Your team has come together, hasn't it?"

We talked about the ups and downs, how hard it had been at first. "Of course, the staff still gets annoyed when I tell them to take their annual leave, or refuse to let them take on more work than one person can manage, but it's better," I admitted, pleased he had noticed how well I did my new job.

"I've got a training-of-trainers workshop coming up in Botswana in a month," said Lee. "Do you think one of your administrative officers can join me? I can't rely on anyone in Gaborone for this and it would make a huge difference if I had someone to help."

After thinking it over, I suggested that I, rather than one of my staff, help Lee in Botswana. I wanted to learn firsthand what my staff's responsibilities were in the field. I thought doing the work myself would help me be a better manager.

Annie and Laurence both thought it was a good idea and were happy to brief me on what the job would entail. As it happened, virtually all my tasks would involve money. If there was one thing I found difficult—was even phobic about—it was money. I hated being responsible for it, holding on to it, paying people with it. I hated any financial transaction at all, even walking too close to a cash register in a department store. If I had a choice, I'd always leave anything money-related to someone else. But in my role as administrative officer, I didn't have a choice. When my staff traveled overseas to help with a course, they carried a huge amount of cash on the plane. Thirty participants in Gaborone for three weeks would each receive one hundred dollars per day for expenses. I would have to carry fifty thousand dollars for participant per diem and another ten thousand dollars for workshop expenses—sixty-thousand dollars in cash on my person on the plane. I shuddered.

Annie told me to wear the cash in a money belt around my waist. When I asked why I should carry cash instead of making a bank transfer from Washington, she replied, "That's the way we've always done it." A familiar refrain.

In June 1988, I arrived in Gaborone alone with sixty thousand dollars in cash and a list of instructions for what to do with it. Without a World Bank resident mission in the city, I had no one to turn to for advice. My first morning, I called the African project manager, who welcomed me to Gaborone and said he looked forward to seeing me soon. I waited for him to tell me when a car would meet me at the hotel. But he never mentioned a car.

Along with my anxiety about anything money-related, I hated getting lost. I was both financially and geographically challenged—not the attributes of your typical World Banker. I gave the address of the project office to the man at the reception desk, and he assured me it was quite easy to get there from the hotel. I should leave by the front door, turn right at the first corner where the shop was, walk another five or maybe eight blocks to the fruit vendor, turn right there, then continue down.

My head spinning, I smiled brightly at him, turned left and began to walk along the hot, dusty road, the bank's project office address clutched tightly in my fist. I made several more wrong turns, and asked innumerable people for directions. What should have been a ten-minute walk from the hotel to the office took me about an hour. When I knocked on the door, the project manager looked up at me, slightly annoyed. "What took you so long?" he asked.

"Oh, I got a bit of a late start," I said, unwilling to tell him the real story. I still had to get the money changed from dollars into the local currency, *pula*. I asked him which commercial bank the World Bank dealt with in Gaborone. Without asking me why I needed a bank, he sent me out on foot once again, with vague directions. Luckily, I had less trouble finding the bank than I did his office. When I arrived, I explained to the teller that I had sixty thousand American dollars that I needed to exchange for *pula*. The teller looked worried.

"Sixty thousand dollars, *Madame*? Are you sure?"

I nodded.

He told me to wait and went to get his manager. I waited, money belt bulging under my cotton blouse. People stared. About half an hour later, the bank manager arrived, led me to his office, and closed the door. I explained my situation. It would take a while to make this transaction, the bank manager explained. He did not keep that kind of money in the branch office.

As promised, it took a while—almost five hours of sitting on a hard chair in the lobby, as people came and went, each staring at me in turn. By the time the manager tapped my shoulder, I was asleep.

"*Madame*, please come to our back room, and we will pull the shades. We have your money for you. You may count it, unobserved."

I did as he asked. On the table in the back room were thirty-thousand twenty-pula banknotes, in three thousand bundles.

Until that moment, I hadn't known the currency rate of exchange: ten *pula* to one dollar. I would be exchanging sixty thousand dollars for six hundred thousand *pula*. It hadn't occurred to me to bring a suitcase in which to carry the *pula*. There was just me and a ton of *pula*, and no security guard to accompany me to the hotel.

"I trust you," I said to the manager. "I don't need to count it."

The manager went into a small storeroom and brought back two large brown plastic bags. "I regret, but this is all we can offer you for carrying."

I stuffed the *pula* into the two sacks, causing them to bulge obscenely, thanked the manager, and waved to the teller, who still looked worried. While it wasn't a long walk from the bank to the hotel, I thought that perhaps he had a good reason to worry for me.

"Are there taxis nearby? "I asked him.

"Oh yes, *Madame,* across the road and down. There is a taxi stand by the big tree."

I thanked him and took off across the road and down, found the tree, and the men stretched out underneath it. Some sat, others slept among banged-up cars parked haphazardly on the dusty ground.

"Excuse me," I said to a man with a shaved head and broad shoulders. "Could you help me find a taxi?" The man stood up, dusted himself off.

"*Madame*, you've come to the right place. We are your taxi stand."

I looked a bit dubiously at the sleeping men and the banged-up cars. I shifted the bulging bags of *pula* from one hand to the other, and asked if someone could give me a ride.

"But of course, *Madame*. We are at your service."

The man snapped his fingers and threw a set of car keys to a skinny boy who looked about twelve. "Take *Madame* to the hotel. Now." He looked sternly at the boy, who lazily pulled himself together to make the trip.

Once at the hotel, I got out and paid the boy the dollar he requested. Inside, I asked the hotel manager for a safe deposit box in which to put the *pula*.

"Certainly," he said. "Come with me."

I followed him to a small room behind the front desk that had one wall lined with safe deposit boxes. He indicated a box, and handed me a key.

"Once you've stored your items, please let me know."

It took me no time to realize that I would need at least four safe deposit boxes in which to put these bundles of *pula*, rather than just one.

Back in my room, I was ridiculously proud of myself for getting to the bank, exchanging dollars for *pula*, and getting back to the hotel with all that money. Still, my work with *pula* wasn't done. I now had to put the *pula* into individual packages for each of the thirty participants, and I had to do it fast because they would be arriving soon.

After lunch, I returned to my room with the *pula* in bags. I pulled out my participant list. Since not every participant would spend the full three weeks in Gaborone, I had to calculate the participants' per diem one by one. I calculated again, just to be sure. Then I counted and re-counted the *pula*. It was agony. I kept counting until I heard a knock on my door. The first participant had arrived and was eager to get his cash. I panicked for a moment and stopped counting. Money was spread all over the bed. I wasn't ready to see anyone. I opened the door a slit as if I had something to hide, like a secret lover naked in my bed.

"You must wait until later," I said as calmly as I could. "Oh, and yes, lovely to see you," I added and, to the participant's dismay, shut the door.

Each time I answered the door, I would have to start counting pula all over again. I'd never have been able to do the job my staff did. Thank God I had Cliff at home managing our money, while I managed people at work.

Nkosi Sikelel' iAfrika

Back in Washington, I talked with Lee about my experience in Gaborone. He reminded me of how important he thought the administrative officer's job was.

"And undervalued. And difficult," I chimed in, still counting *pula* in my head. "I wish your male colleagues agreed with you."

"Not only here," said Lee. "In Africa, as well. It's always the same problem. Men are dismissive of whatever work the women do. No matter how much it contributes to their success."

We kept talking.

"Why don't you include an admissions and participant relations component of your UNEDIL management development program?" I suggested. "It could make the African training institutes much more efficient. Our administrative officers are experts in doing this kind of work. The best. I could ask one of them to develop a curriculum and deliver the training herself."

Lee liked my suggestions and asked me to go with him to Ethiopia the following month to meet with the directors of the African training institutes. They would be deciding which components of the management development program to finance first. My job would be to make the case for an administrative training component.

In the early autumn of 1988, I sat at a large table surrounded by a dozen directors. I was still jet-lagged and had not yet recovered from a stomach flu. It had been a long, tiring trip to Debre Zeit, Ethiopia, from Washington, D.C.

I looked around the table at the formally dressed, middle-aged African men, and was reasonably sure they weren't going to hear a thing I said. Efficient course administration a priority? Fund training for low-level female staff? What had I been thinking? Why had I come?

One by one, each director made a case for his pet program, circulated handouts, and cited the best research. I knew this wouldn't work for me. I'd never win them over with charts and graphs. Rather than do things their way, I began my own presentation by expressing my respect for their work. I admired their strategic thinking. I expressed gratitude that they were willing to hear me out, but supposed they were a bit confused. Why was I making such a fuss about administration and organization? Right? The men nodded. I looked around the room.

"Okay, this will be a tough sell," I said. "So many of you, and only one of me."

The men laughed.

"I've come quite a long way to see you because I want to make your jobs much easier, your programs more successful, your institutions' reputations impressive, and your trainers appreciated. What do you think? Is that worth a long trip and the stomach flu?"

The men looked at one another. They were clearly amused by my offer to make them look good. I knew there was one man in the room who carried more weight than the others. Professor Alfred Mondjanagni, the Secretary-General of the Pan African Institute for Development (PAID), was about fifteen years older than most of the directors. In several cases, he was their boss. I focused my attention on him and spoke French, while an interpreter translated for the English speakers. It didn't escape me that at nine, I'd imagined myself translating for men making their speeches; now men were translating for me while I made mine.

"Professor Mondjanagni, when you attend workshops, do you get grumpy when your flights or hotel bookings are mismanaged, your per diem miscalculated? Does your grumpiness affect how you feel about the class? The instructor?"

The secretary-general leaned back in his chair, smiled broadly. He knew where I was going.

"*Oui, Madame,*" he said.

Then, in English, I addressed the PAID director for English-speaking West Africa. "Sir, how many classes would you say you run a year? Thirty? Forty? And have you ever noticed how often your participants interrupt you when they are not happy? Or how they may arrive late or complain about how much money they need to live? In other words, how grumpy participants make your job harder? And when they fill out evaluation forms, grumpy participants sometimes forget to mention the training itself—the content, the ideas, the conclusions, and the recommendations? Instead, they focus on what went wrong—the flights, the hotel, their per diem?"

"Yes, Madam, it is true," the director said.

I went on, this time addressing the men as a group. "I am here to talk about the 'participant grumpiness factor' and to share my experience as the supervisor of the administrative officers who help trainers plan and organize their courses. My staff in Washington makes our trainers look good. By handling participant administration, my staff allowed the trainers to focus on delivering course content, getting their ideas across, and keeping the participants' attention.

"In Washington, D.C., our administrative officers do a terrific job, but they tend to be forgotten by the men who give the courses. Am I right to think that you may have a similar situation here?"

The men shrugged.

"Professor Mondjanagni, what do you think? Is this a problem that warrants a solution?"

Mondjanagni's eyes twinkled. He knew what I was doing, and he liked it.

"*Madame*," he said slowly. "I think you may be right. I guess none of us has given it too much thought. And it is a shame. And now, here you are." He opened his arms and looked around the room. "To save us from ourselves."

The men laughed.

"Indeed, I am," I said, beaming. "So, you will give it a try? You will include admissions and participant relations as a component of your program?"

"The lady has traveled a long way to see us," said Mondjanagni to the men around the table. "She makes a good point. Shall we vote on it?"

They voted. I had their approval.

I was thrilled that I had found a way to gain more professional status for the administrative officers as trainers. I selected Annie, who was terrific at her job, to train African staff to do her job in their training institutes. My success motivated my staff and got them good press at home. While I knew that I would have been a terrible administrative officer, I felt that I was a pretty good manager. At last, I was in a job I loved and did well.

One afternoon, soon after my return to Washington, D.C., I heard a gentle knock on my office door. I called for whoever it was to come in. When the door opened, I was staring at a man from South Asia, probably Pakistani, with an extraordinarily long beard, wearing a white cotton tunic over long, white cotton trousers.

"May I come in?" the man asked politely.

"Please," I said, getting up.

"You don't recognize me, do you, *Jerroise*?"

"Oh, my God! Arshad!" I jumped up and ran around my desk to hug Arshad Zaman, the man who had eased my way after I lost my mentor and champion Fareed Atabani, the man who had written the evaluation that helped me get a job on the Egypt Water Master Plan, the friend who had long since left the Bank and returned to Pakistan, where he was a senior advisor to the prime minister.

"I see you've survived the Bank," he said, smiling "You are a braver soul than I. And now *you're* the boss!"

"Well, it took ten years . . ."

"But you are happy now, aren't you?"

"Yes, but it's been a long haul, Arshad. You have no idea."

"Perhaps. But let's face it. You were always meant to do more than sharpen a man's pencils!" He was right. But it did me good to hear him say it.

In early 1990, Cliff and I bought a new house, about twice the size of our old one. Although we both loved the house, Cliff was especially excited about how much space we'd have.

"At last," he said, "a proper house, with an office, a study, a library, and even a conference room."

We'd been together for twelve years, yet it came as a surprise for me to learn that Cliff had always dreamed of owning a house like this. A big man needed a big house, he explained.

While Cliff could not have been happier in the new house, both Christian and Adam found the move unsettling. Adam had spent his entire life in the other house, and Christian was raised there, too. The year we moved was also the year of Christian's high school graduation. The spring before he graduated, Christian told us he'd be taking a year off before beginning college. Cliff was not happy about his decision.

"If he doesn't start school now, will he ever go?" he asked me.

I was surprised by Cliff's reaction. Christian rarely gave us anything to complain about. He hadn't been idle all summer. In fact, he'd been working two jobs—making deliveries for a liquor wholesaler during the day, and parking cars at a large parking garage at night. When Cliff told me he didn't want Christian to get too comfortable parking cars for a living, I guessed he might be thinking of Niagara Falls and his father and uncles, who worked for little pay in a factory all their lives. A college education was important to Cliff and he wanted to be sure Christian had one.

One unhappy evening, I returned home from work to find Christian gone. When I asked Cliff where he was, he said Christian had decided to live with his mother, Ellie. When I asked him why, he said he'd told Christian he couldn't live in the house for free now that he'd graduated and was working for a living. He'd have to start paying rent. In response, he packed his bags and left.

Although Christian was certainly old enough to strike out on his own, I hated that his departure was so abrupt, with bad feeling between him and his dad. Right or wrong, it seemed to me like something I should let them sort out. Adam was eight when he became an only child. He adored his big brother, and losing him broke Adam's heart. It broke my heart, too. My first son was gone.

Like Cliff, I loved our new house, but I was nervous, pretty sure it was more than we could afford. Cliff was convinced we could swing it. He wanted to make a good impression on clients. Not only did he want a big house, it turned out, but he also wanted a better, more expensive car. This made me even more nervous. What happened to the Marxist man in Frye boots I loved? He'd become an upper middle-class consultant in a three-piece suit.

But I didn't argue the case for a smaller house or an older car. I let Cliff's decisions stand. I was working long hours, learning a new job, try-ing to be a good manager, meeting with Adam's teacher about his newly diagnosed attention deficit disorder. And we all missed Christian. The three of us still had happy times at Christmas and during summer vaca-tions on the Outer Banks, but Cliff and I were both working more and talking less, while Adam played video games.

Soon after we had moved to the new house, I traveled to Zambia to join my staff member Annie to run a training-of-trainers workshop with participants from several African countries to teach them how to organize workshops, and handle admissions and participant relations as efficiently and confidently as the women who worked for me in Washington.

Annie and I were promoting a new kind of appreciation and respect for African training administrators—most of whom were women. It felt good to advocate for women again. And I loved working in Africa.

The evening of February 11, I was having dinner with a group on the hotel terrace when the receptionist came to our table. There was a telephone call for me.

"It's your husband," he said, "in the United States."

Preoccupied with the day's activity and the interesting dinner conversation, at first I was irritated at the interruption, even by Cliff in Arlington. But as I followed the man from reception back to the lobby, I began to panic. Why was Cliff calling? Was Adam all right? Christian? Had anything happened to my boys? I took the phone. It was disorienting to be in Africa, talking to Cliff. He could probably hear it in my voice, but he clearly had something to tell me and it wouldn't wait.

"Are you watching the television?" he asked.

"Of course not. We don't have television here. Why?"

"Nelson Mandela is walking out of the prison gates." Cliff paused. "Did you hear me? Mandela is free."

My heart skipped a beat. "He's free?" I asked Cliff. I could hear how excited he was to be the first to share the news about Mandela with me, in Africa, no less.

"Yes, he's free. You'd better hang up and tell your friends!"

"It's so hard to believe," I said, shaking my head and wiping away tears with the back of my hand. I tried to pull myself together. I hung up the phone, almost forgetting to say goodbye. A happiness I could hardly contain flooded through me. I would be the first to share the news with my friends from Botswana, Zambia, Ethiopia, Nigeria, Kenya, and Cameroon. I'd be the one to give them the news they never expected to hear.

Stumbling out of the hotel lobby, I raced to the patio where my African friends were all talking and laughing together. I rushed toward them, sputtering. First one, then the next, put down his fork and looked at me with concern. What was it?

"It's happened," I said as coherently as I could. "It's happened. Ten minutes ago. Mandela is free!"

I scanned the group and watched the news register: first shock, then confusion, astonishment, and finally, joy. Then noise! Such noise!

My friends pushed themselves away from the table, chairs clattering behind them. Several ignored protocol, and gave me huge hugs as if it were all my doing that Nelson Mandela was free. The reception clerk joined us on the patio with a large radio. We heard the news. What Cliff said was true. *Nelson Mandela was free.*

As a group, my African friends began to sing *Nkosi Sikelel' iAfrika*, the song that would soon become the new South African national anthem, a song that, since that day, makes me weep whenever I hear it. The day Mandela was set free, I committed myself to Africa in a way that would change my life.

Remembering the moment I learned Mandela was set free still gives me chills.

Reconnaissance

Early in 1990, after I'd been at the Institute a couple of years already, my director knocked on my door for the first time. A tall, angular, British fellow, he usually kept to himself, and wandered the halls with a quizzical look on his face most of the time. I'd barely spoken to him since I joined the Institute, and I had to assume he knew nothing about me.

"Lee has filled me in on the work you did on SWWG with McNamara back in the early '80s. The statistical reports. I'm afraid we aren't much better here than in the rest of the Bank when it comes to the status of women. Senior management is after us to improve our statistics, get more women into our courses and workshops. Like other Bank departments, he said, we need a women in development (WID) committee. Lee thinks you should chair it."

This was excellent news. Chairing the Institute's WID committee meant the Bank would pay me to advocate for women in developing countries, as well as for women in the Bank.

A few weeks later, my director knocked on the door again.

"I'm sure you've noticed," he began, blinking twice and pushing his glasses up on his nose, "we hardly have any women participating in our seminars. Not good, you know."

I nodded.

"Word's out," he went on, "we need to improve those numbers, get more women. And, anyway, hmmm . . . it's the right thing to do, isn't it?"

I nodded again.

"Well . . . what I want you to do is . . . I mean, do you think you could . . . hmm . . . fly to Côte d'Ivoire, and talk to some senior women there. Perhaps Mary Okelo? Maybe she can help us find some policymakers, women, to invite to our courses. What do you think?"

I thought it was asking a lot for me to broach Mary Okelo, senior advisor to the president of the African Development Bank, to help me identify participants for our Institute courses. I didn't know Mary Okelo personally, but I knew her by reputation as an extremely well-respected and influential African woman. I wasn't sure if I had the credentials for Mary Okelo to take me seriously. But my director seemed to think so,

"That's fine," I said, keeping my doubts to myself.

"Good, then," he said. And wandered back into the hall.

Two days later, I was in Africa again, this time in the capital of the Côte d'Ivoire, Abidjan.

Although the director of the Institute had spoken as if it were perfectly reasonable for me to represent the Institute at the African Development Bank in Abidjan, I still wasn't so sure. The African Development Bank may not have been as big and powerful as the World Bank, but it wielded plenty of influence. In many ways, it was the African equivalent of the World Bank. Both lent hundreds of thousands of dollars to developing countries every year, provided technical assistance and policy advice to governments, and financed economic and social development in more than fifty African countries. In terms of international development, the African Development Bank was a big deal.

In terms of women in development, Mary Okelo herself was a big deal. Before joining the African Development Bank as senior advisor to the president, she had worked at Barclays Bank in Kenya, where she became the country's first woman bank manager and co-founder of the Kenya Women Finance Trust. She left Barclays to be the first African representative to the Women's World Banking. Compared to Mary Okelo, my experience working in Africa on women in development was paltry.

As I walked down the corridors of the African Development Bank, looking for Mary Okelo's office, I remembered my first day at the World Bank. What a maze it had seemed like, how unsure I had been that I'd ever find my way. Fifteen years later, in this unfamiliar, important Bank, I felt a bit of my former apprehension.

Mary was waiting for me at her office door. Greeting me warmly, she took both my hands in hers.

"Come in, please," she said, smiling, and showed me to a chair. She ordered tea and immediately got down to business. "Now then, what can I do for you?"

As we sipped tea, I told Mary about the Institute's senior policy seminars, development economics courses, sector seminars, and project management workshops. "Unfortunately, we are a little short on women professionals, both as trainers and as seminar participants," I said.

Mary sighed, then smiled. "It's the same thing everywhere. At least your men are beginning to notice."

We talked easily for an hour, and as we stood to say our goodbyes, she suggested I return the next morning and talk to some senior-level women—the kind the Institute was trying to recruit. "Then you can tell them what you've told me."

I spent the next morning in Mary's conference room with two women from commercial banks, two senior staff of the African Development Bank, and two entrepreneurs. Again, I made my director's case for him.

"The Institute needs more women to train," I said. "Since it offers more senior policy seminars than anything else, we need more women policymakers in our classes."

The women listened politely. They all agreed that the Bank's wish to include more women in its development programs was a good thing, but said little more. It didn't take much to realize the women doubted the World Bank's good intentions would amount to anything. People from international and bilateral aid organizations—people like me—must have been trooping into Mary Okelo's office week in and week out, making the case that I was making.

"I guess you've heard this all before?" I asked.

The women smiled but said nothing.

"But does that mean the World Bank is wrong in trying to recruit women like you?" I persisted.

"Not wrong," said Mary. "But it's a bit unnecessary, don't you think?"

The other women nodded.

"Look at us, here," Mary continued, gesturing around the table. "How much more education and training do you think we need? We've earned advanced degrees. We're senior managers and advisers in our organizations. We'd be happy to travel to Washington or Paris to attend your seminars, of course, but is this a good use of your money?"

I was embarrassed. Had I inadvertently offended the women? Gracious as she was, I felt Mary was saying: "Listen: senior-level women, policymakers are in high demand. Take a number; the line forms at the back."

When the tea and biscuits arrived, I took Mary aside and asked if I was going about this all wrong. "Your friends are polite, but unmoved. Will I have to return to the Bank empty-handed?"

"Not necessarily," said Mary. "After tea, let's talk. I mean, really talk."

When we reconvened the meeting, Mary asked me to tell the women what we'd spoken about during the break.

"Can we start over?" I asked. "Is there anything new we can do together that would make life better for African women that's not a waste of money?"

The women looked at one another. The commercial banker who sat across from me took charge. "Perhaps there is something."

For the rest of the afternoon, Mary and her friends educated me about women in development in Africa. While the women at the table all lived in Abidjan, they had been born in the villages, where their mothers, aunts, sisters, and nieces still lived. No one paid attention to the village women or what they needed, especially not the World Bank.

"Those of us in the room have most of what we need," said Mary, "so why not help our sisters?"

By the time I left Abidjan, I knew I wouldn't be offering guidance on increasing the number of African women in the Institute's senior policy seminars. I would propose instead a new kind of management training program entirely, one designed for the rural women who managed groups and tiny businesses. Rather than a seminar for professional women that would cost about fifty thousand dollars, I wanted a two-million-dollar training program for rural women.

Back in Washington, I wondered what had made me think the Institute would be interested in the ideas I had discussed with Mary Okelo and her friends in Abidjan. To my surprise, however, the director was enthusiastic and suggested I spend a week in Douala, Cameroon, talking with Professor Mondjanagni, who had been so supportive in my efforts to include admissions and participant relations as a training component. We would need an African training partner to help us get a new WID program underway. Perhaps Mondjanagni would share our enthusiasm for the idea and propose that his Pan African Institute for Development (PAID) be that partner.

Before leaving for Douala, I spoke with Lee to see if we could link a new WID program with the UNEDIL women in management (WIM) training offered under his program.

"It won't be easy, but I think you can convince Mondjanagni to take this on. WIM isn't enough," said Lee. "PAID needs to do more WID work. I think Mondjanagni will buy it if it comes from you."

"But you already have Ada working on UNEDIL. She's Nigerian. Why do you need me?" I asked.

"Ada's great at getting the most for African women working in senior management positions in large organizations, true. But I don't think Ada's the best person to work with rural women."

Two weeks later, I was on my way to Douala to meet with Alfred Mondjanagni.

My first day in Douala, I woke up with a throbbing headache. The tropical heat and humidity were oppressive. Between headache and jet lag, I wasn't likely to make a very good impression on Mondjanagni. As if in slow-motion, I showered and washed my hair in water that never got warm. I threw on a cotton skirt and sleeveless blouse, then checked myself out in the cracked bedroom mirror. Unimpressive or not, I'd have to do.

The hotel was shabby, the breakfast buffet tasteless, and the instant coffee bitter. The staff and I were all sullen. I gave up on breakfast, handed my room key to the desk clerk, and pushed through the front door into a blast of air heavy enough to suffocate, hot enough to burn.

In spite of my grumpiness, the secretary-general's driver, George, greeted me with a cheerful hello. He asked if I slept well. He conveyed his wife's and three daughters' good wishes. They all hoped I was in good health. I did my best to greet him in kind, while preparing myself to speak intelligently about African women with an African man.

To build up my confidence, I thought about my last encounter with Mondjanagni at the large meeting of African management training institute directors in Debre Zeit, Ethiopia. I remembered how he had helped me convince his fellow directors to include an administration component as part of their UNEDIL program. Now, though, I'd be meeting him alone in his office to discuss a very different kind of project.

The Pan-African Institute for Development headquarters were in a rather impressive building in a not-very-impressive neighborhood. George pulled the car into the gravel drive under a canopy of palm trees, then parked, and opened the car door for me.

"The secretary-general invites you to go to his office directly," he said.

He and I entered a large, nearly empty room. A small table with assorted flyers on it had been pushed against a wall, above which hung a large, black-and-white photograph of the president of Cameroon. A straight-backed chair stood on each side of the table. We walked down a long hall, passing several small, cramped offices on my way to Mondjanagni's office. George introduced me to the secretary, who ushered me in to see her boss.

Professor Mondjanagni sat at a large desk next to a wall of bookshelves, under a map of Africa. He stood, shook my hand, and invited me to sit at one of the two chairs facing his desk. Tall as I was, I felt small sitting across from him. I also felt foreign, strange, and completely out of my depth. I wasn't sure where to begin. The man had quite a reputation in Washington, D.C. He was cunning and cynical about the World Bank. He wanted things his way. He was stubborn, and, while rarely disagreeable, he was a tough cookie. From my experience in Ethiopia, I also knew that his directors held him in high regard.

I would never be able to bluff this man. He'd know how much I didn't know. Since he didn't speak English, I'd have to negotiate with him in French. I had no secure funding, and little experience in Africa. I wasn't even a WID expert. I wasn't sure if he was genuinely interested in WID. Still, I had promised Mary Okelo to do my best to get a program underway for rural women, and that's what I'd do.

"Good morning, professor," I said, offering him a copy of my activity brief to read.

"Good morning to you, *Madame* Dell," he said, and shooed the brief away. "*Vous avez la bienvenue.* You are most welcome. And perhaps we can dispense with formalities? I am Alfred. Now, tell me why you are here."

I told him about my meeting with Mary Okelo in Abdijan and her six friends around the conference table in Abidjan. Much as I wanted to reach out to village women, I explained, I didn't know how to do it. My work in Botswana and Ethiopia on course administration had not prepared me to initiate management training for illiterate women. Without a respected African training partner, managed by Africans, the program wouldn't have a chance.

I spent the day and much of the evening with Alfred. We talked in his office and continued talking during dinner at his house. We talked as we drove around the back streets of Douala. Alfred climbed in and out of the car to chat with men, who sat on their haunches in small circles around wood fires. Although Alfred was from Benin, he knew enough of the Bantu language spoken in Douala to make himself understood. I got out of the car when he did, but I hung back, and watched from a distance. I wasn't sure why we were there, but it seemed important to him that I join him, even if I couldn't speak the language.

After walking with me along a dirt road, he asked if I'd like to return to his house for a drink, maybe stay over?

"I don't think so," I said, smiling. "But nice try!" Alfred smiled back and shrugged.

"As you wish," he said. When he dropped me off at my hotel, he gave me two chaste kisses, one on each cheek.

The next morning, George arrived at the hotel to collect me promptly at eight. This time, I was in much better spirits. Now that I was no longer jet-lagged, the hotel seemed less shabby and the staff less sullen. When George asked me if I'd slept well, I could reply yes and mean it.

"Okay, *ma fille*, where are we now?" asked Alfred. By then, I was a woman of thirty-nine—hardly a girl. However, rather than being taken aback, I laughed. Almost old enough to be my father, Alfred spoke to me with affection, as he might a favorite niece. I could hardly get angry with him for that. I asked him to tell me what we should do together. He looked at me over his glasses.

"What I mean is—what we should do together to make things better for village women?"

He knew what I meant, of course, but took great pleasure in flirting with me. Maybe he didn't think of me as a niece, after all? At first, this worried me. How much does he care about rural women? Or was he as macho as the men I met at the Bank?

"I respect women," he said. "I was there at the birth of my three children. You cannot watch a woman give birth and not respect and admire her. When my wife died, I built a school in her name. It is a school where girls and boys both learn. African men sometimes forget to respect women. My mother and my wife did not let me forget."

Alfred confirmed what Mary Okelo and her friends had told me in Abidjan. Education and training were not reaching enough African women. Poor women worked in the informal sector, selling food, making crafts, managing small shops. We talked about what kind of training would actually help these women who had so little free time, who could neither read nor write.

"Not only do they have jobs, but the women do all the cooking and marketing. They fetch the water and care for the children," said Alfred. "If you are going to train the women, you have a big job. You will need a new approach."

He suggested that we meet one of his old university friends for lunch at the five-star Rabingha Hotel. Like Alfred, his friend was from Benin, about the same age, and slightly more elegant. Like Alfred, he spoke well and commanded respect and attention.

Not quite adjusted to speaking French all the time, I listened while the men talked. Soon I caught onto their rhythm and followed along. They described themselves and their contemporaries as first-generation post-Independence Africans with advanced degrees, of whom much was expected.

"We failed," Alfred said simply. His friend nodded. "We were supposed to make things better in Africa. But we failed."

I was surprised to hear him say this and assumed it was a bit of false humility. As the conversation continued, I realized it was merely a statement of fact. They *had* failed. They discussed the prevalence of "*Afri-Pessimism*," the confidence they'd had in Léopold Senghor, Senegal's first president after Independence. Like them, Senghor was an intellectual with an excellent education. He was a cultural theorist on the subject of "negritude." When I asked why Senghor had been chosen to lead Post-Independence Senegal, Alfred answered: "France wanted him to be president. That's why. Senghor was more interested in poetry than politics, but he had no choice. He responded to the call."

According to Alfred and his friend, even fifty years after African Independence, France's influence remained huge. Colonialist racism remained well-entrenched. Even now, it was hard for anyone—African or European—to imagine that there could be equality between white and black. Thinking about this later, I realized that Alfred wanted me to understand something important about the African reality, the great deception of his generation.

During my week in Douala, Alfred introduced me to several other impressive people. Joséphine Ouédraogo, former minister of social affairs for Burkina Faso, was the most impressive of all. She was a socialist with a passion for community participation, grassroots development, and women's rights. A sociologist by training, she was appointed Minister of Family Development and Solidarity by Thomas Sankara, Burkina Faso's first Marxist president.

For three years, Joséphine Ouédraogo pushed for an end to female genital mutilation, proposed a national family law, and supported a women's strike. In 1987, Sankara was assassinated and his rival, Blaise Compaoré, took power. As a close friend and confidant of the murdered president, Joséphine was not safe. She went into exile in Tunis, then in Douala, where she coordinated a Canadian-financed women and health program at the PAID in Douala.

When I met Joséphine in her office, I was taken by this tall, slender woman with a Nefertiti neck. She was serious, soft-spoken, and confident. Only two years older than me, she seemed much wiser than I'd ever be. Like Mary Okelo and Alfred, Joséphine believed rural women were being seriously shortchanged by international development organizations.

"These women need to manage their businesses. They must keep records and market their products. It's a matter of survival to them. But donor agencies never approach them for training. Flipcharts that spell out the problem in words or workshops that require profit/loss calculations are of little use to grassroots managers," she said. "Classes offered in French and English are meaningless to rural people. Village women who don't have time, childcare, or transport are the ones who need the training most, and yet are the least likely to get it."

"We'll have to figure out a way, then. That's our job. Yes?" I said.

Joséphine knew I was American, and an advocate for women in development. She also knew I had no experience working in French-speaking West Africa. I hoped she'd show me compassion and give me a chance, even if I did work for the World Bank.

We had a few things in common. We both knew something about sexism in the workplace. Joséphine described the cynicism, indifference, even hostility she had encountered at PAID when she first arrived. Its faculty was overwhelmingly male, counting only one woman among the trainers in each of its four regional institutes. Like the Bank's institute, PAID offered classic economic development courses, which made it difficult for Joséphine to initiate a program on women and health. The directors liked the idea of collaborating with the Canadians on a multiyear program, but they were still far from committed to making women's health a priority.

Joséphine and I spent our second day together talking as Alfred's chauffeur drove us to Yaoundé from Douala and back. We had much to talk about. Fortunately, the trip was four hours each way.

I asked her whether she thought Alfred could be trusted. I asked her what it meant that he always referred to me as "my girl." I needn't worry, she said. It was a term of endearment.

"It's his way of saying you are welcome in Africa. Not every World Banker is welcome, you see. He considers you an exception. One of the family." I hoped she was right about this.

I asked Joséphine what it was like to be in exile. How had her husband taken it? What about her children? Taking them out of school? She shared how hard it had been for all of them. Still grieving for Thomas Sankara, her dear friend, she had had to start all over again. Her husband had been unemployed since they left Ouagadougou. He'd find something eventually, she said, but it would take time.

"When you travel and leave your small son at home, don't you feel a little like you're in exile, too?" she asked.

Taken aback at first, I had to admit it was true. By the time Adam was eight and I was in Douala, I knew all too well what it meant not to travel, to be stuck at my desk in a paper-pushing job in a huge bureaucracy. Traveling for the Bank, I could do work that felt worthwhile. I loved field work. But loving the work didn't mean I felt good leaving Adam behind.

I tried to reassure myself that Adam had a dad who worked from home, and was there for him. I'd arranged for a tutor to help him with his schoolwork. He had dozens of friends to play with. My dad and Kate, my mom, my sister, Katie, and brother-in-law nearby all loved him and were more than willing to spend time with him while I was gone. But even knowing all that, I always missed Adam. And I always felt guilty.

Joséphine nodded sympathetically when I told her that Cliff, who'd always been the world's most supportive husband, was of late far less patient and understanding of all the time I spent traveling for work. He was glad to have left the Bank to be a consultant. He liked the work he did, although he sometimes had to scramble for new clients. Since I'd been promoted, I confided, there were more angry outbursts. I'd put the spoons where the forks belonged. The Tupperware was a mess and it was my fault. The IKEA furniture was missing a piece and was kicked to the curb out front. More and more often, Cliff disappeared downstairs into his study and stayed up late drinking.

"Perhaps he misses you?" she asked.

We talked about our childhoods, our families. I described my socialist grandparents who lived in Bohemian Greenwich Village in the 1910s and 1920s. She raised an eyebrow. A World Banker who grew up with Bohemian grandparents? How did this happen?

"Strange, isn't it? My grandfather wrote novels and my grandmother was a children's librarian. I always assumed I'd do something literary when I grew up. Maybe teach."

"And you end up at the World Bank?"

"That bastion of capitalism." I finished her sentence. Yes, it did seem odd.

A few hours into our drive, while Joséphine rested, I stared out the window at three skinny little boys with shaved heads, runny noses, and eerily grey skin who ran alongside our car. When they pointed and called out *"Toubab! Toubab!"* I asked Joséphine who they were, what they were saying, and why they were so grey.

She said only, *"Toubab* means foreigner," then closed her eyes.

As I kept watching, the children came close enough for me to see the older boy, perhaps eight years old, rubbing something on the smaller child's face, into his cheeks, across his forehead, against his ears and neck—even onto his eyelids.

Now Joséphine spoke again, "Chalk dust."

"But why?" I asked.

"So that they can look like you. The children think rubbing white dust into their skin will make them prettier, better, more important. They want to be white like you."

I felt I should apologize, but for what? For thinking that growing up as a little white girl in a black neighborhood, until my parents moved the suburbs when I started school, should have made us all color-blind?

"Ne t' inquiète pas," said Joséphine quietly, as though she had read my mind. "Don't worry. It's not your fault. You can't help your privilege. You can't help being white." She reached for my hand, touched my wrist.

I thought of the homeless men who slept on grates and in cardboard boxes by the State Department and the World Bank, the soup kitchens that appeared at the end of the day, and the long lines of ragged people waiting to be served. I thought of my father, who gave money to the Salvation Army because if Christianity meant anything, it meant giving food and shelter to the poor. There were many ways to do the right thing, to help people.

By the end of our day together, I'd come to understand that Joséphine was the embodiment of concern and compassion. I knew I could never be Joséphine, but I also knew what was worth doing and how much there was to do. I was tenacious and would work hard. Joséphine was also intuitive and read me well. By the end of that day, I could tell she had decided that World Banker or not, I could be trusted. She would give me a chance.

My last day in Douala, Alfred, Joséphine, and I drew up a list of invitees to a steering group meeting we'd hold a month later.

"Do you know Marguerite Monnet?" asked Alfred.

I nodded.

I'd met Marguerite briefly in Washington, D.C., the year before, when she made a presentation on women in management. Although a clinical psychologist by training, she'd rapidly developed an excellent reputation as a management and gender expert. Senegalese and not yet fluent in English, Marguerite made her presentation in French. Lee encouraged me to attend. Like everyone else in the room, I was wowed. Not only was her presentation full of useful information, but her style was warm and engaging. I understood why Lee and his UNEDIL colleagues were crazy about her and proud to have her on their team.

Marguerite's presentation over, I introduced myself and told her about the work I was doing with the administrative officers and the WID committee. A line of people who wanted to talk with her was forming behind me. I repeated how much I had enjoyed her presentation, how inspiring it was. As I turned to leave, she leaned toward me and said in French, "Let us work together soon."

Thanks to Alfred and Joséphine, Marguerite and I would indeed work together.

For years and years to come.

En Route

Back from Douala, I had my work cut out for me convincing my management to do something new. Rather than design yet another policy seminar that would cost about fifty thousand dollars, I would work with African trainers to develop a multiyear training program that would cost at least two million dollars. Rather than train government officials and CEOs, we'd train trainers to train women in villages all over Africa. We'd need a broad base of support, both in Africa and in Washington, if we were to get the program off the ground. We would also need money we didn't have, which meant finding co-financing partners.

Although I was the program's strongest advocate, I already had a full-time job managing the Admissions and Participant Relations (APRO) unit. To address this, the Institute division chief Bob Lacey offered to assign one of his own staff, Eunice, to work with me on the proposal. Eunice was an NGO specialist with a doctorate. She was also a member of my WID Committee. I quickly accepted Bob's offer.

The following day, Bob invited Eunice and me to lunch. As we ate, he explained the situation to Eunice. Since I'd have to limit my WID work to part-time, he said he'd like Eunice to work with me, to put together a program.

"Okay," Eunice said, looking doubtful.

"Sure," I said, full of enthusiasm. Although I'd come to love my management job, I was eager to learn more about development firsthand. Working on this program would be a good way to go about it. I wasn't sure how working with Eunice would go, but I was willing to try. Meanwhile, Ada, a Nigerian management consultant who'd been working on the UNEDIL women-in-management program with Lee learned about the program and convinced Bob that she should be involved, as well. Since I knew Ada through Lee, I was cautiously optimistic that Eunice, Ada, and I could work well together. At least I hoped we could.

For six weeks, Eunice and I hammered out a proposal, meeting with Ada once a week to talk it over. My optimism began to flag, however, when I began realizing how much time Ada spent closeted in Eunice's office without me. It appeared she preferred to make her contribution to the program indirectly, through Eunice, rather than directly to me. Once the proposal was written and I was ready to discuss it with the new steering group I'd formed with Alfred and Joséphine in Douala, though, Ada saw herself as key to the program's success. When I asked Bob about this, he pointed out that she knew the African "players," which would be a help, and that, after all, she was African herself, and that could be a help, wouldn't it? Perhaps, I thought, as long as she was as comfortable working with illiterate village women as she was with government officials and CEOs.

On my way to Douala in early June, I spent the night in Paris. After visiting an old friend who lived several miles outside of town, I decided to return to the city by metro. It was past midnight when I went through the turnstile and down a long hallway to stand on the subway platform. I was not happy to be the only one waiting for a train. I was even less happy when a weasel-like man in a long, ratty brown coat appeared on the platform, black hair covering most of his face. I turned to face the other way. Perhaps, if I couldn't see him, he couldn't see me. As the man moved in my direction, I clutched my black leather bag tighter against my shoulder. The man kept moving closer. I held my breath until I heard the sound of metal on tracks.

The train slowed to a stop. I took two steps, then stumbled toward the door, the man following. He was close enough for me to smell his stale breath, feel his sweat, hear a growl in his throat as the doors clattered open. I stepped into the train, relieved to be escaping him, but the man rushed for the doors, too, as though trying to squeeze by me. There was no one in the car. I imagined what might happen next. Would he flatten me against the plastic seat? Would anyone five cars away hear me scream? I was terrified. But when the doors shut, the man was still on the platform, still watching me. His mouth twitched in a half-smile.

I didn't get much sleep that night. The next morning, my joints ached, and my head felt as though it were trapped in a vice. Was it the wine the night before? The horrible man on the metro platform? I dressed and went to the breakfast room for brioche and coffee. I was eager to pay the bill, get on the plane, and join Alfred, Joséphine, and Marguerite Monnet in Douala again. But when I reached for my wallet, it was gone. It had held my passport and my tickets, as well as my money. Now, I had no wallet. No passport. No tickets. No money, not even loose change.

"Madame?" inquired the man at the reception desk. *"Est-ce qu'il y a un problème?"*

"Yes," I sputtered. "There is a problem. My wallet is gone. I have no money, and I can't pay the bill."

"Mais ce n'est pas possible," said the man at the desk, who reached nervously for the phone, asked housekeeping to go to *Chambre* 4, check for a wallet.

No wallet.

If I had been thinking that night, of course, I'd have realized that the man in the metro hadn't wanted to rape me, he'd wanted to rob me. I'd been so relieved to see the train that I hadn't noticed how he'd jostled me as the doors shut. I hadn't noticed how much lighter my bag was as I hurried down *rue Christine* to the hotel.

"Happily," said the clerk at reception, "We have your credit card number on file from last night. No harm done."

No harm done? It was early Sunday morning; I had no money for a taxi or a cup of coffee. No ticket for the plane. No American passport or visa for Cameroon. I'd never been so glad I worked for the World Bank. I went back to my friend's house on the outskirts of town, called Cliff, who called a duty officer at Bank headquarters, who in turn called American Express, instructing them to get me a credit card immediately. The card delivered, I returned to the city, and spent the night in the Grand Hotel. The Bank's Paris office would open on Monday, and I'd be able to repair the damage my ill-advised trip on the metro had caused.

On Monday, I sloshed my way from hotel to police headquarters in the pouring rain to report my wallet stolen. I got lost looking for a photo lab to take a picture for my temporary passport. I walked the mile from the embassy to the World Bank office to get new tickets and more travelers' checks. There wasn't enough time to get a new visa for Cameroon. The Bank assured me they'd call Alfred and alert him to my midnight arrival.

On the seven-hour flight from Paris to Douala, I worried. Had they been able to reach Alfred? If they had, would he be able to convince the authorities to let me into the country without the right paperwork?

Once in Douala, I trooped in the dark with the other disembarking passengers down the aircraft steps, across the tarmac, and into the small, dilapidated, airport's passport control. As hot and humid as ever, Douala's weather was more than welcome. I was far from Paris and finally close to where I needed to be. I saw Alfred through the glass, chatting amiably with a man in a uniform. As I presented my passport, Alfred spoke a few words to his uniformed friend, who, in turn, spoke to a passport control agent. The agent scribbled something on my arrival card, and I was free to go.

Having retrieved my bags from the carousel, Alfred steered me toward the car. His driver, George, was waiting. Before climbing into the back seat, I clasped George's hand with both of mine. George gave me a big smile. I was back in Douala again with George and Alfred. I felt safe.

When I arrived at PAID the next morning, the steering group meeting was already underway. From the other side of the door, I could hear a voice in the conference room speaking in clipped, formal English. Through the door's small window, I saw a dozen people: Africans, Europeans, and Americans, about two-thirds of them women. The former ministry official from Lesotho, Mamolete Pitso, sat next to Mary Okelo's sister, Grace Wakhungu, a Kenyan banker. Both women's expressions were serious, almost severe. Across the table sat Eunice, chairing the meeting in my absence. On her left was our Bank colleague, Michael. On her right, Ada, our Nigerian consultant. Next to Ada, Marguerite Monnet, the Senegalese consultant who my new friends Alfred Mondjanagni and Joséphine Ouédraogo admired so much. Although I'd been the one to issue the invitations, I didn't know the others personally. I took a deep breath, squared my shoulders, and entered the room as quietly as I could, hoping no one would notice my late arrival.

As I turned to close the door behind me, I heard someone push a chair back and stand up. Then, the others were on their feet, as well, clapping. I blushed in embarrassment. After all the trouble I'd gotten myself into, the problems I'd caused, they were still glad to see me.

Taking over the meeting, I dispensed with Robert's Rules of Order and sent one question after another out to the floor. I listened to the responses, and wrote furiously on the flipchart.

"Who are the women we want to reach?" I asked: "What do they do? What obstacles do they face? What kind of help can we offer?"

With my encouragement, people stopped waiting politely to be recognized. They stopped speaking in sequence, no longer moved cautiously through a pre-agreed agenda. Instead, we engaged in a kind of call-and-response, which I captured with magic marker on flipchart paper as best as I could.

At the end of the long day, Michael invited me to join him and Joséphine for dinner, and asked if I would mind meeting him alone for a moment first. Privately, he warned me that I should not think twice about having taken charge of the meeting. He was worried that I felt guilty about being late and that perhaps I thought I should have encouraged Eunice or Ada to chair the meeting. Not a good idea at all, warned Michael. Eunice was not up to the job. She'd had the opportunity to impress the participants when I didn't show, but she had not.

"And be cautious with Ada," Michael added. "She smiles. She is friendly. But she is not your friend."

I was afraid he was right. I had wondered from the beginning if Ada resented consulting for an American woman in Africa, rather than leading the program herself. Despite my African friends' insistence that I was the right person to do this job, I could understand Ada's reticence.

"You have the rest of us, though," Michael said. "We trust you not to let us down. Don't be too friendly to your enemies."

I was still too new to Africa, and perhaps too naïve to anticipate people's enmity or recognize an enemy when I saw one. Michael must have known this about me, and I was grateful for his words. But I'd always wonder if I'd been understanding enough to Ada's situation.

When Joséphine joined us for dinner, Michael's mood was lighter, less troubled. Although I hadn't known either of them for long, we talked as old friends talk. They teased me about my American ways, how I would probably jump into a concrete swimming pool without checking first to see whether it was filled with water. How easy it was for me to lock eyes and speak directly with people, even men. Joséphine and Michael were sophisticated in a way I wasn't. Michael's father was one of Cameroon's ethnic kings. Joséphine was a former minister. They were experienced professionals who championed the cause of poor women. But for all her education and authority, Joséphine still lowered her eyes in the presence of a man.

By the third day, all the participants were speaking out. This meeting wasn't a bureaucratic requirement for any of them. They were all there because they wanted the chance to address old problems in new ways. As soon as I saw the kind of energy and enthusiasm we had in the room, the spontaneous facilitation from the floor, I relaxed. I'd invited these people in part because of their diversity—their different nationalities, languages, genders, organizations, politics, and personal styles. It had been a gamble. A diverse group like this could be hard to manage.

Happily, my gamble paid off. By the time the meeting was over, the group had reached consensus in many areas: our goal, objectives, client group, approach, methodology, and evaluation criteria. We had a name for the program: "Women's Management Training Outreach Program" in English, and "*Femmes et Formations a la Gestion Appliquée*" in French. In both languages, the group would be known informally as grassroots management training, or "GMT." Our next step was to form teams in each of seven countries: Cameroon, Kenya, Lesotho, Nigeria, Senegal, Burkina Faso, and Togo.

A week earlier, I'd arrived at the steering group meeting in Douala knowing little about the people at the table, some of whom I was meeting for the first time. But over the course of a week, I'd found allies who were ready to work with me, regional and local training partners to identify the training needs of village women's groups and to design training programs in a participatory way that didn't assume participant literacy. This was no small thing. The success of the steering group meeting gave me the confidence I'd need to promote grassroots management training, and get our program up and running, once I returned to Washington, D.C.

I arrived in D.C. from Douala, still shaken from the experience on the Paris metro, and from what felt like a near-miss at the steering group meeting in Douala. The minute I spotted Cliff and Adam waving at me in

Dulles airport arrivals hall, as they always were when I returned from a trip, my body went limp with relief. I was finally able to relax. I was home.

Back at work, having accepted my marching orders from members of the steering group in Douala, it was up to me to convince my director to get this unprecedented, long-term program for rural women in seven African countries underway. This was not at all the seminar he'd had in mind when he sent me to Abidjan and Douala. When he balked at the price tag, I told him we'd go slowly, and I'd find co-financing partners. When he proposed we pilot the program in English-speaking African countries, I countered that some of our most talented and committed trainers lived in West Africa and spoke French. It would be a mistake to limit ourselves to English-speaking Eastern and Southern Africa.

He asked how likely it would be for university-educated management trainers to successfully train rural women. I explained that we'd train trainers in English and French; these trainers would train the women leaders, who would train the women in their groups in their local language. Our Senegalese consultant, Marguerite Monnet, was confident that our training teams would make it work. During our week together in Cameroon, I had been struck by Marguerite's thoughtful, open-minded, and collaborative spirit. It took me no time to see why Alfred and Joséphine held her in such high regard. She exuded intelligence, strength, and confidence without being pushy. I trusted her judgment. If Marguerite believed in something, so would I.

By the time we were ready to get our grassroots management training (GMT) program underway, Lee Roberts was preparing to move to another division. This meant that I was helping him manage the African management development training program while also managing my unit. Working both jobs was more than a full-time endeavor.

Lee was sure I was the right person to take over his position managing UNEDIL. He didn't expect the director to object. "He knows what you can do. He likes you. He won't be a problem," Lee said.

I was aware of how fraught UNEDIL was on many fronts. I knew the job wouldn't be easy, but my relationship with UNEDIL directors and staff in Africa gave me an edge. I was ready for a change. I told them I was prepared to leave my unit management position to take over for Lee managing the training program for African management development institutes. Bob promised to get the director's approval.

A few days before Lee was to transfer to a new division, he called. "A fly in the ointment," he said. "The director is stepping down and a former Israeli tank commander is taking his place."

"Should I be worried?" I asked, not particularly worried.

"Not sure yet. We'll let you know."

The night before I was to leave for Cameroon to run our first training-of-trainers workshop for English-speaking trainers, Bob called me at home to say that the new director had nixed my taking over Lee's program.

"What? He doesn't know anything about Lee's program, does he? And he doesn't know me. What gives?" I was furious, and I wasn't sure if I was angrier with this new director for refusing to give me the UNEDIL job or with Bob for not standing up to the director on my behalf. Either way, I had another fight on my hands.

"Oh, and another thing," Bob said. "He will be joining you in Cameroon next week to attend your workshop."

Marguerite, Joséphine, and Ada would be at the steering group meeting in Buea, Cameroon, with me. I planned to spend two days in Buea, meeting with the leaders of women's groups from Nigeria, Lesotho, Kenya, and Cameroon to get them working on their presentations, then go back to Douala to meet the new director whom I didn't know but disliked already. He wanted me to then accompany him back to Buea to meet the women.

Unlike my reception in Douala, when the African women around the table had welcomed me warmly, there was a distinct chill in the air in Buea. Instead of smiles and support, I got furrowed brows and caution.

When I called meetings with Ada, and Cameroonian consultant, Yana, they came. When I asked questions, they answered. But that was all. I didn't understand what was wrong.

When we weren't in meetings, I was left alone in my room. Nobody knocked on the door, and nobody explained why. From time to time, I saw Marguerite and Joséphine sitting in the lobby or the courtyard, talking together quietly in French. But even they left me alone.

At night, I heard Ada and Yana laughing in the hall together, obviously enjoying each other's company without me. I began to worry more than a little. If I lost these women, I had no program. I couldn't do it alone, and it was too late to start over. I had fought hard and had the funding we needed to start, but start what? If this meeting didn't get off the ground, my program was sunk. As I wrestled alone with what was going on, having no one to talk to, I remembered what Alfred had said to me as I left the steering group meeting in Douala.

"Okay, *ma fille*. You are winning now. You have disarmed us with your enthusiasm. *Mais attention*. Be careful. It takes more than enthusiasm to succeed in Africa."

I had asked if he thought I couldn't make a success of the program. He wasn't sure, he had responded, we'd have to wait and see. I was beginning to understand Alfred's hesitation.

Despite my worries about Ada and Yana, I reveled in the participants' progress. There were forty-two of them: a group of sixteen African trainers, and twenty-six rural women from Kenya, Lesotho, Cameroon, and Nigeria. Few of the rural women had ever left their own country, much less participated in an internationally sponsored event. Some had never left their village. On the first day of the workshop, these women were nervous, cautious, and quiet. A day later, they'd adapted well, were more relaxed, and were sharing information about their businesses and the problems they faced.

By the end of the week, whatever anxiety the women may have felt at the beginning was gone. The room crackled with excitement, rife with new ideas about leadership, marketing, managing money, people, and projects. Not only did the women lead small group discussions, but at the end of each day, they also led the singing and dancing.

As agreed, in the middle of the workshop's second week, I met my new director in the lobby of the Hotel Akwa Palace in Douala. My new director was an attractive man in a sharp-edged kind of way. He walked fast, leading with his head and shoulders. Although not particularly tall, he was lean and assertive and came across as a big man. Yes, a tank commander who wasn't remotely bothered by what people thought of him.

In the hotel lobby, I shook the director's hand without much enthusiasm. I was still angry about UNEDIL. Although I was happy with how productive the trainers were in Buea, putting together curricula and training materials, I was nervous about what was happening on a more personal level with Ada and Yana. And here was the commander to inspect the troops. I realized that I needed to be direct with him about the situation and enlist his support in advance.

Several minutes into the ride from Douala to Buea, I asked the driver to drop us off at a café along the way. I told him we'd let him know when we were ready to leave. The director frowned. Who was I to be giving orders to the driver when the director was in the car? Ignoring his obvious discomfort, I got to the point as soon as we sat down in the café.

"We are trying to do something we've never done before. It's hard work, and I can't do it without you. Right now, I'm already doing three jobs at once. I can't accept another unfunded mandate. I need you to decide today what it's going to be."

He looked a tad peeved. Who was I, telling him what to do?

"Something's going on in Buea," I continued, "and I think it's about who's in charge. They're testing me. They may think I'm a lightweight, a pushover. Or maybe because I'm not African, and our consultant Ada is. Maybe they are right, and a privileged white American should not be running the program."

The director shook his head. "But we don't hire consultants to manage programs. Even African consultants. And we don't have any Africans on staff to do the job. If anyone's to blame for this situation, it's the Bank, not you."

"Okay, then. I'm willing to do the work, and I'm willing to take charge, but not without being the boss. Am I the boss?"

He looked at me, nonplussed. "Oh yeah? I thought I was the boss."

"If you want me to run this program, I need you to give me the job fair and square, and let the others know that I am in charge."

He gave me a hard look, and I looked back at him, just as hard. I wasn't backing down, and oddly enough, he seemed to understand and even approve.

"Deal," he said finally, and shouted for the driver.

We arrived in Buea midday, a few minutes before the group broke for lunch. After introducing my new director, I handed him over to the women who were waiting impatiently to meet him. Chief Bisi, president of the Country Women's Association of Nigeria, was at the head of the line.

Sitting on the other side of the room with Alfred, Marguerite, and several of the trainers, I watched with delight as Chief Bisi regaled the director with stories about what they'd been doing the previous five days, and the program they were designing for the Institute. I could tell, even from this distance, how energetically and eloquently she was getting her point across to the director. She definitely had him under her spell. Later, Chief Bisi told me how astonished the village women had been initially, and then how proud, later, that the "big men in Washington" had asked them what they did and what they thought. She asked him to please find the money needed to make this training a reality. I couldn't have asked for a better spokesperson than Chief Bisi for this unsteady, fledgling program.

After lunch, we got back to work. The director spent the afternoon at meetings watching sketches and role-plays and listening to testimonials. At the end of the afternoon, he took the floor.

"Friends, I'm only here for the day. But what a day!" The women cheered.

"I must say as I arrived at the airport this morning, I was dubious. Yes, Jerri speaks highly of you. Yes, Jerri believes in this training. Yes, it will be hard, she says, but also worthwhile. I'll be frank with you. I had my doubts." Things got quiet.

"But after lunch with Chief Bisi and her Nigerian team, after tea with Grace, and her Kenyan sisters, after a few quiet words with Alfred, Joséphine, and Marguerite, I'm beginning to believe our Jerri is right about this program. It's a winner. So, let me make it official. As of today, I name Jerri Dell, Women in Development Advisor. Effective immediately, she will direct all aspects of grassroots management training in Africa." Then, he turned in my direction, looked me in the eye, and said, "Right, boss?"

Tall

In February 1991, I arrived, in Ouagadougou, Burkina Faso, to run our second regional training-of-trainers workshop, this time for French-speaking West Africans. Alfred had assured me that his director for French-speaking Africa, Malik Fall, would be pleased to host the Institute's first training-of-trainers workshop for French-speaking trainers. Malik, however, was not at all pleased; he was furious with me and my decision to make Marguerite the regional coordinator for the Institute's francophone Africa program. He had expected one of his staff members, Awa, to play that role. This was definitely not what I had in mind.

Soon Marguerite's team of four Senegalese grassroots management trainers arrived at my door to say they were there to support Marguerite and that they'd return to Senegal immediately if Malik got his way. I took them with me to meet with Malik. Marguerite and I remained quiet, while two of the team, Seni and Boubacar, did the talking. Malik backed down.

Compared to the training workshop in Buea the previous autumn, this workshop in Ouagadougou was a pleasure. Administrative officer Laurence Sage was with me and, unlike me, she was brilliant with details. She took care of everything from hotel accommodations and per diems for the participants to finding a safe place for my wallet and passport.

More importantly, we had the experience of the previous training of trainers workshop to draw on. Malik's management training institute in Burkina Faso was an excellent venue. We had gathered a brilliant group of French-speaking African trainers together in one place at one time. Most of the trainers didn't know each other before the workshop, but they were all professionals and formed teams quickly. In the first week, each country's team shared the results of their training needs assessment. In the second week, groups formed to design four training components: people management, project management, money management, and marketing. All seemed to be well.

A week into the workshop, I learned things weren't well at all. Laurence alerted me to some whispering she'd overheard. It seemed Yana was starting a campaign against me as an American woman with little experience in Africa, who had no business running this program. She was encouraging the participants to insist on being paid consulting fees for the days they attended the workshop. Laurence was as surprised by this as I was.

My staff were always meticulous about participants knowing exactly what to expect in terms of payment. Laurence showed me a copy of the Letter of Invitation, which stipulated that although the Africans participating in the workshop were professional trainers, they would attend the training-of-trainers workshop as participants, not as consultants. Accordingly, they would receive a per diem to cover the cost of travel and expenses, but no consulting fees. Yana never came to speak to me about any of this directly.

If Laurence had not alerted me to what was going on, I don't know what might have happened. A full-fledged mutiny? People packing their bags, threatening to leave Ouagadougou if I didn't relent? One thing was clear, Yana was doing her best to convince our participants that by not paying them as consultants, I was taking advantage of them. It didn't matter to Yana that she and the others had accepted the terms of our Letter of Invitation,

Worrying about how to handle this gossip, I started by asking Marguerite what she thought of Yana. She hedged, then volleyed the same question back to me. "What do *you* think of Yana?"

I wasn't sure, I responded. Wasn't sure I could trust my intuition the way I did at home. I was an American with little experience in Africa but, to me, it seemed to be all about the money. I thought that maybe Yana saw our training as a moneymaking enterprise for herself, her friends, and her family.

"My advice?" Marguerite said. "Trust your intuition." Still, I said nothing right away. I noticed Yana becoming more and more agitated, her eyes darting, her smile pasted on her face like a mask.

The day before the participants were scheduled to leave Ouagadougou, Laurence told me that Yana had asked to be paid in cash to cover the cost of her Cameroonian team's block of rooms. She was outraged to learn that Laurence had paid the hotel directly for the rooms. I knew there was another person with the same last name on Yana's team, and now I learned that this person was her husband. She had expected to be paid for two hotel rooms while only using one. (I learned later that all the African participants knew about her plans, but nobody had said a word.) Yana had also claimed that her flight had been canceled so she would have to cash in her air ticket and drive back to Douala in a friend's jeep. She was furious when Laurence explained that since the Bank paid for the ticket, only the Bank could be reimbursed for it.

I thanked Laurence for all the information and asked her to send Yana to my room.

To my face, Yana was all smiling deference. When she asked why I asked to see her, I smiled back.

"You're out, Yana. This is your last workshops with us. No GMT in Cameroon."

At first, she looked confused; then her eyes went dark.

"For our training to succeed," I continued, "I have to be able to trust every African consultant to tell me the truth. If you won't tell the truth about one of your team members being your husband or if a flight has been canceled, why would I trust you to run a country program for me?"

Yana was outraged, of course, and I knew she'd call Michael, my Cameroonian friend at the Bank, to protest what I'd done. I knew she'd seek out Joséphine and deny my allegations. But I knew that if I couldn't handle Yana, I wasn't the manager to run this program. I couldn't let myself be underestimated or manipulated. It was a tough call, but it was mine to make.

A few months later, in December, I was on a plane making its final descent into Dakar, Senegal's capital. Inside the airport terminal in Dakar, I became part of the jumble of German tourists, French businessmen, American Peace Corps volunteers, and UNICEF and USAID staff, all looking for a line to join and get their passports stamped. As the crowd filled the hall, immigration officials put their jackets back on, straightened their ties, assumed stern expressions, and divided us into two groups: Senegalese to the right, foreigners to the left.

"*Derrière, Derrière*," shouted one of the newly alert officials. "Get behind that line, there, and wait."

Ignoring the people in my line, I fixed on the Senegalese returning home. Businessmen in silk suits stood next to mullahs in long blue robes, city women with gold jewelry, and small children in new Nikes. Market women in red-and-green patterned dresses with matching headscarves and rubber flip-flops on their feet carried bulging cardboard suitcases. Some spoke French, others Wolof.

Once through passport control, I grabbed my luggage from the carousel amidst protests from teenage boys careening around with broken carts, jostling for position. Ignoring the attentions of taxi drivers eager for my business, I pressed on toward the metal gate and scanned the crowd until I saw Marguerite.

After placing two kisses on each cheek in hello, Marguerite and I headed to the car park. It always took a while to get anywhere with Marguerite in public. We would take a step. Stop to say hello and take another step. Stop again. Marguerite seemed to know everyone.

Visiting Dakar meant waiting in traffic with Marguerite as people raced between stopped cars with newspapers, Kleenex, bottled water, plastic kitchen bowls, and baskets for sale. It meant young boys jumping from out of nowhere to wave us into a parking place, wash our windows with dirty rags, guard our car for whatever loose change we were ready to give.

It meant lunches with Marguerite and her three daughters at their apartment, learning the best way to eat a mango. It meant dinner with Marguerite's university friends discussing politics, drinking *bissap*, and eating chicken *Yassa*, fragrant with onion and lime. Most of all, visiting Dakar meant talking nonstop with Marguerite at her apartment, at my hotel, in a restaurant, or in the car.

As she drove, Marguerite told me about her family and her university studies in Paris. We talked about the impact of French colonialism on her country, and how she was a child of Africa's independence from colonial rule. She told me about her work as a clinical psychologist and how she'd become involved in Lee Robert's women-in-management program. She described the Senegalese market women, the challenges they faced, and more about the GMT team she'd put together to help them. She gave me the background I needed to begin my work in Africa, a "crash course" to get me up to speed. As we drove around Dakar, I clutched my small spiral notebook, writing furiously. I had so much to learn.

Two days after I arrived in Dakar, Marguerite and I left together for Thiès, a town about an hour from Dakar. It was important for me to meet the women in Thiès who were participating in our training program there. I needed to see the reality on the ground, who the women were, what they did, and what our training meant to them. GMT was no longer just a program on paper. This was the real deal.

"Thiès is a crossroads," Marguerite explained. "It's a microcosm of Senegal as a whole. The activities women undertake in Thiès are typical of those of women everywhere else in the country. The women in Thiès speak Wolof. There are already many groups running small businesses there. When I had to decide where to start the training, it made sense to go to Thiès, to offer management training to women who had something to manage."

We spent the morning sitting under a baobab tree on the dusty ground, talking with the women. Marguerite translated my questions for the women in Wolof, and translated their answers from Wolof back for me.

"Instead of telling us what to do," one woman said to me directly in French, "Madame Marguerite asks us questions. At first, we didn't understand. She was the teacher, and we were the students. So why didn't she give the answers?" The women laughed.

"*Ah oui,*" the woman said. "Madame Marguerite tells us again and again: *La réponse est dans la salle.* [The answer is in the room.] She trusts us to know more than we think we know. Sharing what we know, we teach each other many things."

The women told me how Marguerite made a video of them on their first day of training, how they kept greeting each other, talked and talked, didn't bother to sit down. When she turned off the video camera, one woman recounted, she told us we needed to think about the time we lost by not getting organized and starting our meeting in a more orderly way.

"Last week, after our training was over, Madame Marguerite showed us the video from the first day. It was horrible. We couldn't believe how much time we were wasting. We told her to burn it!"

Another woman jumped in with her own story, Marguerite translating. "We all are selling fruit. Madame Marguerite took us for a walk in town and pointed out the Lebanese man who also sells fruit. She asked us what we thought, and we all said that he does much better business than we do. She asked us why, and we talked a lot about it.

"We women chase after the cars with our fruit, we knock on the windows, try to get people to notice us. The Lebanese man sits quietly—his fruit arranged in a beautiful display. People like to buy his fruit. They don't like us to chase them. Once we made nicer displays and stopped chasing cars, we sold more fruit. We did better business."

On our drive back to Dakar, Marguerite talked more about the women. "You can't imagine how hard it is to get the women to take the initiative, to believe in themselves. But it is beginning. Imagine what it is like for them when our proverbs reflect how they are perceived. For example: A woman should be as light as a bonnet and as humble as shoes. A woman may make suggestions, but her man makes the decisions. A woman gets her dignity from her marriage. A woman enters heaven only thanks to her husband. A woman without a husband is like a house without a roof."

Marguerite and her team had a lot of work ahead if these women were to believe in themselves, even slightly, for the sake of their businesses.

I remembered asking a group of the rural women who'd joined us in Buea if we should design a management training program for the community at large, men, as well as women. As one, the women roared, "No!" I hadn't expected such an unequivocal response. When I asked about it, one of the women explained that even if there was just one man and twenty women, the man's opinion would be the only one that mattered. Among themselves, the women would learn. In the presence of a man, the women would hang back. I understood. We designed our program for women only.

I respected all the people I worked with on GMT in French-speaking West Africa. But I truly loved the Senegalese team Marguerite put together. Thanks to Marguerite's skill as a manager, this team was exceptional. She made a point of recruiting trainers from more than one organization. For example, the Senegalese *Association Conseil pour l'Action* in Dakar had an excellent reputation. Seni, a microenterprise specialist who knew his way around the NGO community, had worked for several years on a Peace Corps program in Dakar. He was one of ACA's best trainers, and one of Marguerite's first recruits. He developed a participatory approach to training in financial management for pharmacists and doctors, as well as mechanics and tradespeople (most of whom were illiterate). While he had never worked with rural women who managed grain mills, he rose enthusiastically to this new challenge.

She recruited Boubacar, an agricultural economist with a PhD, from the *Ecole Nationale Superieure de l'Agriculture* in Thiès. Boubacar trained agriculturalists but had no experience training illiterate populations or rural women. She brought on three women trainers from *Maisons Familiales Rurales* (MFR), all of whose members were village women who earned what they could selling produce or crafts. They had the experience the team needed to train illiterate women. But they didn't have experience with technical training or agricultural economics.

Seni had much to learn from Boubacar about working with local farmers in rural areas of the country. Boubacar had much to learn from Seni about training populations that could neither read nor write. Both men had a lot to learn from the hardworking woman from *Maisons Familiales Rurales*, with many years of experience with women's groups, about the challenges facing village women in Senegal.

Seni was fast-moving, industrious, and no-nonsense when it came to the work, while Boubacar was more laid-back. Either way, though, they got the job done. They got along well, and introduced me to the endless jokes that the two of them made at each other's expense: "I am your master. You are my slave!" Their talents and their temperaments complemented each other well and contributed greatly to the success of the program. Marguerite's woman trainer smiled less than the men.

One of the unique things about GMT was that the trainer's role was not limited to running a workshop. A few weeks after the training sessions, the trainer would visit the participants where they lived and worked, and see how they were getting along. Were they putting the lessons into practice?

After we visited the women in Thiès, Marguerite dropped me off at ACA in Dakar, so that Seni could take me with him to visit the *boutiques villageoises*. I hung back while Seni greeted the shopkeepers, pharmacists, and a hairdresser. It was easy to see the goodwill Seni elicited from everyone. Even from a distance, I could hear the joking and laughter. Although he was speaking Wolof, I understood that Seni was doing scheduled follow-up with the trainees.

Seni and the shopkeepers looked at the books together; Seni pointed, the others nodded. Seni introduced me to the group. Although I didn't speak Wolof and they didn't speak French, we all smiled. If I was a friend of Seni's, I was okay with them. They loved Seni. It was hard not to love Seni.

At the end of my visit to Dakar, Marguerite had to leave the country for a few days, and left me to meet with Seni and Boubacar on my own. When I let it slip that it was my birthday, they insisted we celebrate together at Boubacar's house in Thiès. For several hours, we sat on the floor and ate *thiéboudienne*, Senegal's national dish of fresh fish, rice, and vegetables, with our fingers, all three of us, from the same broad, shallow bowl.

Our conversation was wide-ranging, and swung back-and-forth from the training to the baobab tree to gender and back to the training again.

"I've been thinking that our program is a lot like the baobab tree," Seni said.

"Why do you say that?" I asked, sipping the ginger juice Boubacar handed me.

"In the rainy season, the baobab absorbs and stores water in its trunk. Not only can you eat the fruit, but also the leaves. Its bark is used for rope and clothes and its seeds to make cosmetics. Nothing is lost, you see?

"Training women is like that. Women make the most of what they learn. Every cent we invest in training them gives at least ten cents back. They aren't like their husbands, who don't see the use of it. The husbands only want money, not training."

I asked Boubacar how things were going with Marguerite.

"They are going well. Marguerite appreciates what we do, how much we know. She is quick to admit she is new to this. Seni has trained illiterate people, I have trained farmers, but neither of us has trained women. Marguerite thinks we both have experience that the women need and can use."

After dinner, Seni and Boubacar confided in me that it was how I had handled things with Yana in Ouagadougou that made all the difference in how they perceived me as a leader. Like Yana, they had initially thought I was friendly, helpful, and perhaps naïve enough to believe whatever Yana told me and to cave in to her demands.

"But you stood up to her," Seni said. "You weren't racist. You expected as much from us Africans as you would expect from your other consultants. "

Boubacar nodded and smiled. "That's when we knew you wouldn't let us down."

On my last day in Senegal, Marguerite returned to join Seni and me in Thiès, to observe Boubacar in action, facilitating a workshop with the village women on product development. At the end of the workshop, as I was leaving, an elderly woman tugged at my sleeve. She wanted to talk; I asked Marguerite to translate.

"When I came here for the first time," she said. "I thought I knew nothing. I was so very small. But when Monsieur Boubacar, a professor, listened to me, I knew I must have something to say."

I encouraged her to continue.

"When Madame Marguerite told us for the first time that 'the answer is in the room,' and wouldn't offer the answer herself, I thought it was strange. I didn't have any answers. What did I know? But now it has been a long time, and many days with Monsieur Boubacar, Monsieur Seni, and Madame Marguerite. I know many things. Now, when I go home, I am not small anymore. I am tall."

Ruptured State

In the spring of 1992, Marguerite and I were together again. This time in Lomé, Togo, where we were part of a five-person World Bank operational mission to prepare the country's first urban development project to address the needs of one of Lomé's poorest neighborhoods, Bé.

After we collected our luggage and emerged in Arrivals, I looked around for a government man holding up a cardboard sign with our names on it. But no government man was waiting; instead, we heard someone calling: *"Madame Dell! Madame Monnet! C'est moi, Alfie!"* We looked over to see Alfie Seddoh, an earnest young Togolese consultant who'd been a tremendous help on a previous mission. He was smiling broadly and waving. He carried our heavy bags to where he'd illegally parked his little white car.

"Wasn't the ministry expecting us?" I asked Alfie once we were moving. Meeting Bank staff on arrival at the airport was a courtesy generally extended by the government, and there had certainly been a government car to meet me when I arrived in Lomé the previous January.

"Yes, yes, Madame Dell! There isn't any problem," he answered. "Do not be afraid, Madame. You are welcome in Lomé!"

Despite Alfie's upbeat demeanor, I still wondered.

After a soggy hour-and-a-half ride from the airport (Alfie's car did not have air-conditioning), I was relieved to arrive at the Hotel Sarakawa, with its two bars, three restaurants, Olympic-sized pool, and sandy beach. But the lobby was virtually empty. A young man stood alone behind the reception desk, looking nervous. He asked for our passports and credit cards. When I asked if the rest of our team had arrived, he pointed toward a double-glass door that opened to a terrace near the swimming pool. *"Ils sont là-bas."*

I was relieved to see the familiar faces: our mission leader, Aubert Dejardin, a Belgian urban planner working in a Work Bank operational department; Olivier, a water supply engineer, also Belgian; and Jacques, a French financial analyst and a colleague of mine from the Institute. Marguerite was the only African among us. The three men stood up from the table to greet us. After shaking hands and kissing cheeks, we sat down. Aubert ordered a round of drinks. We were all tired, but glad to share stories of our frantic last days readying ourselves to leave D.C., unreasonable last-minute requests from idiot bosses, annoyed spouses, troubles over tickets and visas.

I liked the camaraderie among us. It hadn't always been that way. On mission with men in Egypt and Yemen, I inevitably felt like the odd one out. This was changing, and I was glad.

An hour later, we gave in to jet lag and trudged off to our rooms. I couldn't help wondering why there was no one in the pool. The last time I'd been in Lomé, it had been alive with splashing children and relaxed adults. Where was everyone?

The next morning, Alfie appeared at the hotel promptly at 8 a.m. to drive Marguerite and me to meet with the women of Bé. He brought two other drivers with him, one to take Aubert to meetings with the ministry, and the other to take the other men to inspect pit latrines and sewers.

For three days, Alfie drove us wherever we wanted to go. As we bumped along the rugged, unpaved roads, Marguerite and I peered out the windows at the tiny houses, a jumble of rusted roofs and soggy straw. Barefoot children with runny noses wearing torn T-shirts skipped alongside the car, continuing down to the beach to join the pigs who slurped, snorted, and rooted in piles of garbage. Missions to developing countries had prepared me for the impoverished communities, but the kids playing among the pigs was hard to take. From my earlier trip to Lomé, I knew how bad conditions were and why we were preparing an urban project that included water supply and sewerage systems, and enough latrines to accommodate everyone in the community. I knew from just looking around why the children were sick and dying. Unfortunately, their mothers did not.

Six months earlier, on my last trip to Lomé, I'd spent hours talking with the local people in the community center. This time, however, when we arrived at the center with Alfie, it was locked. I asked Alfie what was wrong. Where was everybody?

"Nothing is wrong," he said, without further explanation.

We continued to the same shade tree where I'd met with a large group of women on that previous visit. I remembered how shy the women had been at first, and how they had gradually opened up. They had talked about how it wasn't easy being married to men who didn't work, drank all day, and beat them at night. Year after year, after the rainy season, they had to rebuild their houses and markets.

Alfie parked near the tree, but there was no point getting out of the car. The place was empty, not a woman in sight.

"Where are all the women?" I asked.

"Busy preparing for the rains, I suppose," he said, distractedly.

We had no choice but to return to the hotel.

For the next few days, Alfie drove us around town, then through the outskirts, to see what we could, which wasn't much. So few people were in the streets that I hardly recognized the neighborhoods I'd visited six months ago. Every afternoon, Marguerite and I had lunch and talked with the sanitary engineers, who—unlike us—still had people to meet and latrine sites to identify. Solid and liquid waste were a popular topic over lunch. Marguerite and I did our best to be serious as we followed along.

At the end of each day—miserably hot, dusty, and discouraged—our team would meet on the hotel terrace and compare notes, talk about what we'd seen or not seen, learned or not learned. The community center was empty and locked, I said. No one showed up from the department of public works, Olivier said. Aubert never mentioned anything to us about his meetings with the ministry or their willingness to cooperate with the mission. By the middle of the week, I was convinced that Aubert was out of his depth as our mission leader. He seemed as ill-informed about what was going on in the country as the rest of us, and unprepared to take charge and figure it out.

This was only my second Bank appraisal mission, and I wasn't impressed. All of my colleagues at the Institute complained that our training work was not "mainstream" or related in any important way to Bank lending operations. I didn't agree. The work Marguerite and I were doing with the women in Africa, even on a small scale—especially on a small scale— was gratifying in a way that working on these large Bank projects wasn't. Our training programs allowed us to make our own rules, approach things our own way, make personal connections that we'd never have been able to do on mainstream Bank work. I always knew what needed to be done when I worked with Marguerite on GMT, I rarely felt that when I was on mission doing mainstream Bank work.

At the end of the week, we were no longer sure where to go or what to do. Aubert looked as worn out as I felt. When he asked me to go with him to meet the United Nations Development Programme (UNDP) resident representative, I was happy to go. I wanted to be sure he made our concerns clear to the resident representative.

The halls were dimly lit. The paint on the walls was chipped and peeling, the concrete stairs crumbling. Reports were piled haphazardly on windowsills. After a few wrong turns, we found the resident representative's office. In the early 1990s, the World Bank had resident missions of its own around the world, but in countries where it didn't, the UNDP played that role for us. Monsieur Francois, the resident representative in Togo, was an international civil servant with the rank of ambassador of a foreign state.

Aubert and I perched uncomfortably on two small metal chairs and waited while Francois' secretary announced us. "Monsieur will see you now," the secretary said, ushering us into the inner office, where Monsieur Francois sat at a large empty desk, a well-brushed, white miniature poodle on his lap. He didn't stand to greet us, but flapped his arms in the direction of two chairs facing his desk. "*Asseyez vous, asseyez vous,*" he said, while busying himself with hard candies in a massive cut-glass bowl.

"Ah, *Monsieur et Madame*. I am pleased to see you. You know how much we appreciate your World Bank here in Lomé. All your good work. We admire you."

"*Merci, Monsieur*," Aubert said. "Could I trouble you to brief us on how the government and the international agencies will collaborate on urban development? No one met us at the airport. No one is keeping appointments. The community center was empty and locked when we got there."

"*Oui?*" said Francois, helping himself to more candy. "Well, I don't know why that is, not at all. Is it true? Is no one coming to see you? *Personne?*"

"The point is," Aubert said, "we have a job to do here, and we can't do it."

The secretary opened the door, motioned to her boss. "*Monsieur?*"

Francois scuttled out, his dog tucked under his arm. A few minutes later, he returned, pulled on his cap, grabbed the dog's pink leash, and gave a slight bow.

"Oh, dear, I truly must go. You see, there is an emergency. Do you understand? *Alors, bonne chance, Monsieur et Madame. Bonne chance.*"

Alone in the office again, Aubert and I looked at each other, speechless. Good luck? What was going on? The Bank didn't have an office in Lomé and the UNDP wouldn't help us out? Monsieur Francois had no answers and had disappeared? Things must be worse in Lomé than we realized, but we still didn't know why.

Back at the hotel, the team met again and lamented how far behind we were with our work. So many vacant offices and frightened faces. Still, the earnest Alfie met Marguerite and me in the lobby each morning, as if things were normal.

Aubert had rarely joined us for breakfast or lunch. By the end of the first week, he no longer joined us for dinner, either. Wanting to respect his privacy, nobody asked him about the change in his routine. Nothing about this mission was routine.

Toward the end of our second week in Lomé, sitting in the hotel lobby, I overheard a conversation between two men who appeared to be Europeans. They were speaking in French in muffled tones, scribbling notes on legal pads, and sipping whisky. I coughed, loud enough to get their attention. Then I leaned forward, asked in French if I might interrupt. When one of the men nodded, I said: "As far as I can make out, your mission and mine are the only ones still at the hotel. Could I ask why you are here in Lomé?"

The men looked at each other. "*Madame*, you must know that we are consultants for the United Nations Commission on Human Rights," one responded, and then asked: "*Mais Madame*, don't you work for the World Bank?"

I nodded.

"Don't you know what has been happening here during these past three months? Almost all of the international agencies are gone. No one can do business in Togo with a monster like Eyadéma as president. Our job is to document what he is doing."

"I see," I said. But I didn't see.

"Over the past few months, soldiers have been showing up in neighborhoods like Bé, dragging the men out of their houses, beating them bloody while their women and children look on. Eyadéma's thugs are drowning the men in the lagoon. There have been hundreds of drownings already."

"Bé?" The word caught in my throat.

"Of course," he replied. "Bé is the worst. The people there are well organized. They speak out, protest government corruption, and the lack of elections."

Was he talking about the same people I had worked with when I was in Togo three months before? The people with whom we had cobbled together the community participation piece of our World Bank urban project? Were these people I had interviewed, encouraged, and promised to help all . . . dead?

I stood up from the chair, horrified, and took a step backward. My knees began to buckle. I righted myself, thanked the men for their information, and took the elevator to the fifth floor. I needed to see Aubert. He had to know what was going on. Why hadn't he said anything to us? And if he didn't know, why not? He was the World Bank mission leader, for God's sake. Why were we all in the dark? Still shaky, I took a deep breath and knocked on the door.

But it was Jacques who stepped into the hall from Aubert's room. He closed the door behind him. I asked to speak to Aubert. Jacques said that wasn't possible. "We came to get him for dinner," he explained, "and we found Aubert curled up on the floor of the closet, in the fetal position. But don't worry, we're watching him."

What the hell was going on? Eyadéma's thugs were drowning the men of Bé in the lagoon, and my mission leader is curled up on the floor of his closet?

"Don't worry?"

"We'll take care of it," Jacques said, "We've given him a sleeping pill and put him to bed. One of us will sit outside his door all night." What was he saying? I felt my throat tighten; I could barely speak.

"You're on a suicide watch?" I sputtered. Jacques nodded.

I wasn't ready for this. Any of it. I raced to my room and tried to call Washington, but couldn't get an outside line. I tried to call Monsieur François, but a security guard picked up the phone and said he couldn't be reached. I called Marguerite, who'd been asleep and wasn't quite awake. I decided to let her sleep. I was anxious enough for both of us, and there was nothing she could do, anyway.

"*Ne t'inquiète pas,*" I told Marguerite. "Don't worry, I'll explain tomorrow morning. But have your luggage ready, we'll be leaving Lomé early." I hung up the phone.

I closed my eyes and conjured Aubert's image: a quiet, gentle, conscientious urban planner. Who had he become?

I sat down at the desk and opened my laptop, but wasn't sure what to write. I heard doors opening and closing, then a sharp knock on my door.

"*Restez dans la chambre, Madame.*" Someone was telling me to stay in my room.

"But why?" I shouted through the door.

"The prime minister's residence is burning!" said a man's voice in English. "You must not go out into the street. It is bad to go out."

I finally understood. The people of Togo were fighting back.

I ran to the window. Flames ripped through the black sky less than a block away. My stomach clenched. I tried to stop thinking so hard, to relax my fists, to slow down my pulse. There was nothing more for us to do in Bé. The prime minister's home was probably a pile of rubble by now, and my mission leader was comatose.

The next day, morning crept through the curtains, heavy with heat. Beyond the glass, there were no longer flames, just a smoky sky and empty streets. There were no taxis or cars. No bicycles. I dressed quickly and called Aubert's room. Olivier answered.

"Did you sleep?" I asked.

"Not at all. We were too worried to sleep. Aubert's been moaning, not making any sense. We're not sure what to do."

"Okay, I'll tell you what to do. I've arranged for Alfie to meet us downstairs, with tickets for you and Aubert on the next flight to Brussels. Marguerite and I will fly to Paris, then home."

"But what about the mission? What about the report, the Bank?"

"To hell with the Bank," I said, slamming down the phone. I grabbed my luggage and left the room.

Alfie waited in the lobby, his little white car the only vehicle in the hotel's drive. He greeted me quietly, reached to take my luggage. Then we saw Jacques and Olivier on either side of a wild-eyed, disheveled Aubert, helping him out the door.

At the airport, the departure halls were crowded with frightened foreigners fleeing the country. Air France staff hurried Marguerite and me to the gate. Once on the plane, our seatbelts fastened, we closed our eyes.

I woke to find Marguerite scribbling on the cover of my notebook: *GMT—Saly Portudal, Tunis, Bamako, Rabat, Marrakesh.* Perhaps she was right to think ahead several months, to plan for work we knew how to do in places that would welcome us.

In Paris, after seeing Marguerite to her plane to Dakar, I went to the World Bank office to talk to the Bank's resident representative. Still shaken from the night before, I began to elaborate on the events of the previous two weeks.

"We invented a reality for these people," I said. "We imagined we could save the village." The Bank's resident representative did not look surprised.

"We thought we could fix things in two weeks. Now, these people are more vulnerable to attack than they were before we got there. Our good intentions backfired horribly. Shouldn't I have known that Eyadéma has declared war on his own people? Shouldn't someone have told me? The prime minister's house in flames, the UNDP resident representative fleeing the scene, Aubert cowering in the closet—and no backup?" I gripped the edge of his desk.

"Don't you see? No one was in charge. I was a bit player in all this, but I made it my decision to send the mission home. Doesn't that worry you?"

The Bank man didn't seem worried. He patted my arm encouragingly. "You did what you had to do, dear."

"That's not the point," I said, gathering my things and heading for the door. "Maybe the Bank critics, the ones I've always thought were unfair, are right after all. These are people's lives we are putting at risk. And I want no part of it." I left without saying goodbye.

A week after returning home, I was still furious with the Bank, and wondering what I should do next. Could I go on working for a place that would let what happen to Bé happen? And was I complicit in all of it? Had I had been better briefed, if I had tried harder, would I have known what to expect?

I called Marguerite. As usual, she was philosophical both about Aubert's breakdown and about the Bank's failing to prepare us for the situation we faced in Togo. We'd done what we could, she said. She understood why I was disappointed in the Bank. Still, there was other work to be done. There were things we could do that didn't depend on the good will of dictators or the World Bank keeping track of country conditions.

"Our training programs may be less grand than multimillion dollar World Bank poverty-reduction operations or massive structural adjustment loans, but what we do is practical. We help mothers feed their families and buy their children shoes. Women are waiting for us in many other countries. So, let's go."

I knew my friend was right to be practical, and thought perhaps I was overreacting. She knew the World Bank made mistakes, and that World Bankers weren't perfect; me included. But was it better to walk away when there was still so much work to do?

I stayed.

Sawa Bona

A month or so after I returned from Togo, my father called me at work just as the Bank's general services department finished installing bullet-proof glass in the windows of my office on the second floor. When I told my father about the windows being replaced, he suggested this wasn't such a good sign.

"You work for a place that needs its windows fitted with bulletproof glass? Maybe you need a safer place to work."

He may have been right. It wasn't easy being identified with the World Bank in the 1990s. There were the "bread wars" in Egypt, in which thousands of people protested the World Bank-mandated subsidies of basic food staples, which made the cost of bread prohibitive for the poor. The huge dam projects the World Bank supported in India had displaced thousands of indigenous people. The World Bank made structural adjustment loans that hurt the poor and had no forgiveness for the untenable debt carried by its borrowers. The World Bank was dominated by the United States, which negotiated only with borrower governments, most of which were corrupt. The World Bank didn't give NGOs or villagers a thought.

It took me a while to recover from my experience in Togo. I asked myself again—as I had more than a decade before—why I was still working for the World Bank. Cliff was happier in his job as a freelance consultant than I was as World Bank staff. He was full of advice for me. He talked me down, convinced me to give it some more time. It would be okay.

"Marguerite is right," he said. "Just focus on the things over which you have some control. Forget about Togo."

Sometimes I felt like my work at the Bank would devour me whole. I worked twelve-hour days coordinating and promoting WID and GMT. One of my biggest jobs was to find co-financing to keep the programs float. The Institute was willing to pay my salary and travel expenses, but I had to find other sources—bilateral aid agencies in the Netherlands, Canada, Japan, the Commonwealth Secretariat in London—to finance everything else. And once we got the funding, there were endless terms of reference, back-to-office reports, and evaluations to write. It was all new territory for me, each day more nerve-wracking than the last.

While I was delighted with our progress on GMT in Africa, and the recognition and appreciation we were receiving for the work we were doing, I was less than thrilled when my director insisted that I take the program to India. I knew nothing about India, nor did I have enough hours in the day to think about another program, let alone manage it. As usual, the tank commander knew what he wanted. I would have to make it happen.

Casting about for help with this new program, I contacted a high-energy Australian consultant I knew. John had a lot of experience with the Bank and was familiar with participatory development. He'd spent many years working in South Asia. I was confident he could do the job. He accepted the consultancy, then realized right away that it was too much work for one person. He, in turn, brought in Vanita Viswanath, an Indian consultant already working on NGOs and community development, to work on GMT in India with us.

So, while I focused on Africa, John traveled to India to work with local NGOs to create a grassroots management program suited to the needs of village women in three Indian states: Rajasthan, Bihar, and Orissa. Within a year, this training was being offered by a new non-governmental organization called Udyogini. Meanwhile, I left coordination of the training in Nigeria, Lesotho, and Kenya to Apollonia Kerenge, an earnest, hardworking professional from Tanzania, and a senior management trainer at PAID, who took over as coordinator for grassroots management training in Nigeria, Lesotho, and Kenya.

By insisting we pilot GMT in both French- and English-speaking African countries, I hadn't made it easy on myself. I wanted as much collaboration and sharing among the country teams as possible, but the English-speaking trainers didn't speak French, and vice versa. Whenever I brought the teams together, we had to hire interpreters.

Both Marguerite and Awa, our training coordinator for Burkina Faso, were committed to learning enough English to help me in English-, as well as French-speaking, countries. I was all for it and invited them both to Washington to study English at the Bank and stay with us for a month in Arlington in the spring of 1993.

Although they were at the Bank to learn English, the three of us usually spoke French together. I often forgot to switch over to English when we were home with my family. One evening, as Awa and Marguerite and I sat around the kitchen table talking, ten-year-old Adam rounded the corner into the kitchen. He was blowing a referee's whistle at top volume, galloping around the kitchen, shouting "Language Police! Language Police!"

Both women loved Adam and laughed uproariously at this performing for the guests. But there was something in his performance that forced me to think about how much my work excluded him—not only when I lapsed into French with my friends, but during all the long hours I spent at the office, or the weeks at a time I spent in Africa. Adam never complained, but he must have missed me. A lot.

Cliff missed me, too, and was eager to travel to Africa. Using Bank spouse points, and thanks to Marguerite and Awa's stay in Arlington, Cliff and I were able to plan a trip together to Africa while they cared for Adam. The week before we left, Marguerite spent the evening out with friends, and Awa and I ate at home. During dinner, Awa confided how much she loved the GMT program, but felt there was much more she could do.

"Oh?" I asked, my mind on packing for the trip to Africa with Cliff. "Like what?"

"Well, I could take some of the burden of managing the regional program off Marguerite's shoulders. Make it easier on her."

I must have been too preoccupied to remember our first regional training-of-trainers workshop in Ouagadougou where PAID director Malik Fall had taken me to task for not contracting with his institute as regional coordinator for GMT in Togo, Senegal, and Burkina Faso, and choosing independent consultant Marguerite Monnet instead.

"Does Marguerite consider this work a burden?" I asked, confused.

Marguerite had never suggested anything like this to me. Had she spoken to Awa about it when they were alone together? Was I expecting too much of Marguerite?

"All right, let's talk about it more when I get back from Kenya," I said. After that, I dismissed the matter from my mind.

Cliff and I began our trip to Africa in Tanzania. Although I was curious to learn more about the women's entrepreneurship development training program that I'd inherited from an Institute consultant, my main reason for going was diplomatic. I was there to attend a government-sponsored WID conference. As a Tanzanian, our training coordinator, Apollonia, was keen to communicate to her countrymen the World Bank's interest in WID, in general, and GMT, in particular. I was there as a symbol of the World Bank's commitment to working with the country's women.

From Tanzania, we traveled on to Maseru, Lesotho, where a small, polite man collected us from the airport and whisked us off to Mamolete Pitso's office in town. Although she was a senior government official, Mamolete was unpretentious, thoughtful, and open to new ideas.

She, Cliff, and I talked and drank tea together for about an hour. She arranged for a driver to take us to meet several women's groups in the highlands. When I agreed, I didn't realize that "highlands" meant huge, steep mountains. I didn't imagine it would take seven hours on terrible roads to get there, nor had I considered Cliff's bad back.

The next morning, we found ourselves in a little car without much of a suspension system, bumping and thumping up gravel roads. Cliff held fast to the strap above the seat, trying to steady himself to avoid slipping a disc. The bumping didn't bother me as much as the climb up the narrow road and the tires kicking up dust, which made me queasy.

As we lost daylight, we also lost speed. Although the driver floored the accelerator, we crawled up the mountain in the pitch black, not a house or a shop in sight. I bit my lip as I wondered what would happen if a car were to break down in this place. I looked over at Cliff, who was still holding tight to the strap with one hand, and pointing to the dashboard with the other, where the engine light glowed a bright orange.

I tapped the driver's shoulder. "Is there something wrong?" I asked, pointing to the orange light. "Shouldn't we stop somewhere and check?"

The driver shook his head. "Better not. Once I stop the car, it won't start up again. We'll be stuck on this road. We better keep going."

"But how long until we get to our lodgings?"

"Only three more hours," the driver said, eyes fixed on the road.

Cliff was in pain, and I was nervous, but we did make it to the barracks where we were to spend the night, even if a few hours later than scheduled. Members of the Australian team that worked on the pipeline and lived in the barracks offered us hot stew and cold beer. I left Cliff with the Aussies and collapsed on my bunk.

The next morning, we showered, dressed, and devoured our breakfast, eager to hit the road. Then I looked out the window. What had once been our vehicle was now a few dozen car parts scattered around the yard. We had no transportation to take us to the mountain village where the women were expecting us.

"What do we do now?" I asked the man sorting the car parts.

"You must wait."

Cliff said nothing as I charged out the door. The Australians we had met the night before were piling into their jeep. I shouted for them to stop and lend us a hand.

"We can't stay here indefinitely," I protested. "The women are waiting."

Although they didn't quite understand what women I meant or why they were waiting, the Aussies heard the urgency in my voice. The team leader hauled himself out of the jeep, got on his walkie-talkie, ordered another vehicle to pick them up, and sent us off with their driver in theirs.

Our trip in the jeep was blessedly uneventful. Cliff's back was still sore, and my stomach a little unsettled, but once we got to the village, we forgot our troubles. A crowd of at least one hundred men, women, and children, led by an ancient little fellow blowing a penny whistle, rushed toward us from a stick-and-canvas shelter. Some paraded around in masks; others danced in grass skirts and American T-shirts. Many played instruments.

Only a few of the villagers spoke English, but it was clear how happy they were that we'd come. It was freezing in the highlands. Many of the old women and children who watched the performance sat huddled outside their huts in blankets.

I was there to see GMT in action, but in the flurry of masks, spears, and grass skirts, I didn't learn a lot about our program there. The enthusiasm of the Basotho performers, however, was inspiring. I especially loved one young woman wearing a beret and a T-shirt that read "Girls just wanna have fun." Amid the singing and dancing, the village leader took me aside and reassured me that the training was going well and was much appreciated. I would have to take his word for it.

On the plane from Maseru to Nairobi, Kenya, our next destination, Cliff drank champagne and charmed the flight attendants while I slept. After our plane landed, we collected our luggage and joined Grace Wakhungu, whom I'd last seen in Buea, in a black limousine. Grace put Cliff and me in the back and sat next to the driver. Although I was eager to catch up and ask her questions on the way to our hotel, she made it clear, without saying a word, that I should not. Somehow, she managed to convey that our chauffeur wasn't there only to drive; he was also there to take note of what we said.

By 1992, Daniel Arap Moi had already been president of Kenya for fourteen years. He was one of the African Big Men who crushed political opposition, deepened ethnic tensions, and enriched himself at the public's expense. During his years in power, violence ran rampant and human rights abuses were widespread. Kenya was not a free country.

When we got to the hotel in Nairobi, I thought there'd been a mistake. Grace had booked us into a virtual resort. I was embarrassed, but Cliff was delighted: first, a limo at the airport, then, a five-star hotel.

"It isn't always like this," I said. "Most of the time, I'm with the women in the villages. When I'm not home, there is some hardship involved, you know."

Cliff made a show of looking around the room, clearly unconvinced.

We didn't stay in Nairobi long. After Lesotho, I was eager to meet the women who could tell me something about their GMT program. Many of them lived in Kisumu, about two hundred miles east of Nairobi. Grace arranged to have a small plane take us there to meet with members of one of the Catholic women's groups involved in the training to discuss their training experiences, what they liked most and least about it, and the consequences for them and their families of learning new management skills.

As always, the women laid out the red carpet, sang, danced, and put flower-petal leis around our necks. As we walked into the community center, Cliff, his camera slung around his neck, whispered to me, "Well, Legend-in-Your-Own-Time, guess it's a photo opportunity." I just laughed.

The women accompanied me to the front of the room and helped me into an imposing armchair placed on a platform. Cliff hung back, leaned against the wall, and adjusted the lens of his camera. As usual, he let me take center stage. It wouldn't be until later in the day that anyone even knew he was my husband. They told me later that they'd assumed he was my photographer, a member of my entourage.

The day ended with a dinner prepared by one of the women's groups Grace worked with on her training program. The women had gifts for me: a tie-dyed boubou, which, to their delight, I immediately pulled on over my own clothes, and a turquoise, white, and black cotton apron bearing the group's symbol—an image of a mother and child. After I gave my greeting, the women told me about their training, and I told them how excited we were about the progress they were making. Then, I said, "I'd like to introduce you to this man with the camera." I pointed to Cliff. "This is my husband. If not for him, I wouldn't be here. I wouldn't be doing the work I do. If he didn't stay home with our son, Adam, I wouldn't be able come to Africa at all. If he didn't make our dinners, there might not even be a GMT."

Cliff stood, shifting his weight from leg to leg, hands clasped in front of him.

The women were almost beside themselves with the news: dubious, surprised, confused, and finally, delighted. With nods from the others, one of the women grabbed a second apron, the twin of mine with its image of mother and child and wrapped it around Cliff's waist. The women formed a circle around him and sang the praises of this unusual man.

I loved introducing Cliff to the women. I was proud of him: such a supportive husband, such a trustworthy father. I knew it wasn't easy for him while I was away, but he always seemed to enjoy his father-mother role. It occurred to me in Kenya that I may not have praised him enough for his efforts, and I was glad these women could do the honors for me.

When Cliff and I returned from Kenya, Adam, Awa, Marguerite, and her husband, also a management consultant, were waiting for us. While we'd been in Africa, Adam and Marguerite had become best friends. Cliff and I were glad we'd gone, and thanks to Marguerite, Adam wasn't the worse for our being away.

At dinner, Awa, Marguerite, her husband, and I talked about African culture, economic development, rural women, and GMT. The subject of Marguerite sharing her regional training coordination with Awa never came up. In fact, by then, I had forgotten all about my earlier conversation with Awa.

A few months after my trip to eastern and southern Africa with Cliff, I organized a regional workshop in Senegal for the French-speaking grass-roots management trainers. As usual, I'd been in touch with Marguerite about what we should do. She was prepared and ready to go, and I was scheduled to arrive in Saly Portudal the day before the workshop began. When I arrived, though, Marguerite greeted me with a perfunctory kiss on each cheek and a brief smile, then went on about her business as if I weren't there. When I asked her how I could help, she said she couldn't think of anything and left the room.

Before long, Seni and Boubacar arrived and invited me to join them for dinner. Although I usually ate dinner with Marguerite when we were working together, I accepted their invitation. I loved spending time with them and assumed it would be the three of us. I was more than a little surprised when Awa appeared, kissed me warmly on both cheeks, and joined us for dinner. Our conversation was mostly small talk. Boubacar and Seni didn't know Awa well. They were probably as puzzled as I was about why she was there. They entertained us with their normal riff on their last names Diop and Ndiaye—a kind of ritual rudeness which by then I'd learned was meant to ease tension. Where was Marguerite?

The next morning and the next, Marguerite, the facilitators, and I did what we were in Saly to do. I made my presentation, the facilitators worked with participants in small groups. We ate breakfast, lunch, and dinner together in a big tent. But Marguerite continued to keep her distance and barely spoke to me. Her behavior was so unusual that I felt uncomfortable bringing it up with her. But finally, three days into the workshop, I had to do something. I approached her husband, who'd recently joined us at the workshop, and asked if he could tell me what was going on.

"It isn't my place to say anything," he said. "But I will arrange for us to talk together—you, Marguerite, and me." Then I remembered something Marguerite had once told me: in Africa, two people in conflict rarely resolved their problem without help from a third party. If a couple wanted a divorce, for example, a third person would be invited to discuss this with them and help decide what to do. Was that what was going on? Were Marguerite and I getting a divorce? I was shocked, upset, and confused.

Two hours later, Marguerite and her husband arrived at my door. Marguerite was pale and distant; I was jumpy. We let her husband take the lead. We talked late into the evening, and I was astonished by what I learned.

Marguerite spoke carefully, enunciating each word. Her husband nodded encouragingly; I listened. Marguerite described arriving in Saly to set up the conference room for the workshop and finding Awa already there. The tables, chairs, paper, pens, and water glasses were all where they belonged. Awa had organized the place as if she, not Marguerite, were in charge. Too proud to say anything about it, Marguerite waited for me to arrive to resolve things. When I did arrive, I had acted as if nothing were amiss. To Marguerite, it appeared that I was fine with what Awa had done and that I had accepted Awa as the regional coordinator, displacing Marguerite. So, she had disappeared, hoping I would find her and explain what had changed. But I never did.

"Do you have any idea how I felt?" Marguerite asked me. "Awa there at the head of the room, and me with nothing to do?"

I began to stutter a response but was too dumbfounded to speak. Not only had I been clueless as to what was going on, but now my closest friend, my African big sister, was furious with me.

"Do you think I am someone you can dismiss so easily?" she asked. "Maybe I shouldn't have been so quick to trust you."

"But where did you get the idea I wanted Awa to do your job?" I was finally able to ask.

"Awa told me that you said this over dinner in Washington. She offered to take over regional coordination, and you agreed."

"But I didn't . . ."

"When we were in Washington," she continued, "Awa and I were good friends. When it was time for her to return to Ouagadougou, I drove her to the airport. She never said a word about any of this to me, and neither did you."

Marguerite's husband took it from there. He asked me how I saw things. Had I intended for Awa to replace Marguerite as the regional co-ordinator?

"Of course not," I exclaimed. The conversation with Awa came back to me: she had offered to take over some of Marguerite's work. I had been surprised that Marguerite felt burdened and hadn't told me. But I had never for a minute thought Awa meant to replace Marguerite.

It took three hours, but by the end of the conversation, Marguerite and I were both in tears. Sorry, so sorry, there could have been such a misunderstanding between us. We'd never make such a mistake again.

The following day, I had lunch with Awa and explained the situation. Marguerite—not she—was the designated regional coordinator for GMT programs in francophone West Africa. I expected Marguerite—not her— to take the lead in this regional workshop. More than likely, she'd expected to get me on her side, but when it was clear her plan hadn't worked, she didn't argue.

A month later, I went to Ouagadougou to visit the training team in Burkina Faso. I wanted to get a better sense of how Awa related to them in her role as country coordinator. I was distressed, although not entirely surprised, by what the trainers told me. Awa showed them little respect and paid little attention to their concerns. Apparently, her dissatisfaction with her role as country, and not regional, coordinator was having an impact on her ability to play the role.

Before I left Ouagadougou, I met with Awa over dinner. I said as gently as I could that she might want to find someone—perhaps less senior than she—who would enjoy being the country coordinator in her place. This would free her up to train more policy makers and government officials. She readily agreed and identified the perfect person for the job—a young woman eager to learn, and inspired by the work. Whatever else I felt about Awa, I was grateful to her for turning her position over as quickly as she did.

A few months later, Marguerite, Boubacar, Seni, and I were in Sussex, England, attending an international workshop at the Institute for Development Studies (IDS), where we had been asked to share our experience running management training programs for village women in West Africa. As always, the pleasure I took in the company of my Senegalese friends was palpable. As always, Seni and Boubacar made everybody laugh.

I took advantage of being at IDS to meet Robert Chambers, a leading advocate for putting the poor, destitute, and marginalized at the center of international development. Since beginning his work on rapid rural appraisal in the 1980s, Robert had become everybody's participatory development guru.

When I knocked on his door, Robert greeted me in loose cotton clothes and bare feet, having just returned from India that morning. He asked if I'd mind if he lay on the sofa while we talked.

"So, what have you been up to?" he asked me, his eyes shut.

I told him about our GMT in Africa, and the participatory approach we took to assessing village women's training needs, developing training materials, and offering workshops to help women's groups manage people, projects, and money.

"Sounds promising," he said. "Are you sure you work for the World Bank?"

I laughed.

"I suppose you know by now that I don't have much use for the World Bank?"

I assured him I did know that.

"I facilitated a workshop once on values and incentives at the World Bank," he said. "I left without much optimism that your employer was likely to change its culture or behavior any time soon. Many of your Bank colleagues are powerful, impatient, and have many preconceived ideas. But like Everest," he said, "the Bank is there. So, what do we do?"

"As an outsider," Robert continued, "I have to ask myself: Do we criticize and oppose it from outside? Do we engage with it? Or is it possible to work for change from inside the Bank? That's what you do, isn't it?"

"That is certainly what I try to do," I said. "The training of women managers at the grassroots is utterly different from what other World Bank trainers are doing. Different from what most of our operations staff do. We don't have much of a road map on which to track our progress, though. We make it up as we go along."

As our conversation was coming to an end, I said, "You are the guru. How is it that you succeed at international development when so many others make such a mess of it?"

He sat up abruptly. "No!" he barked. "No one succeeds in international development."

I was so startled by this reaction that I pulled back.

"We all fail," he said, more gently. "But that's not such a terrible thing. Small children learn at phenomenal rates by failing at phenomenal rates.

They toddle, they fall. But they don't mind. We shouldn't mind so much, either. To do anything worthwhile, we've got to be ready to fail. If we are lucky, we'll fail forwards."

For years I'd read Bank documents that extolled my colleagues' "Lessons of Success." I rarely read anything about what our failures taught us. As I had with my mentor Fareed Atabani many years before, I felt more at home talking to Robert Chambers about failing forward than with Bank directors who hopped from one success to the next. All any of us could do was try and fail and keep trying.

By December 1994, we were firing on all cylinders. Six African training teams now had three years of experience designing and running management training workshops for village women in their countries. The Indian team had been running its training in Rajasthan, Bihar, and Orissa for two years.

Since I hadn't been to India myself and had no firsthand experience of our India GMT project, I was eager to meet the key players. I also wanted the Indian team members to share their experience with the African teams. Although each program was customized to its country's reality, the goals and objectives of the programs were the same.

I invited trainers from Senegal, Burkina Faso, Togo, Nigeria, Kenya, Lesotho, Tanzania, Malawi, and India to Bank headquarters in Washington to a workshop I named "Collaborative Approaches to GMT." I was sure they'd have much to learn from one another. I also hoped to interest the Bank operations professionals in what this program was about by learning directly from the trainers themselves. I hoped they might decide to include this training as a component of their own projects.

The morning of our first day together, I walked into the seminar room, made eye contact with each of the twenty participants in turn, and greeted them: "*Sawa bona!*"

Without hesitating, Apollonia Kerenge replied: "*Sikhona!*"

The others remained silent, so I asked Apollonia to explain this greeting.

"Members of the SuZulu tribe in South Africa greet one another this way. *Sawa bona*! means 'I see you.' *Sikhona* means 'I am here.' This is the literal translation, but in fact it means: 'I *am* because of who *we all* are.'"

Everyone listened intently. I explained what I had learned about the African "spirit of Ubuntu"—the philosophy underlying this greeting exchange. The word is difficult to translate literally, but Nelson Mandela came close when he defined Ubuntu as: "My humanity is inextricably bound up in your humanity."

"In the week ahead," I said, "I hope our work together will be infused with the spirit of Ubuntu."

And, for the most part, it was. The only real conflict that arose concerned the feelings the Indian participants had about me. They quickly realized that over the previous four years I'd traveled to Africa many times. I spoke French and was comfortable with the Senegalese, Burkinabe, and Togolese teams. I knew the Africa programs inside-out. But I had designated full responsibility for the Indian program to John and Vanita and had yet to visit India myself. Understandably, they questioned my commitment to their work in India.

From conversations at breaks, I sensed that John hadn't been telling me the whole story about how things were going in India. In fact, there was dissatisfaction with how the program was organized and supervised. There was even dissatisfaction among the Indians with John himself; they found him less than gender-sensitive in his dealings with people. Then there was the Indian NGOs' general dislike of all things World Bank. I had work to do, both to understand the Indians' concerns and to reassure them that I was truly invested in their success.

Although the programs in Africa and India had things in common, they were quite different in many ways. We learned early that one size did not fit all, and the last thing we wanted was to take a cookie-cutter approach to designing training programs in different countries and geographic regions. In Africa, we'd focused on identifying the training needs of village women, developing materials, and offering workshops in people, project and money management, as well as production and marketing to meet those needs.

In India, the team initially focused on capacity building and strengthening several NGOs to work with enterprise support teams, who then would help the village women. Training the women was an important aspect of the program but came a bit later.

While the Indians may have had some reservations about John, they were pleased with the support offered by gender-and-development consultant Kiran Bhatia. Kiran was intelligent, compassionate, and kind. An asset to any program.

We'd planned the sessions well. People seemed pleased with the presentations, materials, and what they were learning. The trainers participated and took an interest in one another's programs. By the third day, there was real camaraderie and warmth in the room.

By the fourth day, we'd made good progress both in plenary and small groups. Several staff members from other Bank departments were joining in the discussions, showing a real interest in ways our training might be incorporated as a part of their Bank operations. Midafternoon, Laurence passed me a note that Apollonia was wanted on the phone. Not wanting to interrupt the presentation, I told Apollonia about the call in a whisper. She left the room and didn't come back. At the break, I asked Laurence if she knew anything about the call, or why Apollonia hadn't returned to the workshop. She explained that during the call, Apollonia learned that her fourteen-year-old son and her niece had fallen to their deaths from Mt. Meru summit near Mt. Kilimanjaro in Tanzania.

When I explained to the group what happened, the room fell silent. I couldn't keep my tears back, and, crying, postponed the last session to end the day early. My grief overwhelmed me. I'd never met Apollonia's son, but as a mother, the idea of my son falling to his death while I was doing my job abroad was too horrible to contemplate. My worst nightmare.

I returned to my office, embarrassed to have shown so much emotion so publicly, but Marguerite and Kiran both came to the office and hugged me. "It's okay," Kiran said. "We are all crying."

I opened the first session of our last day together thanking everyone for their kindness and compassion. The mood was somber, but we continued the work from the day before, everyone doing what they had come to Washington to do. For all the struggle and sadness, we had achieved our purpose: to strengthen and promote our programs by sharing what we knew.

That night, Cliff and I hosted a farewell party at our house in Arlington. It was bitterly cold when Indians in saris, tunics, and loose cotton pants, Africans in *boubous*, business suits, and elegant robes emerged from taxis and made their way up the walk to our house. They were greeted by a cheerful twelve-year-old Adam, wearing the tie-dyed pants I'd brought him from Togo.

Thrilled to see Marguerite again, he gave her a big hug. She called him "*mon fils.*" They were family. After taking everyone's coats, Adam returned to the living room with his ball-python, Jake, draped around his shoulders. He tapped Boubacar on the shoulder to introduce him to Jake. After just one look, my big, brawny friend dashed behind me to hide. When Adam laughed aloud, I had to explain to him that Boubacar wasn't kidding, and it wasn't funny.

The cranberry-red walls of our living room glowed warm. A Christmas tree twinkled in the corner. The scent of cinnamon, mulled cider, and hot buttered rum wafted. Adorned in a gold-and-white Senegalese *boubou*, a gift from Marguerite, I kissed my friends on both cheeks. Cliff was gracious and well turned-out in a slate-gray suit and bright red tie.

After snacks, drinks, and an hour of good conversation, my guests trooped to the dining room, took plates, and helped themselves to slices of rare roast beef and herb-crusted turkey, curried cauliflower and samosas, potatoes *au gratin*, and *poulet chasseur*. For dessert, I served Christmas cookies, cheesecake, pumpkin pie, my grandmother's fruitcake, infused with whiskey and rum, and Laurence's *buche de noel*. People chatted, plates balanced on knees, while Adam demonstrated his version of Michael Jackson's moonwalk. He talked to everyone, encouraging the French-speakers to communicate in English. I loved seeing how much he enjoyed himself with everyone. I so rarely had the chance to have him with me when I was working. I couldn't help thinking of Apollonia, who wasn't with us. I thought of her son Kiro and how lucky I was that Adam was here with me. Safe.

On my way to the living room to join the others, I stopped a moment in the hallway.

It had been a long week. We'd done so much in a short time and put together plans to do more. I was exhausted. But, more importantly, I was proud. Thanks to all the people at my house that night—eating, talking, and laughing—I had begun to make good on my promise to Mary Okelo and Joséphine Ouédraogo. We wouldn't let the women down.

From the hall, I caught Marguerite's eye, and mouthed the words, "*Sawa Bona!*"

She mouthed back, "*Sikhona!*"

Show Time

After a week of meetings with our GMT team in Mali, I went to the Bank's resident mission to make final arrangements for my trip home. As I was about to leave, a Bank consultant I'd noticed working in the mission office asked me to join him for lunch.

"They say you aren't doing typical World Bank work," said the consultant, Mustapha Gharbi. "I'm curious what you do, exactly."

We spent a leisurely lunch eating chicken *yassa* with onions and lemon and I told Mustapha, a Tunisian, about training in Africa and India. He seemed very interested in what I had to say.

"Have you ever thought of taking the program to North Africa?" he asked.

I told him we hadn't, but that my director was eager for me to expand into new countries, which was why I was in Bamako. So far, there'd been no requests from the Middle East or North Africa. After lunch, we said goodbye. I returned home and didn't think much more about the conversation with Mustapha.

My first week back from Mali, the Institute's new director Vinod Thomas called me into his office.

"Have you ever thought of taking your GMT program to the Middle East or North Africa?" I told him I hadn't but was certainly open to the suggestion. Curious, I asked him why he was asking.

"They tell me our new Bank president takes a lot of interest in the Arab world. Maybe you should think about doing something there."

Now, I understood. A few weeks earlier, Jim Wolfensohn, an exuberant investment banker with a mind of his own had been tapped as the next World Bank president. He was to take over in June.

A few minutes later, I made a phone call to Mustapha Gharbi. I gave him the surprising news that we were thinking of taking GMT to the Arab region, after all. He was excited to learn about this. His consultancy with the Bank was about to end, which would free him to help with this new program. Within minutes, we were discussing specifics. This guy didn't waste time.

"Algeria is a little problematic," he told me. "But Tunisia and Morocco would be terrific places to take the program. I'm sure of it."

In no time, Mustapha was occupying the office next to mine in Washington. A few weeks later, we were in Tunis.

Mustapha reminded me of my first boyfriend in Washington, a handsome, mysterious, and appealing Tunisian. I'd always harbored romantic ideas about Tunisia, and I was glad to be there. Working in Tunis was less romantic, and far more frustrating, than I'd imagined it would be. I spoke French, but not Arabic, which meant I had to depend on Mustapha and our local consultant, Mongi, to handle things themselves. It was Mongi's job to get our program started first in Tunisia and then in Morocco. Mongi didn't know much, however, about the Berber craftswomen, nor was he closely connected to the NGO community. Not a problem, Mustapha said. Mongi was smart, efficient, and eager to please. He would be a big help.

Even without speaking their language, I loved the craftswomen I met who made pottery in Sejnane, a Berber village about an hour away from Tunis. These were the same women for whom we'd be designing GMT.

They were the potters who we would help sell their pots via e-commerce on the e-souk site later. For some reason, Mongi and Mustapha chose not to invite these women to our training-of-trainers workshop in Tunis, the way we'd invited the Kenyan village women to our trainers' workshop in Cameroon. It seemed not to have occurred to them how much the Berber women would have contributed to the design of a training program meant for them. I should have gotten more involved than I had. But that realization came later.

Walking with Mustapha in the Tunis market, I remembered walking with Cliff in the Khan el-Khalili in Cairo in 1979. The smell of mint tea and shisha, the vendors eager to sell me rugs I didn't want or need. During those intervening years, I'd raised two sons, traveled to dozens of African countries, managed a unit, and developed several new programs. In 1995, I had every reason to expect things to go smoothly, more easily than when I was first starting out in Egypt. So, what was this discomfort, this lack of confidence I was feeling? Why was I second-guessing myself, wondering why I'd agreed to expand grassroots management training to include women in North Africa?

The hardest part of being in Tunis was not speaking Arabic. It made me feel less like the program manager and more like Mustapha's silent partner. Eager as Mustapha was to get me there, and as much as I liked him, being in Tunisia with him was nothing like being with Soheir in Egypt, or Marguerite in Senegal. Perhaps it was a gender issue; I wasn't sure. But unlike twenty years earlier, I was the manager and Mustapha was my consultant, so I dismissed it as unimportant. Mustapha and I were friends, I'd put my trust in him and Mongi, and had committed to this new program, and it was too late to back out now. It would be fine.

Back in Washington, I knew we'd need to move quickly to build momentum and gain support for our new program. Vinod wanted something concrete to report to the president. Time was short, so I'd have to go back to Tunis during the Muslim holiday of Ramadan, a month devoted to prayer and fasting. Since Mustapha was Muslim and couldn't travel until after the feast of Eid brought Ramadan to a close, it meant I'd need to go on my own. Knowing I would need support there, I asked Marguerite to join me in Tunis the following week.

As regional coordinator for Africa and team leader in Senegal, Marguerite knew the ins and outs of GMT better than anyone. She had experience working with her husband and a Tunisian consultant, Moncef, to develop an NGO training program in North Africa. She was far more likely than I to be able to move things along. More than anything else, though, Marguerite had become one of my best friends. Not only did she care as much about GMT as I did, but she also cared about me. I felt better about working in this unknown territory with Marguerite at my side.

In Tunis, Mongi met me at the airport and took me to the hotel, where Marguerite was waiting. As promised, Mongi was a marvel of efficiency. He organized back-to-back meetings for us with government officials, municipalities, and community leaders. He served as our translator when we met with the rural women who only spoke Arabic.

I knew that Moncef, Marguerite's friend, would be a good contact for us in Tunis, so I was pleased when he invited us to lunch at his home. We spent most of the afternoon and evening discussing our training program and what we hoped to accomplish. Moncef had his doubts about the Tunisian government's commitment to training village women and was surprised to learn that the World Bank was involved in training like this. By the end of our visit, however, he was willing to give the Bank the benefit of the doubt. I was grateful for his offer to help. The more people I could interest in our training, the better.

When I returned to D.C. and recounted the results of my mission, however, I learned that Mustapha was less happy than I was about Moncef's or Marguerite's involvement.

"Marguerite knows West Africa, sure, but she doesn't speak Arabic any more than you do. What do you know about this Moncef, anyway?"

he asked. "Why should he be involved in this program when you've got me?"

Baffled, I asked him to explain his objections to including Marguerite and Moncef on our team. Did he dislike them? No, he insisted, he was concerned for me. He felt I was ill-prepared to work in Tunisia, and he was the one I should trust to help me. No one else. As irrational as this sounded, I backed off and handed the program over to him.

A week or two later, Mustapha was his old self again, engaged, enthusiastic and ready to move the program forward. "Why not organize an international conference where we bring all the Tunisians and Moroccans together with the grassroots management trainers in Africa and India for a few weeks in Tunis? It will make us look good." Mustapha liked looking good.

We didn't have much time to prepare such a conference, where several languages, including French, Arabic, and English, would be spoken and require interpreters. Also, we'd be introducing a complex set of issues. From participatory planning and design to microenterprise development. From new approaches to training illiterate and semi-literate populations to social and gender analysis. But, by June, we somehow managed to get it organized.

We gathered over a dozen grassroots management trainers from Senegal, Burkina Faso, Tanzania, Malawi, Nigeria, and India to share their experiences with a dozen professional trainers and government staff from Tunisia and another dozen from Morocco. I also invited several trainers from Jordan, Palestine, and Israel, who already worked with village women in their countries and were keen to develop similar programs there.

The evening before the conference began, I relaxed over dinner with Mustapha, Marguerite, and several Bank staff and consultants from Washington. Among my dinner companions was Tim, a journalist my director had hired away from the *Wall Street Journal* to run an "Economics for Journalists" course in Africa and Eastern Europe. A few weeks after Tim arrived at the Institute, the director suggested he join us in Tunis, saying GMT was one of the Institute's most innovative and exciting training programs. I was more than delighted to hear this. My programs had always been on the periphery of mainstream Bank work, and it was gratifying to know that was beginning to change.

Relaxed as I'd been at dinner, the next morning, the impact of what I'd committed to doing in Tunis hit me. Hard. Not only had I gathered sixty participants together from thirteen countries who spoke three or more languages, but I'd also brought a whole parade of resource people —American, Australian, and Dutch—to help out.

We spent our days working in small groups, reporting out in plenary, taking field trips, and eating meals in the dining room. In other words, we were together from morning until night. The only time I didn't join the others was for the late-night dancing at the discotheque. By the end of the day, I was too depleted to move.

Although participants all had headsets, and interpreters were there to interpret, sometimes I'd get so carried away that I'd translate my own words from French to English or English to French without realizing it. My friends just laughed. They knew me well and weren't surprised I'd try to do it all.

Sometimes, the conference felt like a three-ring circus and the UN rolled into one. Full of energy, excitement, and, of course, conflict, as well. By the end of our first week, it was clear that Mongi had invited Tunisian and Moroccan teams comprised of government people, whereas the African and Indian trainers were drawn, for the most part, from NGOs or community-based organizations. The Senegalese team, especially my friend Boubacar, felt abandoned; the Indians, whom I didn't know when they got there, felt I'd shown preference for the Africans and given them short shrift. I wasn't prepared for the complexity and conflict inevitable in such a diverse group. Every morning, I showered, dressed, looked in the mirror, and said aloud to myself "Show time, folks," then left to join fifty people for breakfast. I wasn't sure how I'd manage two weeks of this.

When the event ended and the evaluations were in, I was astonished. What had felt like a disaster to me was deemed a huge success by the participants. Even the Indians. Even Boubacar. It helped that I told Boubacar I would recommend to Bank staff working on agricultural projects in Senegal that they include grassroots management training as a component, and that he should be hired to provide the training. It helped that I told the Indian team that I'd go to Delhi, Rajasthan, and Orissa to meet the Udyogini trainers and the village women they trained. It helped that Tunisia's minister of social affairs was on hand the last day to present certificates to all the participants. Maimouna, a former literacy trainer from Mali, who'd single-handedly gotten GMT started with a dozen women's groups in her country, spoke on behalf of the others.

"Madame le Ministre, je vous remercie de la part de tous les participants," she said. "I think you would never believe how much engagement and passion there has been in this room for the past two weeks. We've learned so many new ways to train women. To facilitate instead of lecture. To push the women themselves to talk more and learn from each other. Thank you for honoring us with these certificates. We will now—all sixty of us—go back to our countries and do good things for women, help them in many ways with what we have learned here in Tunis."

The event I had begun to think might doom the program forever had exceeded anyone's expectations. Friendships were forged among black and white, men and women, government officials and NGO representatives, Muslims, Christians, Hindus, and Jews. People shared knowledge, developed new training models, and resolved conflicts.

Once the participants and the consultants left, Mustapha and I packed up, settled our accounts with the hotel, and went for a swim in the Mediterranean. I swam in a big circle, then slowed and floated.

"We did it!" Mustapha shouted, splashing in the distance.

Had we? Really? My mind still raced. I'd put too many people in charge, moved too quickly, tried to do too much for too many. And all those cultures and languages. We tried to cover too much material. But it ended well. Mustapha was calling it a success. Marguerite agreed. We'd be expanding GMT in many new countries with many new women.

It felt nothing short of a small miracle.

I returned from Tunis utterly exhausted. Mustapha and the others may have thought I'd made a great success of the conference in Tunis, but I felt neither great nor successful. I wasn't home an hour before learning that Adam had been caught shoplifting while I was away. By then, Christian was at college in Salt Lake City, and unlikely to return to the east coast any time soon. As for Cliff, after eight years of freelancing as a consultant, he was now casting about for new work. Although he wouldn't see a doctor, I knew his health was bad.

And so, it seemed, were our finances. He never said a word about money, but it was hard to ignore how much time he spent in his office with credit card bills piled up on one side of his desk and a big bottle of red wine on the other. My being gone so much was catching up with all of us.

In June 1995, James D. Wolfensohn took over as president of the World Bank. He was heralded as a "renaissance man." Although he was an American citizen and a successful investment banker when he took the job as president of the World Bank, Wolfensohn had been born in Australia. He grew up in a poor family, got himself a college education at the University of Sydney, and competed as a member of the 1956 Australian Olympic fencing team. In 1957, he arrived in the United States with only a few dollars in his pocket, but managed to earn an MBA from Harvard University and go on to become a prominent investment banker. A philanthropist, as well as an accomplished cellist, he served as chairman of both Carnegie Hall and the Kennedy Center for many years.

In 1980, when Robert McNamara announced he would step down as Bank president, Wolfensohn wanted the job. He wanted it enough to become a naturalized American citizen. He didn't get the job then, but he never stopped wanting it. Fifteen years later, the job was his.

Wolfensohn was well known for his dynamism. He was brilliant, charming, and tireless. He was also an extremely wealthy man with a social conscience and a commitment to ending poverty in the world—an extraordinary combination. Like Robert McNamara, he held strong opinions, was pushy, demanding, and often infuriating. When he became president of the World Bank, he renewed McNamara's focus on poverty. He made it clear that he was committed to making the Bank more inclusive and more responsive to the objections of NGOs and grassroots communities.

Within three weeks of his arrival at the Bank, Wolfensohn had asked each of his directors to give him a one-hour briefing. I was both pleased and surprised when Vinod included me in the briefing. He gave me three minutes to explain GMT. Sure that Wolfensohn would have had his fill of PowerPoint presentations in darkened conference rooms, I kept the lights on and told him a story about a grain mill in Senegal.

"For several years, international NGOs and local politicians had been making gifts of hundreds of grain mills to many women's groups throughout the countryside, including one in the small village of Fadiale," I said. "Although the women appreciated the gift, grain mills needed to be maintained and managed, and the women had never been trained to do either one. The Senegalese countryside became a cemetery of defunct grain mills. Despite their good intentions, these NGOs had substituted one problem for another.

"When the Senegalese training team began their work assessing GMT needs, it spent a day talking with women in Fadiale and quickly agreed that those managing grain mills needed training—specifically, in management and marketing. Since most of the women in the group could neither read nor write, they would need training that took this into account. The grassroots management team went back to Dakar and designed the program the women requested. Within weeks, they were training the women.

"A year after the training program ended, the team returned to Fadiale and met with the women. They found the grain mills in good order and the women's enterprise thriving. The women had been able to save enough money to send their children to school, and to qualify for small business loans from a local bank."

When I finished the story, Wolfensohn beamed. Looking around the room, he pointed in my direction and said: "You see? We need more programs for women, programs like this. We can't keep ignoring communities like the one in Fadiale."

Vinod was nodding enthusiastically, as were a few of his division chiefs, including Isabel Guerrero, who gave me a big thumbs-up. Although my division chief, Barbara Bruns, had been a great supporter of GMT, I'd never been sure what the other Institute managers thought about it.

A few months later, I learned exactly how well my presentation had gone over with Wolfensohn. A friend in the Africa region told me that in discussions with Bank operations staff, he frequently referred to the grain mill of Fadiale. "All you have to do is *see* the grain mill to know that training village women makes perfect sense," he'd say.

When I reported this to Marguerite, she laughed. "*Ma belle*, you seem to have convinced the president that he's actually been to Fadiale himself, and visited the grain mill."

Within a few months of his arrival, Jim Wolfensohn made it clear he planned to learn poverty, participation, and gender firsthand. And to make sure he didn't miss anything, he arranged for his wife, Elaine, to accompany him on every trip he made for the Bank. While the president was meeting with heads of state, government ministers, and scions of finance, his wife, an education specialist and women's advocate, spent her days in villages talking with the women, asking them questions, and in the evenings, reported what she'd learned to her husband. They were a great team.

About six months after the president's first visit to the Institute, during which I told him the story of grassroots management training in

Senegal—the grain mill of Fadiale—my director, Vinod, summoned me to his office. The Wolfensohns would be going to India and would like to meet some of the women who'd participated in grassroots management training. Would I arrange it? He'd like me to be the "advance guard" and prepare their visit.

I arrived in Delhi for the first time, less than a week later. Pleased as I was in the president's interest in our program, I was nervous. Having left the program in the hands of my Australian consultant, I was hardly an authority on it. I'd have to catch up on the fly.

In Delhi, I met with Kiran Bhatia, the gender and development specialist I'd met previously at the Institute during our collaborative approaches workshop. We spent a day together with executive committee members for Udyogini, the NGO that would institutionalize GMT in India. Among the most remarkable of these people was Ela Bhatt, the much celebrated and respected Gandhian founder of the more than one-million-strong Self-Employment Women's Association (SEWA) in India. It was an honor to spend time with this "gentle revolutionary" as she'd been described, this pioneer in women's empowerment and grassroots development. She was pleased the Wolfensohns would be in India and meeting with the women.

"It doesn't always happen this way," she said, smiling.

Early the next morning, I ducked under the whirring blades of a helicopter, barely holding my own against the wind they created as they sliced the air above me. Together with the government official assigned to accompany me to Bhubaneswar on India's eastern coast, not far from the Bay of Bengal in the state of Orissa, I climbed up the steps behind the cockpit, greeted the pilot and copilot, then squeezed into the backseat next to the government man.

Once we were airborne, I realized conversation wouldn't be possible over the roar of the blades. I looked out the window, as dark clouds gathered, going from grey to black, patches of light to no light at all. Then, the rain began. In torrents.

The helicopter rocked, swayed, hovered in place. From where I sat, I saw the pilot and copilot's hands grasped together, knuckles white, shifting gears. I tried hard not to worry, but it didn't work. I was terrified.

The government man pulled out a slip of paper, and wrote in large, block letters: "Monsoon. Do you want to go back?"

Yes. Oh yes, I wanted to go back. I scribbled back: "Think we can make it?"

He wrote "I think so."

"Okay, let's go," I scribbled.

The pilot flew the chopper in circles for what felt like hours, but was probably no more than fifteen minutes, until there was a break in the clouds and the rain lessened. Then, he continued on.

By the time we'd touched down in Orissa, the rain had stopped, and the colonel's wife hurried me off to where the village women were waiting. On our way, I explained my purpose. This would be a kind of rehearsal for the president's visit. I hoped the president would get a feel for our program. The colonel's wife looked offended.

"Of course he will," she said.

Since I didn't speak the women's language, I had to depend on the colonel's wife to interpret. But I also read their body language. And what I read was not reassuring. The women were reticent in a way I'd never encountered in Africa, when Marguerite and I sat with them under the baobab tree.

Was it me? A strange white lady from the World Bank in Washington, D.C., asking question, wanting answers? Or was it the colonel's wife, showing her impatience, pushing them to perform? Even without understanding her words, I could hear the sharp edge to her voice. She held them at arm's length. It didn't feel right. This wasn't how Marguerite spoke to the women in Senegal or Apollonia in Nigeria. Perhaps it was cultural—the Senegalese and Nigerian women were more outgoing and forthcoming than the Indians? Was I exaggerating the problems? Feeling guilty that I hadn't paid enough attention as my consultant designed the program and recruited the director? Maybe there was no reason to be so anxious. Maybe.

About a week after returning from India, Elaine Wolfensohn attended our division meeting to brief us on her trip.

Mrs. Wolfensohn impressed me immediately. About fourteen years my senior, Despite the silver in her hair, she came across as youthfully energetic. She stood tall and carried herself with assurance. She spoke clearly, and, as an educator for many years, she knew how to make her point. Once she'd been introduced, she told us how very glad she'd been to meet the women in Orissa.

She thanked me personally for arranging the visit. 'I've heard that you braved a monsoon for us," she said.

While the others laughed, I shivered, the memory of that trip in the helicopter still fresh in my mind.

She went on to tell us that she thought the program's objectives were marvelous. She'd been surprised, and pleased, to learn that the World Bank was supporting a program like this.

I was relieved. Yes, it was a good program. I'd been wrong to worry so much.

"This said," she continued, "I have some concerns I want to share."

I shifted in my seat.

"The head of the program is a colonel's wife. Isn't that right?" She looked at me.

I nodded.

"So, what does a colonel's wife know about the needs of scheduled tribal women in Orissa? And yet, this woman speaks as if she knows it all. When she told the women to speak, they wouldn't look up. When they did speak, it was as if they'd memorized their answers."

All too true, I though, wishing I were someplace else.

"I was impressed with Ela Bhatt, of course. I'm glad there is a SEWA connection. But I wonder if there isn't a bit of a disconnect between what Ela Bhatt supports and this Bank program. Will this colonel's wife be able to actually bring the women in, get their full participation? From what I can tell, she talks down to them. She doesn't ask questions. They do what they are told to do. I'm just not sure about it."

I'd been right to be worried. Mrs. Wolfensohn had picked up on what was wrong right away. Had I screwed up on India so badly that the president would be soured on GMT now?

As soon as I got back to my office after the meeting, I met with my Australian consultant, John, and asked what he thought of the remarks. Not fair, he insisted. She hadn't understood what we'd been doing. I didn't agree. I thought she'd understood perfectly.

I remembered a conversation I'd had in Washington with Kiran Bhatia, who'd warned me that John wasn't as sensitive to gender issues as he needed to be. I was talking to Vanita about caste and class, and the impact of this on programs intended for scheduled tribal women. Had I paid more attention, things might have been different. It would be up to me to fix it. The program was too Delhi-centric, and too identified with the World Bank. John did things the World Bank way. He'd hired someone to run the program who he thought would impress international financing partners. But the colonel's wife was not the right person. I spoke to Kiran, who spoke to Ela Bhatt, who suggested the names of a few people to run the program.

A week after Mrs. Wolfensohn joined our division meeting, I invited her to lunch. I wanted her to know that I heard what she'd said, how disappointed she'd been in the program, and that I took responsibility for the ways in which it fell short. I'd planned for us to eat in the executive dining room.

"No," she said, "I spend too much time in executive dining rooms. Let's go to the cafeteria."

After waiting a few minutes outside the cafeteria door, I peered down the hall and saw my luncheon companion—well-dressed in worsted wool and low-heels—racing toward me, laughing, and waving in my direction like a young girl, oblivious to all the people staring, surprised to see the president's wife heading for the staff cafeteria. I laughed, too, directed her to the trays, silverware, food, drinks, and dessert.

Once I'd paid, found a table, and we'd started eating, I launched into a full-throated declaration of gratitude and apology. "Mrs. Wolfensohn, I want to thank you, and I'm so sorry that . . ."

She waved my words away, "Elaine, call me Elaine. And please don't apologize."

I began again. I thanked her for her visit to meet the women in Orissa. I thanked her for the briefing on her visit, and for having been so honest about it. She was right to be concerned, I said. I'd been so preoccupied with my work in Africa, I'd not focused enough on what was happening in India. The colonel's wife was indeed not the best person to manage the program or work with the women. I explained that as a result of her briefing, I'd asked Kiran to identify a more gender-sensitive, participatory director. Also, I'd shifted responsibility for the program from John to Vanita. She would be a much better fit for the program.

"Oh dear," she said, "I hope you didn't think I was too harsh."

When I shook my head no, and began to speak, she interrupted me.

"And please don't think I don't like your grassroots management training. I do like it. It has so much potential for doing so much good. That's why I worry about it in India. Millions of women need GMT, don't you think? They should have it. But people like the colonel's wife shouldn't be in charge."

I must have been frowning because she reached across the table and patted my hand.

"Don't worry," she said, "I believe in what you're doing. I'll give you all the help I can."

And she did.

Spin

As time went on, I invited my Tunisian consultant, Mustapha Gharbi, into my life. Not only were we colleagues at work, but we were also friends. So, when I learned his wife and daughter planned to join him in Washington, I took him house hunting in the neighborhood where I grew up. I helped them paint their new house, and they helped me paint mine. When his in-laws came to visit—all five of them came for Christmas dinner. I'd always taken my work personally and was happiest when colleagues became friends—whether in Cameroon with Alfred and Joséphine or in Senegal with Marguerite, Seni, or Boubacar. Sharing a passion for community development and GMT made this easy to do.

Mustapha seemed enthusiastic and was eager for me to take what we'd learned elsewhere into his part of the world. He cultivated a new team of trainers and brought new energy. As overwhelmed as I'd felt during the conference in Tunis, I was grateful to him for helping me expand the program. We went to Paris to meet with the man who'd developed a "e-souk"—an internet-based marketplace from which the Berber women living in the High Atlas Mountains could market their pottery.

In 1996, the internet itself was quite a new phenomenon. Internet-based markets like eBay were barely up and running, so the e-souk was pretty amazing for the time. Although I lacked any computer skills myself, I was intrigued by the promise of an online market like this for these desperately poor craftswomen. Mustapha was all for it. It would catch people's attention, he said. Mustapha was all about catching attention. He made the most of every opportunity.

In October 1996, Mustapha and I went to Rabat, Morocco, for a training-of-trainers workshop, to which we'd invited the Tunisian and Moroccan trainers who had been at our conference in Tunis the year before. I was encouraged by these trainers' eagerness to get GMT going in their respective countries. I was less encouraged, however, by the male consultants, including Mustapha. As before, I didn't understand enough Arabic to follow what was going on, but it was clear there was jealousy and competition among the consultants, and a lot of drinking at night while I slept. Hangovers were much in evidence every morning. I was glad to have invited Marguerite to join me there. I needed her voice of reason to keep me focused on my job.

Three days into our workshop, Marguerite told me that Maimouna— the coordinator of a new program in Mali who'd been such an asset at the Tunis conference—had called from Bamako, asking if I could spend a few days in Mali. The Bank's resident representative wanted to know more about our management training for village women, and Maimouna thought she might be willing to find funding for the program for the members of her women's groups if we moved fast. I liked moving fast. I looked around the table at the young Moroccan and Tunisian trainers, all bright, motivated, and ready for what came next. Even if the male consultants were still hungover from the night before, I was sure that Marguerite had everything under control. I wasn't worried. I left for Bamako.

It was midnight when I arrived at the Grand Hotel in Bamako. I was exhausted from the long flight from Rabat and looked forward to collapsing in the room I'd reserved and prepaid. I was dumbfounded when the desk clerk told me that my room had already been taken.

"*Je suis desolé*," he apologized. "*Mais Madame*, didn't you notice how busy Bamako was tonight?"

I thought back. Yes, maybe I should have noticed how long it took for my taxi to get from the airport to the center of town. Maybe I should have wondered about the huge crowds of people with backpacks and blanket rolls walking down the dusty road alongside my taxi. Now, I also recalled seeing what looked like a tent village in what had been an empty gravel lot the last time I was in Bamako. That's when I realized that my visit coincided with an international music festival, the biggest cultural event hosted by Bamako once a year.

"My room is already taken? By someone else?" I said, stuttering stupidly.

"*Oui, Madame*," said the clerk, nodding in the direction of a nattily dressed European, triumphantly holding a key up high over his head.

"Unless, of course, Monsieur would like to offer you his room. Or perhaps share his room with you." The clerk gave me a wink. The man with the room key looked at me a moment, eyebrows raised.

"Never mind." I turned, suitcase in hand, and headed for the door, unnerved and furious. In my haste to get away, I almost bumped headlong into the tall, slight, elderly-but-energetic Maimouna as she entered the front door of the hotel. Despite my jostling, she smiled, helped me right myself and said, "*Ca va, Madame Jerri?*"

"*Non*," I said, and shook my head. "There's no room. They gave it to someone else." She looked at me blankly, clearly baffled. This sort of thing didn't happen to people coming to Bamako from the World Bank in Washington, D.C.

"Don't worry," she said and directed me to a rattletrap taxi on the street outside the hotel. She leaned into the cab, said something to the driver in Bambara, then reassured me that they'd find me a place to stay. A fine place, she said. We both got into the taxi, and, for over an hour, we drove from one end of the city to the other, looking for a hotel. No rooms available, anywhere. Not even for a World Banker.

It was well after 1 a.m. when Maimouna directed the driver down a dark alleyway far off the main road to a tiny pension. We were greeted by a tired old woman in slippers, wearing a threadbare *boubou*. Maimouna spoke to her rapidly in Bambara, then looked at me uneasily, and said the woman would take care of me.

"It is simple, but it is safe," she said. "I would ask you to stay with me, but you've been to my home before. You know that we are seven in one room and sleep on mats. I don't think I can invite you there, can I? This is better. It is not much, but it is better."

I thanked her and followed the tired old woman down a short dark hall into the room where I was to sleep. The door was half off its hinges. The paint was peeling and although there was a skimpy mattress on a wobbly frame in the room, there was no sheet, pillow, or towel. There was a toilet with the seat missing; the bowl was red with rust. A bare light-bulb hung sadly from a shredded cord above the bed. The smell of smoke came from fires burning out in the alley, where people were still drinking tea and talking.

There was so much street noise it was impossible to sleep. There wasn't enough light to read by, so I lay on the skimpy mattress thinking one grim thought after another, wondering what kind of place this was, what kind of people these were. While it was better than sleeping in the street—Maimouna was right about that—how much better was it, really? My sweaty back stuck to the bare mattress. The heat was horrific.

Before dawn, I heard a small cough, then someone humming, and clicking his tongue against his teeth. A small boy, nose running, eyes wide, shirt misbuttoned, and feet bare stood at my door. He looked at me, then punctuated his tuneless hum with what I suspected was one of the few French words he knew: *"Madame?"*

"Attends," I said. *"J'arrive."*

He nodded and continued to stare as I stood at the rusty sink and splashed water on my face, combed my tangled hair as best I could, then stumbled out into the hall. I followed his lead to a weary-looking old man with bare feet who sat at a small, rickety wooden table. The man pointed me to a second chair at the table and then at a plate with a crust of baguette and a single, greasy, fried egg, which was clearly waiting for me. Breakfast. Chickens clucked and pecked underfoot. Two more old men and four more children of assorted sizes stared at me curiously, asking the same one-word question: *"Madame?"*

Although I spoke French fluently, I didn't speak Bambara. We smiled and pointed. The children seemed fascinated with my white skin, so I let them touch my face. It was nearly an hour later when I heard Maimouna's voice as she clambered out of a taxi and came to find me. She wore a simple, tie-dyed, yellow-and-green cotton *boubou* and plastic flip-flops that squeaked when she walked. As she appeared in the kitchen's half-light, her eyes darted from the old men to the chickens to me. Then she went back to the street and signaled the driver to come closer and wait.

"Allons," she said, with some urgency. "We'll get you out of here, now." Embarrassed about the mix-up at the Grand Hotel the night before, Maimouna tried to hurry me out as quickly as she could. This *pension* was no place for her World Bank boss to spend the night.

When I protested that I was still eating my breakfast, she ignored me. We said our goodbyes to my hosts and hurried out the door. As the driver pulled away onto the gravel road, I looked back at the tiny hotel in the alleyway. The little boy was still standing there, laughing, waving, and calling, *"Madame! Madame!"* I missed him already.

The next day, a room became available at the Grand Hotel, and with no fanfare this time, I moved in. Maimouna kept me busy for the next three days, taking me from house to house, shop to shop, meeting to meeting with the women who'd participated in her training. We visited dusty corners of tiny yards where the women melted wax and spread muslin, dyed long strips of fabric, then hung them on lines to dry. We went to the market where the women sold their tie-dyed fabric. Maimouna told them who I was and where I worked. The market women were in business. They showed me their cloth, eager to share what they'd learned from Maimouna about marketing.

She introduced me to her training team and arranged for me to meet with the Bank's resident representative, whom she seemed to know well. It was a pleasure to talk with this young American woman running World Bank operations in Mali. She had a terrific reputation as smart, practical, and innovative. Her interest in our training was genuine and it did my heart good to hear the enthusiasm in her voice. We agreed that Maimouna would give her a proposal and she'd do her best to find more funding for the new program in Mali.

During our week together in Bamako, Maimouna and I talked about our work and our families. She listened sympathetically when I told her how hard it was to leave Adam so often. How sad and guilty I felt. She agreed I was lucky to have a husband I could count on to take care of things at home. She understood when I described how my job had started to crowd out everything else, including my family. But I didn't tell Maimouna everything. I didn't mention Cliff's drinking, his anger, or how he'd stopped paying the bills, how his legs had started to swell for reasons he wouldn't explain. I didn't tell her my marriage was teetering on the edge.

Once I left the Bank office and our business for the day was done, Maimouna informed me that we had another visit to the market still to make. She remembered my mentioning how my son loved African music.

"We must get Adam a djembe drum and a balafon," she said. "I know where to go."

"Maybe one or the other, Madame, but both?" The balafon—a gourd-resonated xylophone—was two-feet long, fourteen-inches wide, and stood a foot off the ground. The djembe drum was two-feet tall, with a twelve-inch drumhead. A bit cumbersome to carry, to say the least.

"Oh yes!" she said. "I can get you a very good price. Especially if you get both together."

True to her word, she got me the best price for the African instruments. But it wasn't obvious to me how I'd get them home on the plane.

"*Pas de problème,*" said Maimouna. She carried the balafon, gave me the drum, took my hand and we dashed through traffic, down an alleyway, past a dozen squawking chickens to a shed where a young friend of her oldest son was waiting for us.

"This is Madame Dell of the World Bank. She must return to the United States and take these things with her for her son." She placed the instruments on the counter.

"*Bien sûr,*" said the young man, and pulled out two large plastic zippered bags, white with blue-and-red plaid stripes, each four times larger than either the drum or the balafon. I knew these bags from the hours I'd spent in airports, where African women working in the informal sector filled them with shoes or jeans or T-shirts from neighboring countries to sell at home.

"But the bags are too big," I began to protest.

Maimouna consulted the young man in Bambara and out of nowhere he produced a machine that allowed him to shrink-wrap the parcels for me. Shrink-wrap in Bamako?

Maimouna was the most generous, hardworking, and efficient woman I'd met since Marguerite and I had started the GMT program. She was a village elder. Elders command respect in Africa in a way they don't in America. "When an elder dies, a library burns," goes the African proverb. Maimouna was one of Mali's finest libraries.

The next morning, I returned to Rabat to rejoin Mustapha, Mongi, Marguerite, and the North African trainers. They applauded as I entered the room and presented me with a banner that read: "*Bienvenue, Madame Jerri!*" Everyone had signed it with little drawings and a word or two of friendly appreciation. Later, they threw a big party in my honor, complete with a sumptuous buffet and much dancing. I admired the shining, blue-black hair of the women, the glitter of their beaded bodices, the men so ready to please as they ushered me here and there, reporting back to me on all the work they'd done while I was gone. I was honored, of course, and pleased at this warm reception. Still, my mind kept returning to Bamako.

In the World Bank, we worked in poor countries, but usually at a remove from the daily reality of the poor. I felt lucky that our training programs made it possible for me to spend time in villages rather than government ministries. Still, as Bank staff, I was usually spared any discomfort. In Mali, I hadn't been spared. While I'd been anxious and unable to sleep most of the night, I would always be grateful to the little boy with the runny nose and his family. It was a privilege to have been invited into their lives, even briefly.

The Mediterranean Development Forum (MDF) took place in Marrakesh in May 1997, the first-of-its-kind regional conference sponsored by the World Bank and organized by the Institute. With more than six hundred fifty participants, it included a large number of workshops on many topics, including: financial market development; capital flows; water management; education reform; management and financing of small enterprises; economic management training; economic journalism; telecommunications; fiscal decentralization; global integration and trade; and investment and trade promotion. The works.

It was Mustapha's "e-souk" that had snagged me an invitation to the MDF.

In Marrakesh, the conference hotel was alive with people and activity. The ballroom was a mass of tables, booths, and electronic equipment. Amid all this sat a Berber woman, a potter from the High Atlas, beaming at the e-souk website, where her pottery was featured for all the world to see. The star of the show.

Conference organizers and Bank staff escorted the president and his wife, Elaine, from table to table, booth to booth. I watched Elaine touch her husband's arm, point to the Berber woman, the computer screen. They lingered, staring at the screen, then called others over to look. I made a point of keeping my distance, let the Wolfensohns take it all in. Elaine caught my eye and waved.

"This is what I'm talking about . . . this sort of thing," said Jim Wolfensohn.

I couldn't help but remember introducing the president to the grain mills in Fadiale. Neither, I thought, could Elaine. She gave me a wink. If I'd been paying more attention, I'd have seen Mustapha standing nearby, waiting to be introduced to the Wolfensohns. But I didn't. No doubt, much of Mustapha's interest in GMT may have had to do with my connection to the Wolfensohns. At last, he had the chance to connect with them, too, and—however unintentionally—I'd quashed it.

Toward the end of our first week in Marrakesh, Mustapha alerted me to a visit he'd organized for us to meet a group of women potters in the High Atlas Mountains. Several senior Moroccan government officials, including a former minister of agriculture, asked to join us and arranged for transportation to get us there. We met the officials and their four-wheel drive vehicles in front of the hotel one morning. To the officials' dismay, an enormous storm the night before had flooded the banks of the river we'd need to cross to visit the women. The roads were bad—probably impassable. They asked me for guidance.

"These are sturdy vehicles," I said. "I'm sure we'll be fine. We promised the women we'd come. We can't let them down, now. Let's go."

I doubted this was the guidance they'd hoped for; nevertheless, we all piled into the vehicles and headed off. It was soon clear that a drive that normally took about two hours was going to take considerably longer, and the officials grew restless. After a few hours on the road, while we were still far from where the women were waiting, the driver said something in Arabic to the man next to him.

"To cross the river in the jeep will be too difficult. We must turn back," the man translated for me. "We'll return another time."

I knew there wouldn't be another time. The only reason the government officials were making the trip was to please the Bank people, who would return to Washington as soon as the conference was over.

"You go, then," I said, "Mustapha, the minister, and I will stay. Ask one of your drivers to return for us in three hours."

The driver of one of the government cars told Mustapha in Arabic that he'd fetch a donkey to help us with the rest of the journey. The men could walk, he said, and I could ride the donkey. The driver would wait in his jeep for us and take us back to the hotel when we were ready.

I had no interest in riding a donkey. At the river's edge, the minister of agriculture rolled up his pant legs, removed his shoes, and, hand in hand, we crossed the river. Barefoot. The water wasn't deep, but the stones were sharp. I winced. The Minister looked concerned. Had I changed my mind? Did I want to go back? I shook my head. He tightened his grip. We continued to step gingerly—and painfully—on the rocks in bare feet until we stumbled our way to the other side to wait for the others. Meanwhile, Mustapha rode the donkey.

Once our group was together again, we climbed a steep hill to get to the community center. I did the best I could in my soaking, squeaky shoes to get to where the women waited.

As we approached, I saw one of the women standing, watching for us. The minute she saw us, she clapped loudly, then let out a high-pitched trill with her tongue—"*lalalalala*"—announcing our arrival. A dozen women—the potters—came out from a makeshift community center to greet us and shepherd us into the one large room. There was great commotion as they sat us down at a long table, set it with plates and utensils, then began scurrying in and out, bringing us one dish after another. We ate goat—lots and lots of goat—and couscous. Honey cakes. Mint tea. They listened attentively as Mustapha spoke to them in Arabic, telling them about our adventure getting there. They seemed delighted and astonished that we were there at all. They wanted us to be glad we came.

Communication was a bit slow going, but we grinned at one another and that seemed enough.

The meal over, the women paraded us to their pottery studios to see the plates and bowls on display. Mustapha told them about our interest in artisan enterprise, about the e-souk and how it could help them find new markets for their products. As he talked, the women crowded in close. The more he talked, the more amazed they looked. A discussion of internet marketing with a group of Berber women who rarely, if ever, left their village may have seemed far-fetched, but the women couldn't have been happier.

"You'll help us, then?" asked one woman in Arabic.

"We'll try," replied Mustapha.

I thought about the government officials who hadn't made the trip. Those were the men we needed to convince that artisan enterprise was worth supporting. I hoped the cause was not already lost and the women would not be disappointed.

We climbed back down the mountain to where our driver waited for us in the jeep. When we got to the hotel, I was all mess and mud as I crept through the fancy lobby. I opened the door to my room and found Cliff waiting for me.

A few months earlier, I'd seen how eager Cliff was to visit Morocco. After our travels together to Egypt, then to Europe and East Africa, he looked forward to making another trip with me. But he didn't speak French, and I'd be running in several directions at once. There were so many people and so much to do. It wasn't Cliff's fault, but I was worried: could I manage all my work and take care of my husband, too?

For some reason, I'd not told Mustapha, yet, that Cliff would be joining us in Marrakesh. Although he'd spent a lot of time at our home and knew Cliff fairly well, I got the feeling Mustapha wouldn't be thrilled to see him in Marrakesh. North Africa was Mustapha's domain, and I knew he'd prefer not to share his influence over me with Cliff. But what may have worried me most of all was the anger that I'd been feeling toward

Cliff about the taxes. How he'd gotten us into such terrible debt. I'd done my best to forget about it. But it hadn't worked. I wasn't even sure I wanted Cliff there.

But there he was. I gave him a hug, changed my clothes, and led him to the reception in the grand hall, by which time, the story of my fording the river barefoot over sharp stones had gotten out. At cocktail hour, there was much applause, telling, and retelling of the story. Cliff wasn't surprised. He was used to his wife getting a lot of attention, and he was happy to be part of it. As the evening wore on, I noticed people pointing to Cliff and approaching him with questions. Journalists asked him his view about globalization and its impact on the world economy. Why would Cliff's views about economics (even though he had many) be of any interest to Moroccan journalists? This interest in Cliff seemed odd to me.

Later that night, we learned that my large, broad-shouldered, grey-haired, bearded husband bore a striking resemblance to the World Bank chief economist—and soon-to-be-Nobel-Prize-winner—Joseph Stiglitz, who was on the trip with us. An hour later, when we recounted the story to Joe, he laughed out loud.

"Cliff," he said, "Go ahead and field those questions. Maybe they'll leave me alone!"

Later that evening, Cliff and I found our way to a restaurant in the Medina, dark and infused with the fragrance of orange blossom, incense, and shisha. Ten of us sat at a low table on cushions of ruby brocade: Moroccan officials, World Bankers, a few wives, Cliff, and me. We ate roast lamb and couscous, and drank mint tea. For dessert, we were served pastries with crushed pistachios and a flaky crust. I'd been charming in French for three hours and was ready to collapse. I looked at Cliff and shrugged. He nodded his sympathy.

Just then, the man to my right said, "Look, here comes the entertainment." He pointed toward a low, empty platform a few steps from our table.

I heard the flute first . . . then the drum . . . then the tambourine. I could barely hear them in the din. But the sounds swelled, the voices hushed, and slowly, three men in wide, white skirts and tall hats—Sufis—emerged from the shadows onto the stage. Swaying in time to the music, they began turning, left to right, back to front. Within minutes, I found myself on the stage, swaying alongside the men. My feet were bare, and my arms extended. Like the men, I began to spin. I knew the Sufis spun to be one with God, to reach perfection and abandon desire.

The men's skirts rustled against their ankles and legs; my silver caftan twisted around my knees. I did not feel one with God. I was alone and spinning. There was no husband. No unpaid taxes. No enormous debt. No jealous or demanding colleague. No mountains or flooded riverbed. No women waiting. Lost in orange blossom, incense, and shisha, melding in with heavy drapes, gold rope, brocade, the saffron air, I no longer felt tired or trampled. I was ecstatic, however Godless and imperfect.

Eventually, the music slowed, the Sufis slowed. I could feel my feet beneath me again. My eyes fluttered open.

By the time we returned from Marrakesh, Mustapha was barely speaking to me. I could only guess what had made him so angry. Was it my failing to introduce him to the Wolfensohns? Or failing to tell him about Cliff? My celebrity for fording a river in my bare feet, while he rode the donkey? Cliff being mistaken for Joe Stiglitz and getting so much attention? In the end, it hardly mattered why; the fact was that he was finished with me.

Only a short while after we returned from Marrakesh, the division chief I liked so much, Barbara, transferred to a new position, and was replaced with French education economist, Michelle. Barbara was sure I'd like her, and she'd like me. Barbara was wrong.

From the moment we met, Michelle was as ill at ease with me as I was with her. As an economist, she didn't know what to make of my programs or my new ideas about gender analysis, community development, or GMT. When we were together in Ottawa on a co-financing mission, she chose not to advocate for any of my programs with the Canadian International Aid Agency.

Meanwhile, Mustapha no longer showed any interest in the training we'd been doing together When I asked him about the programs in Tunisia and Morocco, for which he was the lead consultant, he answered, "Who knows? Guess it's time for you to take over." The man I'd considered an ally and a friend was neither. Clearly, I'd served my purpose by then. He was on the lookout for a new patron, ready to move up.

Within a month or two, I noticed Mustapha was often closeted in an office, deep in conversation after-hours with Michelle. Although I wasn't privy to the conversation, I could imagine him saying, "GMT isn't much of anything, she gets more attention that she deserves. Believe me." He'd tell her she'd be much better focusing on other things—social safety nets, for example, if she wanted to succeed in the division. Then he'd sell himself as a social safety nets expert. Michelle avoided me, cut our meetings short, and showed no interest in anything I had to say. I felt too exhausted by the situation to confront either of them.

It was hard to accept Michelle's indifference and Mustapha's abandonment of the program in North Africa. Things had gone so well in Africa and India. My intuition and my judgment of people had always stood me in good stead. I'd always been a little worried that there wasn't a woman on the team I'd handed over to Mustapha in Tunis or Morocco. Now, it seemed that I'd had reason to be worried. The women I'd been working with in Africa found our work inspiring. I wasn't prepared for someone like Mustapha, for whom GMT was just a job. A World Bank assignment to put on a résumé. Hiring Mustapha had been a mistake.

While things were bad at work, they were just as bad at home. Cliff's temper was getting worse, and there were more and more angry outbursts. Especially when I asked him about the liter-sized bottle of red wine, two-thirds empty, that I found in his desk drawer. And when I asked about the pile of unopened envelopes from the IRS on his desk. And when I pestered him about going to see a doctor about the swelling in his legs and feet.

"It could be diabetes," I said, watching him pour half a bottle of chocolate syrup into his glass of milk.

"So?" he replied, licking the spoon.

And then I worried about Adam who, at fifteen, seemed spaced out most of the time. He spent less and less time at home and was evasive when I asked where he'd been. He continued to do poorly in school. Against my wishes, Cliff let him have a television in his room, and bought him a cell phone, a rarity for a fifteen-year-old in 1997. What did a kid need a cell phone for, anyway?

I didn't have the energy to fight with Adam, Cliff, and Mustapha, as well. I asked my director to give me another job. My tenacity had finally failed me. Vinod was surprised, but willing to do as I asked, and moved me from Michelle's division to the community empowerment and social inclusion team. These were people who knew my work, shared my concern for women working at the grassroots level, and were glad to have me. I wouldn't be working with the GMT teams in Africa, anymore, but I could be useful. And I could stop hyperventilating. At least at work.

At home, I stayed in denial as long as I could. This was made even harder when I learned from the Bank's personnel department that Cliff hadn't paid our federal income taxes for a full year, which put us into debt to the Internal Revenue Service by over a hundred thousand dollars, and the US government wanted to put a lien on my Bank salary. Since I was an employee of an international organization, the government wouldn't be permitted to do this, but I was being investigated for *fraud*.

This was more horrible than anything I could imagine, and yet, Cliff refused to take responsibility, insisting it wasn't that big a deal. Had my managers not vouched for my honesty, Cliff could have cost me my job at the Bank. Between the taxes, the drinking, and the uncontrolled anger, our marriage was all but over. But I was afraid to be a single mother, or to have to juggle work and home alone, and for lack of nerve, I denied it all. And held on for dear life.

Atinchik

Early in 1998, six months after I transferred into my new division as part of the community-driven development team, a lean, deeply tanned man with a Pancho Villa mustache and a ponytail appeared at my door. Dressed in jeans, poncho, and sandals, Peruvian consultant Juan Arce didn't look much like someone who'd work for the World Bank. But with Jim Wolfensohn in charge, lots of things looked different at the World Bank.

To permit the Bank to make smaller, faster, more targeted loans for indigenous community development in Peru, Wolfensohn had thrown his support behind a five-million-dollar "Learning and Innovation Loan" (LIL). Juan Arce was helping the World Bank team develop a participatory approach to strategic planning with indigenous communities.

"The Bank's new resident representative in Peru, Isabel Guerrero, is enthusiastic about this work," Juan said. "Do you know her?"

I remembered Isabel as the division chief who gave me two thumbs-up when I made my presentation as part of the Wolfensohn briefing three years earlier.

I learned from Juan that Isabel Guerrero was back in D.C. from Lima for a week. I was more than a little curious about her LIL project. Her visit would be a chance for me to learn more about it from her directly.

I always had fun talking to Isabel, who was a warm, bubbly, and brilliant woman. After answering a few of my questions, she insisted I tell her where things stood with GMT programs. I described our new programs in Mali and Morocco. I mentioned that Bank staff working in Senegal, Burkina Faso, and Gambia were keen to include it as a component in their rural development projects.

"Fantastic," she said. "Now, what about Peru? When are you coming to Peru to get your training started with indigenous and Afro women?"

I told her that I'd love to, but I didn't speak Spanish.

"No excuses," said Isabel. "You can learn enough Spanish to get along, especially if you let Atinchik take the lead."

I knew from talking with Juan that Atinchik was a consulting firm that he and his wife, Rocio Lanao, had created. It specialized in facilitating local development in the Andes and the Amazon. Before Isabel returned to Lima, I agreed to work with Atinchik. In fact, I decided to go to Lima that summer and study Spanish.

Still hurt and angry with Cliff for not paying our taxes, and ashamed that I'd let it happen, I needed space and time to lick my wounds and figure things out.

I spent the summer of 1998 in Lima with Juan Arce, his wife, Rocio, and their two sons. They'd converted their garage into a studio apartment—a perfect home for me. They arranged Spanish lessons for me and provided a young driver to get me there and back.

When I'd arrived in Lima, I'd been depleted from troubles with Mustapha in North Africa and from everything I didn't seem to be able to fix at home. Adam was sixteen, and, like many parents of many adolescents, I'd been put through the ringer, learning about his continuing poor performance in school, and the trouble he'd been getting into with friends.

He didn't want to talk about it. Meanwhile, Cliff continued to deny he had a drinking problem. I hoped he'd eventually figure it out and do something about it. But I couldn't save his life. And I didn't want him to take me down with him. I needed a break from everything in my life, and a summer in Lima felt like the perfect opportunity.

Living in Lima with the Arce-Lanaos was magical. From the moment I walked through the door, Rocio acted as if I'd always been there. Her laughter echoed in Lima's fruit and flower markets. *"Mira! Mira!"* she would call, and the boys and I would come running. I felt surrounded by an abundance of love and fresh produce. In the car, Rocio sang songs from her high school days, as she bounced up and down in her seat, her boys continuing to shout, *"Mira! Mira!"* from the back.

Rocio had a genius for making people feel good. She was a born storyteller. Her eyes crinkled when she smiled. Earthy and exuberant, she infused her house, Atinchik, and the training center in Pachacamac with warmth and affection. She was someone who understood things without my ever having to explain.

I didn't speak Spanish well enough to be part of dinner-table conversations, but it didn't matter. The Arce-Lanaos' hugs and smiles, and the stories they translated for me made up for it. From the first, Rocio called me *hermanita* ("little sister") and joked that I was the "lost Lanao," the sister who'd disappeared but was suddenly back as if she'd never been gone.

I let my hair grow long and curly. I wore jeans and a sweatshirt. In my late forties, I felt like a kid.

At the Atinchik office, Rocio explained the origin of her firm's name. "Atinchik" was the Quechua word for "Together We Can." This was a perfect description of their objective as a company, and a perfect description of the work I'd been doing with women's groups in Africa and Asia: communities working together to make things better. Over the summer, I learned enough about Atinchik to know it would be the perfect partner for us in Peru. Isabel was right, my lack of Spanish didn't have to be a big problem. I could trust Atinchik to do the work well and carve out a less demanding role for myself this time.

Rocio's brother, Mario, also an Atinchik consultant, joined our training team and soon became our team leader in Peru. Both Lanaos were enthusiastic about GMT and keen to adapt their training in management and marketing along the lines we'd been using in Africa and India. They were certain that the women they'd been working with would benefit. They wondered whether a different kind of training they'd used with these communities before might be valuable, as well: *Facilitation de Desarroyo Local* (FDL) or "Strategic Planning with Local Communities," through which the women would gain confidence in themselves as facilitators, first, and then be trained to offer GMT to the women in their groups. I was all for it. Happily, so was Isabel.

Mario and Rocio learned from our experience in other countries how to create their program, while also making it uniquely Peruvian. Improving the lives of poor women was a Lanao family business. Years earlier, Rocio's father and mother had founded a village banking organization in Ayacucho. One of Rocio's sisters had founded another NGO to help indigenous communities in the Amazon cultivate, process, and market products made from Brazil nuts. Rocio, Juan, and Mario had worked in international development since they were students. Even Rocio's twenty-year-old niece worked for Atinchik, accepting the torch for the next generation. By joining forces with Atinchik, I was able to draw on their multigenerational development experience and wonderfully high spirits. I could let them do it and I could watch what they did.

Casa Atinchik, the firm's training center, was in the small town of Pachacamac, about an hour outside of Lima. On one of my first visits, I spent a week at the center. In the large conference room, the Shipibo women from the Amazon sat on the floor in the back, looking down, avoiding my eyes. The Quechua women from Cuzco and Ayacucho in the Andes, sitting in chairs on the other side of the room, looked nervous.

The Afro-Peruvians sat by the door at a round table, as far away from the trainers and me as they could get.

Seeing how the women had separated themselves and were avoiding me and the trainers, I worried—even more than usual. But I needn't have. Predictably, Rocio and Mario got the women working together in no time. Between their collective wish to learn, the participatory approach the trainers used to get the work started, and the cheerful way Mario cajoled, and Rocio comforted each participant, the atmosphere changed quickly. Rocio invited the women to join her outside at sunrise and together they made offerings to *Pachamama* (Mother Earth.) At the end of the day, Mario built a fire, and he invited the women to sing their songs and tell their stories to the rest of us.

In the classroom, the Lanaos encouraged the women to put their heads together and create an image of the reality they wanted, and a vision of how they would help their communities get there. With pieces of large paper, colored markers, and endless rolls of masking tape, the women began to define their vision, their plan, the activities they'd need to undertake, and the support they'd need to complete these activities. By the end of the week, the initial anxiety and distrust that originally predominated had been replaced with excitement and enthusiasm.

During class, the women used role playing to show what they were up against at home. One of the Quechua women, Rosa Maria, began. In her village, the men hold community meetings twice a month. Women are not invited. Women make dinner and care for the children. It is men's work to make decisions for the community.

"But the men can't agree on anything," Rosa said. "They always argue, and they never make decisions. All of their meetings get us nothing."

The other women in the room nodded their heads. They knew what she meant.

Lucila, an Aymara, told another story. "My friend and I were at the shopping plaza in Lima, dressed as we always are—in our hats and dresses, with packs on our backs. A security guard approached us, told us to 'Get out and go home.'"

No one in the room seemed surprised by this.

"But we stayed put. We demanded the name of the security guard's supervisor. We took out a paper and pencil, wrote the name and asked the guard for his identification number. We stared at him. After that, he left us alone."

The women burst into applause for Lucila and her friend. They'd stood up for their rights. If they could do this, maybe the others could, too.

Hilda, a Shipibo woman dressed in an embroidered sarong and a pink satin top, her black hair long down her back, took her place in the front of the room. Shyly, she told the group that in her village, the women had plenty of responsibility. Unlike the Quechua, the Shipibo society was matriarchal, and women played an important role in their communities. But with so many responsibilities, they felt they never had enough time to take on new projects, generate new ideas, or solicit help from the local government.

Sofia was the last to speak. A broad-shouldered, powerfully built Afro-Peruvian, Sofia was the group's natural leader. She described the Afro community where she lived, in Chincha, on the coast. She told the group how often she had waited for hours to see a local politician in his office, but no matter how often she visited or how long she waited, she wasn't taken seriously. Either the politician never opened his door or, if he did, he paid little attention to what she said.

"Nothing ever changes," she said directly to Mario. "What are we doing wrong?"

Mario and Rocio worked with each of the groups to answer this question. Together, they identified what mattered most to them and created action plans to solve their problems and achieve their goals. They sat together in a circle, heads together, figuring things out. It was remarkable how much like the Senegalese, the Nigerians, and the Indians these women were. They knew what was wrong, and they were ready to fix it.

Sitting in Casa Atinchik, I remembered why I was doing this job, I remembered the thrill of sitting with Marguerite and the women on a hot day in the shade of the baobab tree. Atinchik and the FDL women helped me heal.

I was back.

Reward

Nine years after my meeting with Mary Okelo, the WID Advisor at the African Development Bank in Abidjan, we had eight GMT programs well underway. Management training institutes, non-governmental organizations, and government departments were offering our training as a regular part of their programs in Africa, India, and more recently, Peru. I was proud of what Marguerite and I had accomplished, meeting the goals we'd set for ourselves at the steering group meeting in Douala in 1990. We'd created something brand new, and nine years later, grassroots management training was a reality. We had trained a few hundred trainers in several countries, and already thousands of women had benefited either directly or indirectly from those early training-of-trainers workshops.

Now, I felt ready for something new. At night, I'd been reading *The Artist's Way—A Spiritual Path to Higher Creativity* by Julia Cameron. After my twenty-five years at the World Bank, a book liked this seemed a bit hokey, but I persevered. I wasn't sure about the spiritual part, but I knew I was creative, and the idea of reading something that was not another World Bank report was a relief. Fascinated, I read Cameron's book from cover to cover, twice. Then I did all the exercises Cameron suggested to find "the artist within."

According to Cameron, it is important—even lifesaving—to pursue a creative dream, be it painting or poetry or writing. A person's passion for art must be acted upon, not ignored. I'd never been an artist myself, but I loved art, and wherever I went, I felt linked to the women who dyed cloth or fired pots or wove shawls. I had spent hours wandering the markets of Dakar, Ouagadougou, Tunis, and Marrakesh, admiring the beautiful objects. All the women I worked with in Africa and Peru made their livings with their hands, either as farmers or artisans. I knew their crafts would never be a lucrative business for them, but I was sure they could be paid better for their work. I loved the women's crafts, not only for their beauty, but for how they represented each artisan's culture and tradition, passed down from mother to daughter.

I believed artisan enterprise had the potential to increase income for women and that I should promote it. Most of the women I was already working with were artisans. We'd been using approaches specifically designed for women's groups. Both FDL and GMT were well suited for artisan entrepreneurs. But beyond teaching the craftswomen themselves, I realized I should also reach out to policy makers, buyers, and sellers in middle-income and high-income countries. The next step beyond GMT might be to link culture, community, and craft to create a more conducive environment in which craftswomen could be more successful microentrepreneurs.

An "artisan as entrepreneur learning program" would be an odd thing to ask the World Bank to finance, but everything I'd done since joining the Bank had been a bit odd. If I were to capture anyone's imagination, however, I couldn't depend on the Bank's normal way of communicating—memoranda, reports, PowerPoint presentations—to make my case for artisan enterprise. I didn't need more words; I needed pictures— lots and lots of pictures that would bring the craftswomen and their craft to life. I needed photographs.

I couldn't imagine a better photographer for this project than my college boyfriend Larry Merrill, whose pictures had traveled with me from house to house for twenty-five years. I dug a smudged card with Larry's phone number out of my desk drawer, called, and asked him to join me in Dakar to take photographs of artisans. Surprised as he was to hear from me after so many years, he enthusiastically agreed.

In April 1999, I was back in Dakar. This time, Marguerite and Larry were with me at the Soumbédioune craft market. I loved the noisy chaos of the place, the vendors' high-pitched come-hither, the shouting of young boys making deals, running from stall to stall, the squawk of chickens on the street. We zigzagged to avoid the open drainage ditch and the greasy brown water. On our way to the artisans' makeshift stalls, we brushed against plastic bottles and bags stuck in wire fencing, stepped carefully around thin men in tattered clothes lying along the side of the road. Women in cotton *boubous* sat on their haunches, tended fires, and roasted peanuts. I nearly collided with a donkey cart piled high with lumber, plastic mats, and muddy boots. I realized that even when I was in Washington, writing World Bank reports in perfect bureaucratese, running meetings, and commuting to my comfortable house in Arlington, in my head I was in this market.

Fatou, a cheerfully confident doll maker with a moist, black face and gap-toothed smile, stood proudly among the dolls in her stall. Seeing us, she threw her head back, reached out, then kissed me and Marguerite on both cheeks, extending her hand for Larry to shake.

"*A bon, la Banque Mondiale*" she said. "You are welcome. *Viens, viens!*"

As Fatou presented her display of lifelike ladies in fancy dress and simulated gold, I remembered a chubby baby doll my grandmother B. Marie had given me as a small child, a Tiny Tears of dark-brown rubber, with limbs that moved and eyes that opened and closed. When I was growing up as a child in Washington, D.C., all the fancy lady dolls had pink-and-white skin and synthetic yellow hair, but it was the black baby doll that mattered most to me. When I told Marguerite about this doll, she said she wasn't surprised. I was just that kind of white girl, she said.

Once Larry had captured Fatou and her dolls in photos, we moved on to a shack where a young apprentice bookbinder wearing a bright-pink, sleeveless top was running a press: turning the wheel in the near dark. She leaned forward, shoulders squared, eyes bright, as she focused on her task. I looked at her paint-spattered press, unbound pages piled high, pots of paste on the dirt floor. I found myself strongly drawn to this workshop, a place nothing like my office at the World Bank with its large windows and beautiful views of the monuments. I liked the warmth, the spicy smell, and the intimacy of this small space. I admired the industriousness of this young woman in pink, working hard to please the master, an old man with a frown who followed her every move. She reminded me a bit of the little girl in corduroy overalls I'd been in New Hampshire forty years earlier, head down, fists clenched, marching with purpose up Whipple Hill Road. Or the World Bank secretary, twenty years after that, trying hard to prove myself worthy among the frowning men who followed my every move. Like this young woman, I'd kept my shoulder to the wheel and pushed hard.

Before leaving, we approached a boy sitting next to an old woman on a bench against a wall of rusty, corrugated tin, cracked cement underfoot. The boy made djembe drums for a living: hollowing out tree trunks with hand tools; carving, pounding, and shaping the wood; stretching animal hides taut over the top; winding and knotting the string to get the sound just right.

When he realized we were headed his way, the boy jumped to his feet and asked in rapid-fire French if this was my first trip to Dakar, and did I play drums? Disappointed when I shook my head, his face brightened when I told him that my son, Adam, did.

"*Ah oui, Madame*," he said. "Adam is like me. And I have many drums for him."

When I asked if Larry could take his picture, he grinned.

"*Mais bien sur, Madame.* I am photogenic."

He led me back to a bench where a blind, sick, old woman sat still, hands in her lap, flies buzzing around her eyes.

"My grandmother," said the boy. "She is a widow. I bring her along when I work. Isn't she beautiful? You must take her picture, too."

I saw my son, Adam, in this tall, kind, and gregarious boy. Like him, Adam loved his grandmother, who wasn't blind but was crippled with rheumatoid arthritis, and had tubes of oxygen flowing permanently into her nose. Her face and arms were dry and wrinkled now, but once she'd been my beautiful mother, a jazz singer who lost her voice to a two-pack-a-day habit. Adam never thought of her as a sick, old woman. She was Grandma, who was home with him when I was gone. And I was so often gone.

Later that week, Marguerite, Larry, and I drove to the Senegalese village of Ndem, where the main source of income was making and selling patchwork clothing, wall-hangings, and quilts. Larry took pictures of the artisans in their studios, then we met with a large group of women sitting on benches in the village square, where I spoke at length in French, full of encouragement and admiration for the work they were doing. As I ended my speech to enthusiastic applause, I caught a glimpse of Larry on a far bench. He was clapping, too. Clearly, he approved of the speech I'd made in the middle of nowhere.

Four months later, I met Larry again, this time in Peru, where he would photograph artisans in the Andes. After giving us a day and a night to adjust to the new country, my friends at Atinchik sent a driver to take us to Pachacamac, where Larry met Rocio, Mario, and Juan. We walked the grounds and enjoyed Juan's exotic gardens. The following day, Mario drove us to Ayacucho in the Andes to meet his father, a man they called Wiracocha, which means "God" in Quechua. Although neither Larry nor I spoke Spanish well enough to hold up our end of the conversation, Wiracocha—at eighty years old—was so engaging and energetic that we couldn't help but understand his eagerness for us to meet the crafts-women in Ayacucho. The women were clients of the village bank he and his wife had created years before, and he was excited that Larry was going to do them the honor of taking their pictures.

After Ayacucho, we continued to Cuzco, where Larry photographed women in braids with big hats, fruit sellers wearing multiple petticoats and skirts, boys painting pottery plates, and women doing piece-work appli-qué—the same Quechua women I'd met during the summer of 1998 at Casa Atinchik. With every trip we took together, Larry's photos got bet-ter, and I was ever more convinced that I'd been right to get him involved. We didn't need more reports; we needed more pictures to tell our story. And Larry's pictures were terrific.

Thanks to my work with craftswomen in Africa, the Amazon, and the Andes, I was invited to attend an unusual conference, which the organiz-ers called *Culture Counts!* an unusual collaboration of the World Bank, UNESCO, and the government of Italy. In October 1999, a hugely di-verse group of participants—dancers, musicians, government officials, el-ders of several indigenous communities, and leaders of powerful international organizations, like Jim Wolfensohn—gathered in Florence to consider the cultural dimension of sustainable development around the world.

The highlight of the event for me was Wolfensohn's speech. He began by describing what it was like to grow up in Australia, where he learned nothing about local—Aboriginal—culture. He was taught British history, which didn't interest him. He took refuge in music, through which he made friends, which led to him eventually running Carnegie Hall in New York and the Kennedy Center in Washington, D.C. It was clear to him that culture was the thing that united people.

He described his first trip to Africa after becoming president of the World Bank, when he met with a group of young Malians, saw them dance, and talked with them about Mali's ancient past, their birthright. He and his wife, Elaine, then visited a school where Malian children studied French. On the walls were posters showing an ambulance pulling up to a car that had just hit a fire hydrant. One of the children in the poster was calling out: "*Au secours! Au Secours!*" (Help! Help!) But the poster had little significance to these children, who had never seen either an ambulance or a fire hydrant. Few had even seen a car. French was a language from another planet. It had nothing to do with their lives.

"So now," Wolfensohn continued, "the Bank and the Library of Congress are working to preserve indigenous languages and put libraries into villages and towns that relate to the local culture. In developing as well as developed countries, there is a world that must be preserved, a world of richness, a world in which people need to build on their heritage. Culture is not an adornment, not a luxury, not elitism. Culture is humanity."

Listening to him speak, I not only felt proud of my president, but I also felt proud to be part of the movement toward making the unusual a more accepted part of World Bank work under Jim Wolfensohn.

The World Bank's "development marketplace" was one of many Wolfensohn initiatives. His idea was to build a marketplace for antipoverty plans, through which innovators and funding sources could network in a way that the Bank's formal, top-down review process usually discouraged. The World Bank—the epitome for many of a slow, cumbersome bureaucracy—was eager to listen, it said. It was ready to fund new approaches to reduce poverty. Unlike World Bank multimillion dollar loans to governments, development market grants would be small—between $50,000 and $250,000—and given to non-governmental and local organizations in developing countries. Ushered in by an enthusiastic president and hundreds of highly-motivated staff, the development marketplace would give people whose voices were usually ignored an opportunity to put forward their ideas and compete for funding. It would be a way for a large organization to make space for radical, low-cost innovations.

By 2000, Marguerite, Rocio, Mario, and I had been working on a small scale with NGOs and local organizations for ten years. GMT, facilitating local development, and the artisan as entrepreneur learning programs were all innovative, pioneering projects for the institute and our partner organizations in Africa and Peru. The development marketplace was a natural fit for us. But we knew that competition for the grants was steep. The total purse was five million dollars. It was likely that no more than fifty grants would be awarded. Any assumption that we could win one of them was probably unrealistic. Still, it was worth a try.

Our first step was to prepare a grant proposal that outlined the goal, objectives, activities, training partners, participants, anticipated outcomes, budget, and financing plan, which we would submit to the development marketplace committee. Our proposal to create an artisan enterprise institute in Peru was one of nearly twelve hundred proposals for the committee's consideration.

To my delight, our proposal was accepted as one of two hundred seventy finalists. Each finalist was tasked with creating a booth, in which the project would be presented visually—a kind of story board—and a presenter would be available to answer questions. The night before the DM opening, hundreds of us worked furiously to get our booths up and ready for the next day's judging.

The morning of February 9, 1999, the atrium buzzed with excitement as we waited for the judges to begin their trek from one booth to the other, asking questions and discussing the projects in more detail than the story boards allowed. By noon, the judges had finished making their rounds. They spent the afternoon discussing the projects and determining who the winners would be, while Bank staff and others were invited to visit the displays and talk to the presenters.

This meant the development marketplace was not just a potential source of funding for our programs, but also an opportunity to showcase our training programs. The World Bank was rarely identified with small-scale development projects, in general, or training programs in particular.

We welcomed the opportunity to publicize our programs as widely as possible and to make others aware of the benefits of the programs and the results we were achieving. This was its own reward, whether we won a grant or not.

At four o'clock, a huge crowd gathered in the atrium: judges, presenters, Bank staff, and the public. On the landing above the floor on which our booths were located, the judges stood next to Jim Wolfensohn, who would be the one to announce the winners.

Waiting with me was a large group. It included Marguerite and Mario, Laurence and Annie, administrative officers from my old unit; my division chief, and my director. I'd never competed this way for the money we'd need to continue our programs. But we'd been named finalists, at least, and that was good. But we'd learned that only forty-four grants would be awarded. We waited.

One by one, the president called out the prize-winning project's booth number, the amount of the prize, the name of the project, and the name of the presenter. One of the first grants to be award was awarded to a Zimbabwean who had developed a process that produced gel from rubbish to use as fuel for cooking and heating to build a small plant. Another went to train judges in Guatemala about the culture, languages, and traditional approaches to dispute resolution of Indians descended from the ancient Maya. Wolfensohn continued to invite the winners to the stage. When he announced: "Booth #241, fifty thousand dollars for the e-souk, an e-commerce site to market North African craft, Mustapha Gharbi, presenter," I clapped enthusiastically. For all of my struggles with Mustapha, I didn't begrudge him this honor or the money that went with it. The Berber women would benefit, and that was what mattered.

When they announced a "roundabout play pump," a system that used energy created by children playing to operate a water pump, the South African team broke into a celebratory dance. Their chanting rang through the atrium. Wolfensohn announced project after project, and then I heard him say: "Booth #117, a hundred thousand dollars for an artisan enterprise institute for indigenous craftswomen in Peru, Jerri Dell, presenter."

I gasped, then broke into a run, heading up the steps to where Jim Wolfensohn waited for me.

"Well done," he said, handing me the envelope with a big smile.

In my excitement, I gave him a big hug, provoking laughter at my audacity from the audience. Also on the landing, but out of sight of the audience, stood Elaine Wolfensohn. As I caught sight of her, she lifted two thumbs up and mouthed, "another winner!"

Later that year, I used some of the development marketplace grant money to organize an artisan as entrepreneur learning fair at Bank headquarters. My purpose was to reach out to World Bank management and staff with ideas about artisan enterprise.

The centerpiece of the day's activities was a panel discussion that featured representatives of several NGOs: SERVV, Ten Thousand Villages, and Aid to Artisans. They spoke about indigenous cultures and the global market, and about investment in artisans, commerce, culture, and alternative fair trade. We invited a few Bank staff who managed projects in Romania, Morocco, and Bhutan to offer insights from their experiences as well.

The panel discussion was introduced by Elaine Wolfensohn. She began: "Ever since Jim became president, I've been privileged to travel to every corner of the globe. Wherever we go, we seek out inspiring new development programs with a direct impact on poverty that reach women, improve the lives of indigenous people, and take local culture into account. All of Jerri's programs do this. Grassroots management trainers train local women to manage their tiny businesses more efficiently. Facilitating local development empowers indigenous and Afro-Peruvian women. Now, the artisan as entrepreneur program will show how artisan enterprise can contribute to economic development."

As always, Elaine did a great job helping me to do mine. It was wonderful to hear her say publicly what she'd said to me privately so often. Elaine Wolfensohn was my not-so-secret weapon to fight the Bank's traditional way of doing business.

One of our panelists, Todd Crosby, a former Peace Corps volunteer, spoke about the Mali "Culture Bank," which served both as a village bank and a village museum. Villagers in Dogon could qualify for small loans by offering a family heirloom or a cultural artifact as collateral for the loan and as an addition to the museum's collection. Once the loan was repaid, the villagers could retrieve the artifact, or leave it in the museum as collateral for another loan. Meanwhile, foreigners paid an entrance fee to visit the museum. The museum preserved the village's cultural heritage and boosted the local economy at the same time.

Both before and after the panel discussion, artisans demonstrated their crafts throughout the large hall. Guests talked with weavers like Rosa Maria from Peru and Bobo from Ghana, with a Tibetan paper maker, with a woodworker from Haiti, and with Peruvian Tiberio Gonzales, who carved stones and made jewelry. A djembe drummer circled the room. People admired Larry's large-format photographs of Senegalese, Peruvian, and Haitian artisans on display.

Soon after the learning fair ended, I traveled with Larry and his camera again, this time to the Amazon to take pictures of the Shipibo craftswomen. Our first morning in the Shipibo village of San Francisco as I was preparing to meet Larry downstairs for breakfast, the phone rang. It was Cliff.

He didn't even say hello. "I want you to know that our son is totally out of control, and I won't put up with it anymore. I kicked him out of the house."

"You kicked him out? Unilaterally? When I'm in the Amazon?"

He hung up on me before I had a chance to hang up on him.

I hardly had a moment to absorb what Cliff had said when the phone rang again. This time it was Adam.

"Dad kicked me out of the house, Mom. I don't know what made him so mad. Maybe you can help me out. What do you think?"

"How should I know?" I asked, trying to control my rage. "I'm in the Amazon."

I didn't know who made me madder, my husband or my son. Maybe it was myself I was mad at. Why hadn't I seen this coming? Would this have happened if I'd traveled less and spent more time at home?

I hurried downstairs to breakfast, where Larry was waiting. I told him about the calls. He listened quietly, taking in my anger and alarm. He made no excuses and gave no advice; instead, he reached across the table, patted my arm, and said, "Home can be hard sometimes. Maybe you need to focus on work for now?"

"Perhaps," I said. "But why should it be so hard?"

Not a question Larry could answer.

My success in the development marketplace—not just the first one in 2000, but a second one in 2002, in which three of my proposals were grant winners—meant that Bank operations staff came to know something about what we were doing. Perhaps for this reason, I was invited to run a series of panel discussions on grassroots management, gender, and community empowerment. Microfinance and GMT were covered in the last of this series.

I held these discussions in one of the Bank's auditoriums. As the audience gathered, and the panelists prepared themselves, I spotted a familiar face in the back row. I left the well-lit stage and walked to the back of the darkened room.

"Welcome," I said, shaking Robert McNamara's hand. "So good to see you again."

At eighty-two, McNamara had aged, of course, but he still stood tall and erect. He wore his signature wire-rimmed glasses and was still recognizable as the man I'd come to admire so much. No matter what anybody said.

"Why are you sitting way back here? There's plenty of room in the front," I said.

"No thanks," McNamara said. "I'll stay here. Learn something about microfinance."

So even Robert McNamara had come to realize bigger was not always better.

Happy and surprised as I was to see him there, I had to get back to the stage and get things started. I gave him a quick hug and hurried away. Robert McNamara settled back in his seat, in the dark, and listened to what I had to say.

At Fifty

In early spring, the Bank person responsible for putting together an urban project in Bhutan called and asked Larry and me to be part of a mission she would be fielding the following month. She wanted her project to reflect an appreciation for Buddhist culture, architecture, and craft. She remembered the artisan as entrepreneur learning fair and Elaine Wolfensohn's enthusiasm for the work we were doing. She'd been impressed by Larry's photos.

The Kingdom of Bhutan wasn't an easy country for a tourist to visit. Druk was a tiny airline, and there were only a few flights to Bhutan from anywhere. Visitors were only allowed to travel around the country in groups accompanied by a Bhutanese tour guide and were obliged to spend at least two hundred fifty dollars per person per day. I realized immediately how lucky I was, not just to be traveling to Bhutan at the World Bank's expense, but to be traveling to Bhutan at all.

Studying up for the trip, I learned what an amazing country this was. A tiny Buddhist kingdom in the Himalayas wedged between two giants—China and India—isolated from the rest of the world until the 1970s,

Bhutan had not joined the World Bank until 1981. By the time I got there, tourists had only been allowed in for ten years.

In 1996, Bhutan was the first country to officially measure its socio-economic progress by anything other than the Gross National Product. Its measure was "Gross National Happiness." No one working in international development had heard of such a thing. When the representative from Bhutan first announced this at the United Nations, the audience laughed, thinking it was a joke. Gross National Happiness, indeed. Bhutan, however, was deadly serious about happiness, keeping its environment pristine, educating and finding decent livelihoods for all of its people, preserving its cultural heritage, promoting traditional art and craft. I couldn't have been more grateful for the opportunity to explore, up close, a country in which craftspeople were considered national treasures.

Other than a few meetings with government officials, Larry and I spent most of our time with artisans, individually or in groups, always accompanied by Karma Jimba, our Bhutanese guide. We met young men and boys who painted intricate patterns on large canvas, an art known as *thangka* painting. We met young women and girls who wove cloth for traditional clothing. We climbed up into a tree where the King's bootmaker lived with his family. We watched a wood turner at his primitive lathe.

Despite a push for higher education, there weren't enough professional jobs in this small country. This was one reason why citizens were encouraged to become artisans and pass the tradition down from parent to child. To reinforce pride in Bhutanese traditions and culture, as well as to guarantee regular employment for Bhutanese weavers, the King decreed that all Bhutanese citizens were to wear traditional dress at all times.

As we traveled from place to place, we learned more about the "Land of the Thunder Dragon." For example, if Bhutanese parents cannot afford to feed or care for their children, the state arranges for them to be raised by others, such as monks in monasteries or artisans at Zorig Chusum, the National Institute for Traditional Art and Craft.

Larry was thrilled to be in Bhutan. Any photographer would have been. The people, the architecture, the craft, the extraordinary landscapes. The photos he took in Bhutan would eventually hang in the Globalization Institute at Yale University. Of course, I was thrilled, as well, to see such a magnificent country at close range, to indulge my passion for art, culture, and craft, as well as international development.

Soon after we returned from Bhutan, I learned that the Bard alumni office was planning a thirtieth reunion for Larry's class in May. I contacted the alumni director, told her about our trip to Bhutan, and described Larry's photos. She jumped at the opportunity to include us in her program for the reunion. We'd combine an exhibit of Larry's photos with a presentation that I would make on artisan enterprise in Bhutan. The prospect of our showing up together at Bard, thirty years after graduation, sounded like fun. We accepted her invitation.

Meanwhile, I organized another event. To celebrate my fiftieth birthday, I took my family and twenty of my closest friends for three days to a lodge in Cacapon State Park, near Berkeley Springs, a historic spa town in West Virginia about ninety minutes from Washington. It wouldn't just be a birthday party, though. It would also be a workshop, complete with flipcharts, plenary sessions, and breakout groups. Our workshop objective was to figure out how I could continue my artisan enterprise work—both with and without the Bank—to plan for my retirement, whenever that might be. As usual, I had a hard time telling work from play. It was energizing and exciting to have everybody together at the lodge.

Six months earlier, after Cliff kicked Adam out of the house while I was in the Amazon, I wasn't sure there would ever be peace between father and son. When Adam told me he'd been invited to Mississippi to stay with some friends, I took him to a nearby mechanic to give his car a tune up, and then got him a membership in the AAA, in case he ran in to trouble on the road. He'd been living to Mississippi for several months when Cliff called to tell him about my fiftieth birthday party. The months

apart had eased the tension between my husband and son, and I was relieved. Adam was at the party. Christian was there, too—home from Wy-
oming for the event. My best friend from childhood, Lois, and her
husband were there from New York, as were Laurence, the first person I
ever recruited, and Tim, who had helped me through my exhausting experience in Tunis. Ghislaine, my first friend at the Bank, came from Montreal, Mario from Peru, and, of course, Marguerite made the trip from
Dakar. I also invited Cliff's protégé, August, a tiny, twenty-eight-year-old
redhead who—like me at her age—wanted to save the world and had
made it her goal to exceed everybody's expectations.

Since I believed every workshop needed a skilled facilitator, I offered
Cliff the job. He was one of the best facilitators I knew. For three days,
he asked questions and got people talking. He wrote their conclusions on
the board. I was grateful that it was Cliff and not me running this meeting,
so I could simply enjoy imagining this future others were designing for
me.

For three days, my friends sat at tables and came up with ideas. I circled the indoor space where groups were huddled together hammering
out a plan. I went outdoors where other groups were spread out at picnic
tables, magic markers and flipchart paper at the ready, considering the
possibilities. At the end of each day, Cliff called the groups back to the
main cabin to report. I could hardly believe my good luck. All these smart
people coming up with ideas for me—not for village women or trainers
of village women or task managers or team leaders. For me.

Late afternoon on our last day, Cliff summarized the workshop results.
They'd decided we'd need to create a non-profit organization to carry on
the artisan enterprise work I'd started at the Bank, an organization called
"Arteco." Some favored a grander name: "The Arteco Institute for Artisan Enterprise," for example. Others thought it should not be limited to
training, but serve as a gallery, or a publishing company, producing books
about artisans and their craft.

Once the groups had finished reporting, Cliff called me to the front of the room and asked for my comments. I told them how grateful I was for their thoughts and reflections, for their friendship, for all the work they'd each helped me do. My sons who had put up with my absence. Cliff, who had given me his wise counsel for so many years. And, yes, I'd be happy to run with this plan of theirs.

After much clapping and cheering, Ghislaine and Mario got the pisco sours started. Marguerite and Laurence put dinner together, while Lois and Tim helped serve.

Once we'd finished dinner, we pulled tables and chairs back toward the walls to make space for the flamenco dancer. Her stomping feet, swirling skirts, and clicking castanets set the stage for an evening of drunken dancing, briefly interrupted by a show Ghislaine had put together, featuring Cliff and me as bigger-than-life puppets, which had the crowd on the floor in hysterics. Lois's husband played many choruses of "I'm So Glad" on the guitar; Adam played his djembe drum, and then, I twirled my baton for the first time in thirty years.

The talent show over, diminutive August jumped up on a table, holding a scroll from which she read a testament to my successes as an oddball World Banker, a mentor and a friend. My heart swelled.

At midnight, someone whispered to someone else, then sat me down at a table. The room went dark, I closed my eyes. When I opened them again, an enormous cake was on the table in front of me, covered with enough flaming candles to burn the lodge down. I still have a photo of that moment; I am clapping my hands, a huge smile on my face, surrounded by friends, thrilled to be fifty, optimistic beyond words. In the photo, everyone is laughing. Everyone except Cliff, who is sitting on a stool, stroking his beard, looking pensive.

The first weekend after my birthday celebration, I left Cliff and Adam in Arlington and drove to Bard to attend Larry's thirtieth reunion. Although my plan had been to meet Larry there, a close friend of his died suddenly, and he attended the funeral in Cincinnati, rather than the reunion at Bard. I didn't want to do the Bhutan presentation without him, so I canceled the presentation but went anyway. Once there, I wandered around campus in the rain on my own, wondering why I was there.

On my way to the alumni dinner, which was held outdoors under a huge canvas canopy, I ran into Larry's old friend, Terry. Unlike most of the people I met on campus, Terry remembered me. And I certainly remembered Terry. Thirty years earlier—after just one afternoon and evening driving around together in his car, talking nonstop, I was crazy about him. Two days later, Terry graduated, I went home for the summer, and that was that. A happy memory of a boy who'd been kind to me, once, when my boyfriend wasn't.

"You look great," Terry said, after giving me a hug. At dinner in a crowded tent, rain pounding on the roof, I was wedged in between Terry on one side and a stranger on the other. I ignored the stranger and talked to Terry. I told him about my work with the same excitement I'd felt during my birthday weekend. I entertained him with plans for Arteco and extolled the Culture Bank in Mali, Gross National Happiness in Bhutan. I described my trips with Larry to Senegal, the Andes, and the Amazon.

Although a bit less ebullient than me, Terry also had things to say about his life as a woodworker. He told me about living on Martha's Vineyard and building the arts-and-crafts house he'd wanted to build for so long. His mason had gathered stones for his chimney from hard-stacked stone walls in Maine. Now he wondered if he'd done the right thing. Perhaps taking stones from one state to build a fireplace in another was no better than Belgians taking Mali's cultural artifacts home with them. He'd never thought about that before. We couldn't stop talking.

After we finished a bottle of wine between us, we decided to head to Blithewood, an elegant mansion on the Hudson River that had been a girl's dormitory when I went to Bard but had been transformed into the Levy Economics Institute for Graduate Programs in Economic Theory and Policy since then. When I'd attended Bard in the 1970s, there was only one professor of economics. Now there was a whole institute devoted to the subject. Outside, Blithewood was strewn with tiny, twinkling white lights and tables, at which we could continue our conversation in the open air.

Aware of no one else and a little blurry with drink, Terry listened intently as I exploded with words. It was as if, all at once, we both remembered the impossible crush we'd had on each other thirty years before when he was living with the girl he would later marry, and I was with Larry.

"You were my hero," I said, thinking back on the afternoon we'd spent together, how he'd taken me back to my dorm room, kissed me good night and left, never asking for more. I'd yet to meet a Bard boy who didn't ask for more.

"Not a hero," he said, "A coward. I wasn't brave enough to even hope for a woman like you."

The next day, a large group of us traipsed around campus together in the rain. Many of the old buildings were still there. But there were many new ones as well. Something about Bard made me both happy and sad. I knew I should probably leave early in the morning to get back to my family and my real life. Terry offered the group of us a lift to the dorm where most of us were staying. As I headed to the door of the building, Terry jumped out of the van and caught up with me. He asked if we could talk in the morning. Much as I wanted to keep talking to him, I knew that it would be smarter to say no. I had to leave early, I explained. I had to get back.

"Please stay," he said, touching my arm. I shivered.

"Well, maybe," I said, and ran inside.

The next morning, packed and ready to go, I was pretty sure Terry wouldn't—shouldn't—show up. Did I want him to, or not? What nonsense was this anyway? I was fifty years old. I had a husband and a family.

As I rolled my bag over the gravel towards my car, Terry pulled his van into the drive. "Hey," he said, jumping out. "Don't leave yet."

We returned to the room. I only had an hour before I had to return my room key to Security and get on the road for the trip home. I tried for small talk, chattering about one thing, then another. It wasn't working. There was something between us that needed to be said.

"How are you?" Terry asked, leaning in close. "How are you *really*?"

Just as the words about my work had spilled out the night before, they spilled again. This time about Cliff and me. Suddenly, I was telling him things I'd never told anyone else—how self-destructive Cliff had become, how he'd mismanaged our money, how much wine he drank and how he denied it, how he wouldn't talk about any of his problems. I still loved my husband, I said, and would never leave him, even if our marriage was now more friendship and professional partnership than romance. Terry told me about his own marriage, which hadn't been happy for a long time, either.

I began to sob uncontrollably. Terry crossed the room, sat on the bed beside me, and took me in his arms.

Empodermiento

Early in May 2001, Isabel Guerrero, who was still the Bank's country director for Peru, asked me to speak about our FDL training program at a conference the Bank and the Peruvian government were organizing on the outskirts of Lima. She handed me a brochure with the conference synopsis. I read: "This international conference will bring together economic development professionals from international and bilateral agencies and government officials to reflect upon the multidimensional character of empowerment; the importance of bi-directional dynamics of empowerment processes; the design and implementation of, and access to, legal services; local governance; and macro, economy-wide choices."

God, no, was my first thought. Not another one of these.

"I can't do it." I said, and handed the brochure back to her. "I'm willing to attend the conference, if you want, but I won't speak for the women about FDL."

"Why not?" she asked. "Isn't this the chance we've been waiting for? This audience of men who don't understand women or community empowerment at all? Aren't they the ones we need to reach?"

"Yes, they need to be told, but I'm not the one to tell them," I said. "The women don't need me to speak for them; they can speak for themselves. That's what our work for the last two years has been about."

Not convinced, Isabel asked if I thought it fair to send them off to a conference like this to face all those men in suits. Fair or not, it wasn't up to me to decide for them.

"Invite some of the FDL women to speak and pay them consulting fees."

"Consulting fees?"

"Yep. And cover their travel costs, too."

I knew I was pushing my luck in setting these conditions for bringing the women to the conference, but I also trusted Isabel to understand.

"Okay," she said. "Let's do it!"

Three months later, I was at the El Pueblo resort waiting for the indigenous Afro-Peruvian women to join me. Some would be coming from the Amazon by canoe; others on buses from the Andes; still others on flatbed trucks up the coast from Ica and Chincha. I heard the women before I saw them.

"*Hola, hermanita! Hola!*" called Rosa Maria.

Suddenly the lobby was a crush of round bodies, black braids, felt hats, handwoven shawls, petticoats and overskirts, cotton shifts dyed brown with tree bark, headbands, and bright feathers, pink and aqua satin tops, and embroidered sarongs. Before I got a chance to wonder where the Afro-Peruvians were, I caught a glimpse of Sofia dressing down the doorman. Her friend smiled at me, shrugged, and rolled her eyes. Rosa Maria grabbed my hand to bring me into the circle the women had formed not far from the reception desk. As we smiled, swaying and swinging our arms, Rosa Maria gave a loud "whoop." When we were ready to settle into our rooms, the twelve women and I clambered into the hotel shuttle bus, a small pickup masquerading as an Andean cart. Our driver kept turning around to look. He shook his head, clearly amused by the sight of us. The driver and Rosa Maria bantered in Quechua as we rumbled our way along the cobblestones. At the first corner, the truck swerved to avoid hitting a tall blonde woman walking in the middle of the road, struggling to stay upright on her three-inch heels.

"Oh look," she squealed to her companion. "Our dancers, our dancers!"

This time, the women and I all rolled our eyes.

The next morning, I was relieved to see Rocio and Mario arrive in time for breakfast. The women knew and trusted the Lanaos, and we were all calmed by their presence. We made our way as a group to the hotel's large conference room, already crowded with government officials, academics, World Bank staff, and conference organizers. As the chairman urged people to take their seats, Isabel waved at me from across the room. I took a chair between Lucila and Hilda. I could see the other women—in traditional dress, bags tied to their backs, hats perched on their heads—scattered among the more than one hundred conference participants.

Once the chairman called the meeting to order, it all became drearily familiar. Economics professors spewed poverty statistics, outlined research results, and distilled policy implications. International agency staff congratulated themselves on money they'd raised for communities in Peru. The deputy minister of economy and finance boasted of the many programs his government had instituted to address the needs of his country's indigenous people.

Eyes glazed, heads drooped, and stomachs rumbled. It was lunchtime, and although they'd been on the agenda for the morning session, none of the women had been asked to speak. I saw their confusion. Was it possible that the chairman forgot them or had dropped them from the program? I tried to look reassuring.

Once the chairman adjourned the morning's meeting and started gathering his things, I joined him at the podium and said slowly in English: "You left the twelve indigenous and Afro-Peruvian women out of this morning's program."

Staring at me blankly, he checked my World Bank badge and coughed. "Madame Dell, you must understand that we have the deputy secretary of state for finance and economics scheduled to speak first and then there are—"

Before he finished his sentence, I said quietly, "When we return from lunch, you will ask the women to speak. Yes?"

He hesitated a moment, nodded, and left the room.

Lunch over, conference participants dawdled and yawned, stretched their legs, and finally grudgingly stumbled back to the conference room.

"Ladies and gentlemen," the chairman began. "Please join me in welcoming our special guests."

Without offering any real introduction, he stepped away from the podium and sat down at the table. I nudged the women on either side of me to stand and approach the front of the room. Seeing them, the other women rose and followed.

As the women made their way towards the front, the whispering and coughing stopped. I could hear the rustling of petticoats and the soft slapping of bare feet as the women passed. These unusual World Bank consultants—some wearing black bowler hats, others in feathers, beads, and embroidered sarongs—lined up on the raised platform. Sofia moved the podium to the side and introduced the women, one by one. Each offered a greeting in her own language, then stepped back.

"We understand that you are here today to discuss community participation and empowerment," Sofia said. "We have been asked to join you in the discussion."

A few raised eyebrows.

Sofia continued, "We understand that you wish to reduce poverty and believe in empowerment."

A few nods.

"A month ago, our friends at Atinchik told us about your research and your report on this subject and they said Señora Guerrero wanted our help. We read the report, but we found it hard to understand." She looked out at the crowd.

"Our friend Mario insisted we not give up on what the report says or on what you want to do. So, we talked more about it with Mario. It turned out that we did know what you were talking about, after all. This afternoon, we will talk to you about empowerment."

Stepping back, Sofia pointed to a flipchart with a bullseye in the middle, surrounded by three concentric circles. "In our meetings with our communities, we women help the men to understand that the center of something is a vision—the thing that matters most."

"As we see it, your vision is community participation, poverty reduction, and empowerment." She wrote the words in the center of the bullseye.

"At Atinchik, we learned that to realize a vision, we must have objectives. As we see it, you have four objectives."

She divided one of the circles into four: access to information, social inclusion, accountability, and local organizational capacity.

"To realize your vision and to reach your objectives, you need projects." She divided the third circle into twelve sections. "Unfortunately, in your report you only go to the second circle." In our communities, we go further than this. We come up with many activities to keep our children healthy, educate our girls, manage our businesses, market our crafts."

Sofia asked Rosa Maria to give an example of a community vision, objectives, and projects, which she did. Once Rosa Maria sat down, each of the other women gave their own example. Sofia returned to the stage.

"When you officials talk about empowering communities, we sometimes wonder what you mean. How do you empower us? Isn't it we who must give ourselves the power to decide what matters? Isn't your job to ask us, and for us to tell you what that is?" She looked at her audience for a long moment.

Now, Sofia backed up, joined hands with the other women. Holding their hands high they said as one, in Spanish: "We are empowerment!"

As the women stood together holding hands, the room was still. Then, slowly, one by one, the people in the room stood and cheered. "Yes!" "Bravo!"

I looked across the crowd at Isabel who was looking at me, both thumbs up. It had been a struggle. For almost ten years now, I'd been learning from women like Sofia what empowerment looked like. If the women could stand up and be counted, empower themselves, then so could I.

though he, like the others in my family, wasn't surprised. But I was especially dreading telling Christian because he was so far away in Peru.

The month before I left Cliff, the Lanaos had invited Christian to stay with them in Lima for eight weeks. It was a generous gift from a generous family, and a great opportunity for Christian. He would be back for Thanksgiving. A week before he was due home, I called.

"Something's happened," I said. "I won't be at the house when you get home. I won't be there for Thanksgiving. I'm living in Maryland now. And I'm not alone."

"I'm sorry, Jerrs," said Christian, "I was afraid this might happen."

As would be true for everyone in my family, Christian was sorry for Cliff and me, but he wasn't surprised.

The day after Thanksgiving, which they spent with Cliff, Christian and Adam came to see us in Silver Spring. We spent the evening eating and talking, while they took Terry's measure. As they were leaving, I walked them to the car. I had to ask the question that had been weighing on me for months.

In a small voice, I said: "Can you ever forgive me?"

Christian put his arms around me and whispered, "There's nothing to forgive. You and Dad did the best you could. For each other and for us. You'll always have two sons who love you."

"That's right, Mom," Adam said, taking my hand. "Always."

Never for a moment did I imagine my sons would understand, let alone forgive me for leaving their dad. For years, I'd been afraid to leave. Afraid to hurt Cliff and the boys. But I'd done it, and my sons understood.

For all the fear generated by the terrorists on 9/11, the sadness and guilt I felt about leaving Cliff, the unfamiliarity of a new love and a new house, I was ecstatic to be starting this life with Terry. And the following year, I decided to leave the World Bank. I'd spent almost thirty years doing what I could to put women first in development, but I knew my work at the World Bank was done.

When I gave notice I'd be retiring, my division chief asked me to reconsider. She offered me a promotion and a salary increase. "We need you," she said. "No one else is doing the kind of work you do." I wasn't tempted to stay.

By the time I decided to leave, Marguerite had been living in Washington and working full-time at the Bank for two years. I knew she would carry on the work and the spirit of community and of gender and grassroots management in Africa. She would continue to develop GMT with artisans in Mali and community-driven development in Uganda, and to expand the gender dimension of AIDS prevention and maternal and child health. By the time I left the Bank, a world of people knew what an extraordinary trainer, facilitator, and consultant Marguerite was. She now had close friends all over Washington just as she had had in Dakar, when I first met her, and colleagues at the Bank, who couldn't do without her any more than I could.

But when I told her I'd given my notice, she said, "You can't just leave us like this. At least once more we must travel together, work together. Once more before you leave."

I knew how disappointed she was by my decision to leave. I had to do as she asked.

Three weeks before I retired, I went with Marguerite to Kampala to train a group of twenty-four CDD trainers from four African countries. As always, when Marguerite was in charge, the workshop was a great success. I loved feeling the thrill of enthusiastic, talented young African trainers learning something new. And how eager they were to help communities develop differently—from the bottom-up rather than from the top-down. I loved the camaraderie, the meals together, the comfort of working one last time with Marguerite.

On the flight home from Kampala, Marguerite and I sat side-by-side. As always, we talked, laughed, and remembered the other places we'd been together. As I drifted off, my friend reached over and touched my arm, her eyes bright with tears.

"Ma belle," she said. *"Tu l'as terminée en beauté."* She wanted me to know, I'd brought my work at the Bank to a beautiful close. I had done well. And the work? It had been beautiful, indeed.

Three weeks later, I was alone in my office, clearing out my bookshelves, packing boxes, and saying goodbye to colleagues who came by. I'd been at it for a week, and I had the rhythm down. I pushed the flattened cardboard open from the center, folded the flaps in to create the box, ripped the tape, reinforced the seam at the base, and made it strong enough to carry the ton of stuff I had collected over the past thirty years. I'd already emptied two of my three bookcases and filled most of what were called "burn bags" with papers I wouldn't need again, but which the World Bank considered too important to risk circulating.

Over the previous week, I'd thrown hundreds of terms-of-reference, project briefs, and back-to-office reports into the grey recycling container. Such a quantity of bureaucratic prose telling of steps forward and back, recalling disappointments, triumphs, and fallings short. Among the items I chose to keep, though, was one I'd been given by the World Bank children's center board in celebration of the childcare center's tenth anniversary—a cup with the WBCC logo I had designed seventeen years ago etched into the glass.

I took down from the wall my enlargement of Larry's photo of the young Senegalese book binder in the pink top with whom I so identified in Dakar. And other pictures, too: a framed photo of Cliff in Kenya, a turquoise, white, and blue apron around his waist, a dozen village women dancing around him in a circle, singing his praises. One of Marguerite and me in Saly Portudal, both dressed in boubous and headscarves, the evening after we made up for our one big fight.

I reached for the training manuals we'd published in English, French, Arabic, and Spanish, and a program from the FDL commencement where Elaine Wolfensohn and I had presented certificates, performed an abbreviated can-can, and serenaded the indigenous and Afro-Peruvian women with a chorus of "You Are My Sunshine," astonishing everyone.

The three documents still on the shelf, side by side, made me smile: the 1980 *Status of Women Working Group* report, in which I thanked Robert McNamara for his help, next to the personnel department's report, *Equality and Excellence*, produced twenty years later, next to *Engendering Development—Through Gender Equality in Rights, Resources and Voice*, dated 2000. I hadn't written the last two, but I was proud of them, anyway. The Bank had made some serious progress on gender and development. Not as much—or as quickly—as I might have liked, but probably more than I could realistically have expected.

I felt around the top of the bookcase for the ceramic blue hippo that my British division chief Peter Naylor bought for me in Cairo and gave me as a baby gift when Adam was born. I found her—Taweret, ancient Egyptian goddess of childbirth and fertility, the fierce protector of children. Looking at her now, I wondered: had I protected the children fiercely enough? My own children—Christian? Adam? And the others who needed better care, who needed mothers who could afford shoes for them to wear to school and immunizations to keep them well?

I hoped so.

It was late. The phones had stopped ringing. The hallways were quiet, and the conference rooms empty, just me left—grubby and disheveled in jeans and work shirt—eager to have my work behind me.

Still stowing things in boxes and throwing others away, I sensed a shift in the air behind me, someone at the door. I wasn't surprised, people who couldn't come to the farewell party Elaine would be hosting for me later had been dropping by all day. My back to the door, I heard a discreet cough—a slight clearing of the throat. I recognized this tiny sound. I peered up from the dusty packing at a figure standing in the doorway. Fareed Atabani, my old boss when I was a secretary—my hero whose weak heart sent him packing for Sudan and away from the World Bank decades earlier. He'd gained a little weight and lost most of his hair. But he still wore a starched white shirt and a suit from Savile Row. His face was still the color of charcoal and the shape of a ripe pear. His brown eyes were as dark and warm as ever. He was the same distinguished fellow he'd been when we sat in his office together as I ranted about the men at the Bank, or when I joined him at coffee with the economists and listened to what they said about my new employer.

It didn't seem possible. Any of it. Me packing my boxes to leave or Fareed Atabani showing up out of the blue to say goodbye. I rushed to the door and hugged him fiercely as I'd done when I was twenty-five and he was leaving the Bank for the last time.

"How did you know?" I asked, struggling to find the words. "That I'd be retiring? That today would be my last day?"

"I've still got a few spies around the place." He smiled.

"But why in all these years did you never come back to see me?" I knew I sounded like a plaintive child, but I didn't care.

Fareed took a moment to reply. "Do you remember once, after my heart attack, when you asked me how I could let the World Bank almost kill me?"

Of course, I remembered.

"You were right. If I hadn't left, the Bank might well have killed me, so I stayed away. I knew you'd be okay. You didn't need me."

"But I did. That first year after you left was awful."

"I'm sorry," he said, taking my hands, as tears got the best of me, and his image blurred.

When I asked him if he'd go with me to my farewell party, he shook his head. He had to get back to his wife, Bodour, who was waiting for him in the lobby.

"You remember her, don't you?" he asked.

Although it had been more than twenty years, I still remembered Bodour as she greeted me at the door of his hospital room, wrapping her *thawb* around me, making me a part of her family. Such a tall, lovely woman.

"So now she has her PhD," he said. "Now I'm retired and she's the big shot." I laughed at the word, "big shot."

"You must be proud of her."

"I am," he said. "She's almost as determined as you."

As I watched Fareed walk down the corridor toward the elevator, I realized that like my grandparents and my father, he'd always expected big things of me, and my accomplishments came as no surprise. But maybe Fareed was right. Even as a child of nine at the United Nations, a woman of twenty-three walking into the World Bank for the first time, a professional twenty years later creating a kind of "mini UN" for myself in Tunis, I'd always been bound and determined. Despite the cynicism that ran rampant in the World Bank, I believed anything was possible.

Sitting at my desk, alone in my office, again, I reached for one of my favorite books—*In Her Hands: Craftswomen Changing the World* by Paola Gianturco—and found the foreword in which Alice Walker speaks of African, Turkish, Guatemalan, and Peruvian craftswomen who lived on less than a dollar a day. Walker described their "dauntlessness of spirit," women who are "giving life everything they've got." As always, I found her plea that we rich Westerners stand with these women, learn their stories, and recognize their worth and understand how much we owe them for working so hard, and not giving up. That they teach us the meaning of love, sacrifice, practicality, creativity, and courage.

So many women—so many friends—from whom I learned so much. Soheir, Amal, Joséphine, Marguerite, Maimouna, Binta, Apollonia, Kiran, Vanita, Rocio, Sofia and Rosa Maria, women making pots along the Ucayali, growing cassava in Sanmatenga, repairing fishnets in Bhubaneswar. It was these women who drove those of us in the World Bank to do things in new and different ways. How lucky I was to be invited into that circle of women Alice Walker wrote so beautifully about. The women who taught me optimism, persistence, and solidarity.

And dauntlessness. That, too.

CPSIA information can be obtained
at www.ICGtesting.com
Printed in the USA
LVHW022200151121
703391LV00006B/1062